**Berliner ökophysiologische
und phytomedizinische Schriften**

Hrsg. von Christian Ulrichs und Carmen Büttner

Lebenswissenschaftliche Fakultät,
Humboldt-Universität zu Berlin

Band 41

Hrsg. von

Dr. Susanne Huyskens-Keil
Humboldt-Universität zu Berlin

und

Dr. Arnold M. Opiyo
Egerton University, Kenja

Pre- and postharvest treatments for the quality assurance of African indigenous leafy vegetables

Dissertation
zur Erlangung des akademischen Grades
Doctor rerum horticulturarum
(Dr. rer. hort.)

eingereicht an der
Lebenswissenschaftliche Fakultät
der Humboldt-Universität zu Berlin
von Elisha Otieno Gogo
geboren am 15.10.1984 in Kitale, Kenia

Präsidentin
der Humboldt-Universität zu Berlin
Prof. Dr.-Ing. Dr. Sabine Kunst

Dekan
der Humboldt-Universität zu Berlin
Prof. Dr. Bernhard Grimm

Gutachter
1. Prof. Dr. Dr. Christian Ulrichs
2. Prof. Dr. Jens Pape

Tag der mündlichen Prüfung: 20.10.2017

Bibliografische Information der Deutschen Nationalbibliothek
Die Deutsche Nationalbibliothek verzeichnet diese Publikation in der
Deutschen Nationalbibliografie; detaillierte bibliografische Daten sind im Internet
über http://dnb.d-nb.de abrufbar.
1. Aufl. - Göttingen: Cuvillier, 2017
   Zugl.: Berlin, Humboldt-Universität, Diss., 2017

© CUVILLIER VERLAG, Göttingen 2017
   Nonnenstieg 8, 37075 Göttingen
   Telefon: 0551-54724-0
   Telefax: 0551-54724-21
   www.cuvillier.de

Alle Rechte vorbehalten. Ohne ausdrückliche Genehmigung des Verlages ist
es nicht gestattet, das Buch oder Teile daraus auf fotomechanischem Weg
(Fotokopie, Mikrokopie) zu vervielfältigen.
1. Auflage, 2017
Gedruckt auf umweltfreundlichem, säurefreiem Papier aus nachhaltiger Forstwirtschaft.

   ISBN 978-3-7369-9650-2
   eISBN 978-3-7369-8650-3

Table of contents

	Page
List of tables	iii
List of figures	v
1. Introduction	1
2. Scientific background	4
3. Analysis of postharvest loss along the supply chain of African indigenous leafy vegetables	20

Gogo, E.O., Opiyo, A.M., Ulrichs, Ch., Huyskens-Keil, S., International Journal of Vegetable Science – submitted (Ref: WIJV-2017-0047).

4. Nutritional and economic postharvest loss analysis of African indigenous leafy vegetables along the supply chain in Kenya	36

Gogo, E.O., Opiyo, A.M., Ulrichs, Ch., Huyskens-Keil, S., 2017. Postharvest Biology and Technology 130, 39-47. http://dx.doi.org/10.1016/j.postharvbio.2017.04.007.

5. Impact of direct-electric-current on growth and bioactive compounds of African nightshade (*Solanum scabrum* Mill.) plants	54

Gogo, E.O., Huyskens-Keil, S., Krimlowski, A., Ulrichs, Ch., Schmidt, U., Opiyo, A., Dannehl, D., 2016. Journal of Applied Botany and Food Quality 89, 60-67. http://dx.doi.org/10.5073/ JABFQ. 2016.089.007.

6. Postharvest UV-C treatment for extending shelf life and improving nutritional quality of African indigenous leafy vegetables	71

Gogo E.O., Opiyo, A.M., Hassenberg, K., Ulrichs, Ch., Huyskens-Keil, S., 2017. Postharvest Biology and Technology 129, 107-117. http://dx.doi.org/10.1016/j.postharvbio.2017.03.019.

7. Hormic postharvest UV-C application to improve health promoting secondary plant compound pattern in vegetable amaranth	93

Gogo, E.O., Förster, N., Dannehl, D., Frommherz, L., Trierweiler, B., Opiyo, A.M., Ulrichs, Ch., Huyskens-Keil, S., Postharvest Biology and Technology - submitted (Ref: POSTEC_2017_437).

8. Discussion	116
9. Conclusion and recommendation	123
10. Summary	124
11. Publications	127
12. References	128
13. Acknowledgements	142
14. List of abbreviations	143

List of tables

	Page
Table 2.1: Leaf yield and nutritional value (per 100 g fresh edible portion) of selected Kenyan African indigenous leafy vegetables (AIVs)	5
Table 2.2: Postharvest losses, storability and treatments of selected Kenyan African indigenous leafy vegetables (AIVs)	5
Table 2.3: Summary of studies on pre-harvest application effects of electric fields on vegetables during production	10
Table 2.4: Summary of studies on postharvest application effects of electric fields on fresh vegetables	11
Table 2.5: Summary of studies on postharvest application effects of electric fields on vegetables during processing	12
Table 2.6: Summary of studies on pre-harvest UV-C application effects on vegetables	15
Table 2.7: Summary of studies on postharvest UV-C application effects on morphology and physiology of vegetables	16
Table 2.8: Summary of studies on postharvest UV-C application and their effects on secondary metabolites and antioxidative properties of vegetables	18
Table 2.9: Summary of studies on postharvest UV-C application effects on microbiological properties of vegetables	19
Table 3.1: Sociodemographic profiles (%), as means ± standard deviations, of farmers cultivating African indigenous leafy vegetables in Kenya (n = 45 for each county)	24
Table 3.2: Production, harvest operations and causes of losses at harvest (%), as means ± standard deviations, of the main African indigenous leafy vegetables cultivated in Kenya (n = 45 for each county)	26
Table 3.3: Seasonality, postharvest treatments, and preservation (%), as means ± standard deviations, of African indigenous leafy vegetables in Kenya (n = 45 for each county)	27
Table 3.4: Transportation and causes of losses during transportation (%), as means ± standard deviations, of African indigenous leafy vegetable in Kenya (n = 45 for each county)	29
Table 3.5: Marketing and causes of market losses (%), as means ± standard deviations, of African indigenous leafy vegetables in Kenya (n = 45 for each county)	30
Table 4.1: Weather conditions during the supply chain evaluation of African nightshade leaves from the main producing counties in Kenya	43
Table 4.2: Causes of postharvest losses (%) of African nightshade leaves during supply from the main producing counties in Kenya (n = 45)	44
Table 4.3: Economic loss during postharvest supply chain of African nightshade plants in Kenya	50
Table 5.1: Effect of different electrical voltages on growth of African nightshade plants	62

Table 5.2: Effect of voltage applications on chlorophylls and carotenoids content (mg/g DM) of African nightshade plants.. 65

Table 5.3: Effect of voltage applications on mineral element and heavy metal content (g/kg DM) of African nightshade plants.. 65

Table 6.1: Effect of postharvest UV-C treatments on macro- and micro nutrient contents of vegetable amaranth leaves during storage at different temperature regime 81

Table 6.2: Effect of postharvest UV-C treatments on macro- and micro nutrient contents of African nightshade leaves during storage at different temperature regime 82

Table 6.3: Effect of postharvest UV-C treatments on structural carbohydrate contents (g kg^{-1}) of vegetable amaranth and African nightshade leaves during storage at different temperature regime 83

Table 6.4: Effect of postharvest UV-C treatments on chlorophyll and carotenoid contents (g kg^{-1}) of vegetable amaranth leaves during storage at different temperature regime 85

Table 6.5: Effect of postharvest UV-C treatments on chlorophyll and carotenoid contents (g kg^{-1}) of African nightshade leaves during storage at different temperature regime 86

Table 7.1: Effect of postharvest UV-C application dosage on phenolic acids content, on dry matter basis (mmol kg^{-1}) of vegetable amaranth leaves during storage 107

Table 7.2: Multiple correlations of secondary plant compounds and antioxidant capacity of postharvest UV-C treated vegetable amaranth leaves during storage at 20 °C... 110

List of figures

Figure 2.1: Schematic representation of the effect of electric current or UV-C on molecular, biochemical and physiological changes in vegetables 7

Figure 3.1: Postharvest evaluation on the visual appearance (A = Yellowing, B = Wilting, C = Foreign bodies, D = Mechanical damage, E = Disease damage, and F = Insect pest damage) of African indigenous leafy vegetables along the supply chain in Kenya. AH = At harvest, BT = Before transport, AT = After transport and AM = At the market. Values represent means±standard deviations, (n = 45 for each county) 32

Figure 3.2: Assessment of postharvest loss of African indigenous leafy vegetables along the supply chain in Kenya. Values represent means ± standard deviations, (n = 45 for each county) 34

Figure 3.3: Shelf life of African indigenous leafy vegetables under farmers' ambient conditions in Kenya. Values represent means ± standard deviations, (n = 45 for each county) 35

Figure 4.1: Cumulative fresh produce loss (A) and dry matter content (B) of African nightshade leaves during postharvest supply chain analysis in different counties of Kenya. Means ± standard deviations across the counties and along the supply chain followed by the same letter are not significantly different ($p < 0.05$) according to Tukey's HSD test 46

Figure 4.2: Mineral element contents of African nightshade leaves during postharvest supply chain from the main producing counties in Kenya. Dry matter content corresponding to specific mineral element measurements from harvest to market was 95.6, 95.2, 95.7, 94.8 % from Nakuru; 94.3, 94.9, 95.1, 94.7% from Kisii; and 94.6, 94.9, 95.3, 95.0% from Kakamega. Means ± standard deviations across the counties and along the supply chain followed by the same letter within an element are not significantly different ($p < 0.05$) according to Tukey's HSD test 47

Figure 4.3: Protein contents of African nightshade leaves during postharvest supply chain analysis from the main producing counties in Kenya. Dry matter content corresponding to the specific measurements from harvest to market was 95.6, 95.2, 95.7, 94.8% from Nakuru; 94.3, 94.9, 95.1, 94.7% from Kisii; and 94.6, 94.9, 95.3, 95.0% from Kakamega. Means ± standard deviations across the counties and along the supply chain followed by the same letter are not significantly different ($p < 0.05$) according to Tukey's HSD test 48

Figure 4.4: Total chlorophylls contents of African nightshade leaves during postharvest supply chain analysis from the main producing counties in Kenya. Dry matter content corresponding to the specific measurements from harvest to market was 13.5, 12.0, 9.4, 9.1% from Nakuru; 12.9, 11.4, 8.2, 8.0% from Kisii; and 13.9, 12.4, 9.9, 7.6% from Kakamega. 48

Figure 4.5: Total carotenoid contents of African nightshade leaves during postharvest supply chain analysis from the main producing counties in Kenya. Dry matter content corresponding to the specific measurements from harvest to market was 13.5, 12.0, 9.4, 9.1% from Nakuru; 12.9, 11.4, 8.2, 8.0% from Kisii; and 13.9, 12.4, 9.9, 7.6% from Kakamega. Means ± standard deviations across the counties and along the supply chain followed by the same letter are not significantly different ($p < 0.05$) according to Tukey's HSD test 49

Figure 5.1: Microclimate condition during greenhouse production of African nightshade plants 57

Figure 5.2: Changes in current flow on African nightshade plants during production as influenced by DC intensity. Means (± standard deviation) followed by the same letter are not significantly different according to t-test ($p < 0.05$) 60

Figure 5.3: Effect of different voltage applications on leaf area of African nightshade plants. Mean values (± standard deviation) followed by the same letter are not significantly different according to Tukey-test ($p < 0.05$) 62

Figure 5.4: Effect of different voltage applications on fresh (A) and dry (B) weight and marketable and non-marketable leaves (C) of African nightshade plants. Mean values (± standard deviation) within a specific variable followed by the same letter are not significantly different according to Tukey-test ($p < 0.05$) 63

Figure 5.5: Effect of different voltage applications on different structural carbohydrates on leaves (A) and Stems (B) of African nightshade plants. Mean values (± standard deviation) within a specific variable followed by the same letter are not significantly different according to Tukey-test ($p < 0.05$) 66

Figure 6.1: Greenhouse microclimate conditions during production of vegetable amaranth and African nightshade plants in 2014 and 2015 (June to July) 74

Figure 6.2: Effect of postharvest UV-C treatments on fresh weight loss of vegetable amaranth (A) and African nightshade (B) leaves during storage at different temperature regime. Means ± standard deviations followed by the same letter within a storage temperature regime and a vegetable are not significantly different according to Tukey's test ($p < 0.05$) 78

Figure 6.3: Effect of postharvest UV-C treatments on protein content of vegetable amaranth (A) and African nightshade (B) leaves during storage at different temperature regime. Means ± standard deviations followed by the same letter within a storage temperature regime and a vegetable are not significantly different according to Tukey's test ($p < 0.05$) 80

Figure 6.4: Effect of postharvest UV-C treatments on microbial counts on vegetable amaranth leaves at 20 °C storage temperature. Means ± standard deviations followed by the same letter within individual microbes are not significantly different according to Tukey's test ($p < 0.05$) 88

Figure 7.1: Greenhouse microclimate conditions (A-2015 and B-2016) during the production of vegetable amaranth at Humboldt-Universität zu Berlin, Germany..... 96

Figure 7.2: Effect of postharvest UV-C application dosage on vitamin E content on dry matter basis of vegetable amaranth leaves during storage. Means ± standard deviations followed by the same letter within storage temperature regime are not significantly different according to Tukey's test ($p < 0.05$) 102

Figure 7.3: Effect of postharvest UV-C application dosage on carotenoid content on dry matter basis of vegetable amaranth leaves during storage. Means ± standard deviations followed by the same letter within a carotenoid type and storage temperature regime are not significantly different according to Tukey's test ($p < 0.05$) 103

Figure 7.4: Effect of postharvest UV-C application dosage on flavonoids content on dry matter basis of vegetable amaranth leaves during storage. Means ± standard deviations followed by the same letter within a flavonoid type and storage temperature regime are not significantly different according to Tukey's test ($p < 0.05$) 104

Figure 7.5: Effect of postharvest UV-C application dosage on quercetin to kaempferol ratio of vegetable amaranth leaves during storage. Means ± standard deviations followed by the same letter within a storage temperature regime are not significantly different according to Tukey's test ($p < 0.05$) 106

Figure 7.6: Effect of postharvest UV-C application dosage on total phenolic content on dry matter basis of vegetable amaranth leaves during storage at 20 °C. Means ± standard deviations followed by the same letter are not significantly different according to Tukey's test ($p < 0.05$) 108

Figure 7.7: Effect of postharvest UV-C application dosage on Trolox equivalent antioxidant capacity (TEAC) on dry matter basis of vegetable amaranth leaves during storage at 20 °C. Means ± standard deviations followed by the same letter are not significantly different according to Tukey's test ($p < 0.05$) 109

Figure 7.8: Effect of postharvest UV-C application dosage on glutathione peroxidase (GPOX) activity on dry matter basis of vegetable amaranth leaves during storage at 20 °C. Means ± standard deviations followed by the same letter are not significantly different according to Tukey's test ($p < 0.05$) 109

1. Introduction

African indigenous leafy vegetables (AIVs) are currently referred to as 'underutilised species' (Virchow, 2003). Public awareness of these species has continued to increase since they were first brought into the limelight in 1992 by the Convention on Biological Diversity and the Global Plan of Action for Plant Genetic Resources for Food and Agriculture (Virchow, 2003). Since then, a number of organisations and most recently the German ministry (BMBF/BMZ) funded project Horticultural Innovation and Learning for Improved Nutrition and Livelihood in East Africa (HORTINLEA), under the funding initiative "Securing the Global Food Supply – GlobE". HORTINLEA is focussing on investigating and promoting these crops as a strategy to improve livelihood and nutrition of the rural, peri-urban and urban inhabitants in developing countries, especially Kenya.

AIVs referred to in this case might not be indigenous to the country, but are associated with traditional production systems, local knowledge and usually have a long history of local selection and usage. Their role in improving living standards of resource-limited communities has long been recognised by ethno-botanists who have even documented traditional knowledge associated with these species (Maundu et al., 1999). In the past, AIVs (e.g. African nightshade (*Solanum* spp.), vegetable amaranth (*Amaranthus* spp.), spiderplant (*Cleome gynandra* L.), cowpea (*Vigna unguiculata* (L.) Walp), Ethiopian kale (*Brassica carinata* L.), were to be found only in the back-streets and in a few open-air markets. Today, marketing and consumption of these vegetables, in Kenya have changed. Currently, they are competitively sold in most supermarkets and municipal markets of major towns and cities, in increasing quantities on a daily basis alongside the most commonly consumed exotic (introduced) vegetables. These exotic vegetables include cabbage (*Brassica oleracea* L. var. *capitata* f. *alba*), chard (*Beta vulgaris* subsp. *cicla* (L.) W.D.J. Koch); commonly known as spinach in Kenya and collard greens (*Brassica oleracea* L. var. *viridis*); known as sukumawiki or kale in Kenya (Chelang'a et al., 2013; Onyango and Imungi, 2007). In Kenya, the most consumed AIVs (e.g. African nightshade and vegetable amaranth) serve as useful sources of vitamin A, Fe, and Zn. Malnutrition and the global nutrient problem known as "hidden hunger" are associated with deficiencies in these micro-elements (Gogo et al., 2016). They are also reported to be rich in proteins, fibre and minerals such as Na, P, and Ca (Abukutsa-Onyango, 2003). Recently, attention is being directed to these vegetables because of their high contents of bioactive secondary compounds such as carotenoids, flavonoids, phenolic acids, and other phenolic compounds (Castrillón-Arbeláez and Délano-Frier, 2016; Nana et al., 2012; Noori et al., 2015). These substances possess strong antioxidant and possible anticarcinogenic properties and have recently been implicated in health promotion (Kasote et al., 2015; Nana et al., 2012; Noori et al., 2015; Odongo et al., 2017).

In many cases AIVs are well adapted to the agro-ecological conditions, thrive well under minimum resource conditions, thus have a comparative advantage in marginal lands over exotic vegetables and may contribute to low-input sustainable production systems (Abukutsa-Onyango, 2003).

Overwhelming demand of AIVs has stimulated many entrepreneurs, especially women and youth, to grow and trade these vegetables on a small-scale basis (Chelang'a et al., 2013; Muhanji et al., 2011). Opportunities exist in Kenya to use AIVs to expand the local food base, improve nutrition and health of the population, enhance food security and generate income. Therefore, AIVs fit well in the achievement of the sustainable development goals (SDGs), especially the first three (no poverty, zero hunger and good health and wellbeing). The commonly produced and marketed AIVs include African nightshade (*Solanum* spp.), vegetable amaranth, spiderplant, cowpea, Ethiopian kale, slender leaf/rattle pod (mitoo) (*Crotalaria ochroleuca* G. Don. and *C. brevidens* L.), jute mallow (*Corchorus olitorius* L.), and pumpkin leaves (*Cucurbita maxima* L. and *C. moschata* L.) (Baldermann et al., 2016; Maundu et al., 1999). However, for most of these species, documented scientific knowledge is either rare or only beginning to emerge, especially on postharvest losses, further complicating the intervention process.

The main constraint to increased production, marketing and consumption of AIVs is its high perishability and low storage capacity in fresh form (Onyango and Imungi, 2007). AIVs display high metabolic activity after harvest hence, liable to faster postharvest deterioration in quantity and quality. Currently, the magnitude of postharvest losses of AIVs in Kenya can be as high as 50%, depending on the species (Gogo et al., 2016). These losses are attributed on one hand to pre-harvest factors (e.g. inadequate nutrition, irrigation, crop protection); affecting yield, harvest and postharvest quality and on the other hand to postharvest factors (e.g. inappropriate postharvest handling and treatments); resulting in rapid physiological deterioration, loss of nutritional quality and microbiological decay during the supply chain (Onyango et al., 2009; Onyango and Imungi, 2007). The commonly used postharvest treatment methods include air-drying, solar-drying, blanching, and fermentation (Gogo et al., 2016). However, despite their wide adoption for many years, these methods are reported to result in significant loss of nutritional product quality (Muchoki et al., 2007). In the past few years there has been increasing interest in the rediscovery of traditional postharvest treatments (e.g. sun/solar drying, blanching, fermentation), on one hand and on the other hand, on new emerging pre- and postharvest technologies (e.g. electric current, UV-C irradiation, modified film packaging). Numerous studies have shown the beneficial effects of these postharvest treatments to control insect pests, prevent fungal rots, and inhibit undesired acceleration of ripening and senescence or even to promote the synthesis of health promoting compounds during storage and marketing (Artés-Hernández et al., 2009; Chairat et al., 2013; Dannehl et al., 2011; Huyskens-Keil et al., 2011; Khalili et al., 2017). These easy-to-apply postharvest treatments can prevent quality losses effectively and can substitute chemical preservation with non-damaging physical treatments that meet hygienic requirements; to develop new food safety regulations for AIVs and to prolong their shelf life as well as their storability. In addition, based on the challenge of availability, reliability and cost of electricity these postharvest treatments might be applicable instead of cooling facilities (Yadoo, 2012).

Aim of the present study was to assess the situation of postharvest losses during AIVs supply chain (from smallholder farmer to consumer), determine the amount of postharvest loss (quantitave and nutritional) along the supply chain in Kenya. Thereafter, a series of studies were conducted on pre-harvest (electric current) and postharvest (UV-C irradiation) treatments to determine their effects on primary compounds (chlorophylls, mineral elements, proteins and dietary fibre) and secondary metabolites (carotenoids, flavonoids, phenolic acids, phenolic compounds, glutathione peroxidase (GPOX), and vitamin E) and microbial status as well as antioxidant capacity, in order to strengthen a product quality and safety oriented food supply chain. The study focussed mainly on two commonly consumed AIVs i.e. Vegetable amaranth (*Amaranthus cruentus* L. cv. Madiira) and African nightshade (*Solanum scabrum* Mill. cv. Olevolosi).

2. Scientific background

2.1. Traditional pre- and postharvest handling, treatments and losses of AIVs in Kenya

Pre- and postharvest treatments of agricultural produce are one of the central problems developing countries are facing resulting in low yield and poor quality AIVs, including Kenya (Table 2.1). Owing to the lack of and/or inadequacy of pre- and postharvest treatment technologies, large quantities of urgently needed food, especially AIVs, are lost (Table 2.2). Major postharvest losses reported in Kenya are due to insufficient pre-harvest conditions, insect pest and diseases, poor storage conditions, and poor handling along the supply chain (Gogo et al., 2016). These unfavourable conditions are even more serious during rainy and dry seasons where the vegetables exist in abundance and scarcity, respectively. During this period when AIVs are scarce, many rural, peri-urban and urban dwellers have a limited availability of leafy vegetables; which contributes to lack of dietary diversity or malnutrition of the local populations. Postharvest handling and treatments (e.g. cleaning, sorting, grading, cold storage, packaging, blanching, drying, and fermentation) in Kenya have been reported to improve shelf life and quality as well as reducing microbial contamination of AIVs (Ayua and Omware, 2013). On the other hand, other studies indicate that drying and blanching may reduce quality of AIVs (Chege et al., 2014; Kasangi et al., 2010). However, farmers in Kenya still rely on traditional postharvest treatment methods; including sprinkling cold water on leaves to maintain freshness, sun-drying, unconventional packaging (gunny bags and non-perforated polythene bags). In Africa and Kenya in particular, the lack of and/or inadequacy of postharvest treatment technologies exists with many vegetable varieties (especially AIVs) resulting in wastage during the in-season (late March to June) and limited supply during the off-season (December to April) accompanied by high prices (Habwe et al., 2008), because most locally available vegetables are seasonal and not available year-long. AIVs cannot be marketed fast enough when they are in-season owing to their high perishability and thus, limited shelf life and storability. This forces farmers to sell soon after harvest (Shiundu and Oniang'o, 2007). Onyango and Imungi (2007) reported 3.1%, 3.5%, 4.2% and 5.5% losses of spider plant, African nightshade, cowpeas and vegetable amaranth, respectively, due to wastage as a result of excessive wilting, in Nairobi groceries alone. Accordingly, market sellers and supermarkets strive to sell all the supplies on the day of delivery and whatever remains at the end of the day may be discarded as having lost saleable value. This was reported to be a major problem of AIVs sold in urban centres contributing to heavy postharvest losses (Onyango and Imungi, 2007). In addition, wilting was also indicated to be a challenge as AIVs deteriorate faster especially at ambient retailing conditions where trading of these vegetables is mostly done. Appropriate pre- and postharvest treatments and adequate storage methods are necessary in order to ensure quality and the availability of these nutrient-rich foods all year round (Habwe et al., 2008).

Table 2.1: Leaf yield and nutritional value (per 100 g fresh edible portion) of selected Kenyan African indigenous leafy vegetables (AIVs).

Scientific name	Harvesting stage (weeks)*	Yield ton ha^{-1}	Crude protein (g)	ß-Carotene (mg)	Vit. A (mg)	Vit. C (mg)	Ca (mg)	Fe (mg)	Dry matter (g)
Vigna unguiculata (L.) Walp.	4-8	5.4-10	-	6-8	5.7	70-100	152-400	10-15	15-20
Solanum spp.	4-8	30-80	3-6	8-10	8.8	40-140	250-442	5-17	18-22
Cleome gynandra L.	4-8	10-13	5-10	6-19	8.7	130-180	262-434	11-15	15-20
Amaranthus spp.	4-8	45	4-5	5-10	10.7	90-160	480-800	5-15	11-15

*Weeks from sowing to harvest.
Source: Abukutsa-Onyango, 2003; Gogo et al., 2016.

Table 2.2: Postharvest losses, storability and treatments of selected Kenyan African indigenous leafy vegetables (AIVs).

Scientific name*	Shelf life (days)**	Quality loss symptoms	Storage temperature (°C)	Postharvest treatment***
Vigna unguiculata (L.) Walp.	3	wilting, yellowing, rots	-	Yes
Solanum scabrum L.	3	wilting, yellowing,	-	Yes
Gynandropsis gynandra L.	4	wilting, yellowing,	-	Yes
Amaranthus spp.	3	wilting, yellowing,	5	Yes

*The AIVs are marketed in the open and closed markets (ambient conditions) as well as supermarkets (cold storage) and consumed fresh.
**At ambient conditions, all listed ALVs can only keep for one day. Shelf life indicated is for fresh AIVs.
***Most common postharvest treatments (preservation) are traditional (e.g. blanching, fermentation, drying).
Source: Gogo et al., 2016; Onyango and Imungi, 2007.

According to Smith and Eyzaguirre (2007), there is a need to develop and promote appropriate handling and processing technologies to minimize postharvest losses and ensure quality and safety during the supply chain in rural, peri-urban and urban centres. Just like other leafy vegetables, AIVs should be prepared for market or preservation as soon as possible after harvesting. Since these vegetables are highly perishable, the likelihood of spoilage increases rapidly after harvest, as time passes. Therefore, these vegetables need to be transported to a nearby shade or cold store within the shortest time possible. Majority of farmers producing these vegetables are resource limited (Yadav and Sehgal, 2002); hence cannot afford conventional cold stores. Most farmers normally prepare their vegetables under a tree shade or ordinary (traditional) stores. Some farmers sprinkle cold water on the vegetables in order to quickly remove field heat and maintain freshness for a longer time. At this point, these vegetables are sorted, cleaned and packed using farmer and consumer specific requirements. Cleaning (or washing) is necessary to remove any dirt or residues. Unfortunately, many farmers forget to dry leaves after washing and therefore encounter higher prevalence of disease development, especially moulds (Gogo et al., 2016). However, at supermarkets these vegetables are stored in cold shelves at about 5-10 °C together with other vegetables and fruits. Knowledge of low temperature storage of AIVs along the supply chain is still limited. Very low temperatures (< 5 °C) have been reported to cause chilling injury to AIVs (Nyaura et al., 2014). Mixing of these vegetables with ethylene producing fruits and vegetables (as in the case of most markets and supermarkets) will hasten their deterioration rate. In most cases, if these vegetables are not sold within 24 hours after harvest, the likelihood of deterioration is imminent. In the case of the remaining AIVs from the previous sale, some farmers have tried to sprinkle water on the vegetables and leave them in the open overnight. However, problems of disease development and thus microbiological contamination still hamper their effort. Moreover, nutritional quality is also highly affected by the different postharvest temperatures. For example, it has been demonstrated that ascorbic acid declined by 88% in vegetable amaranth when kept at room temperature (20 °C) after 4 days of storage while the lowest loss was observed at 5 °C (55% loss) after 23 days of storage. Based on this study, Nyaura et al. (2014) suggested that shelf life extension and nutrient preservation of vegetable amaranth can be achieved through storage at temperatures of 5 °C. These problems are further aggravated by the increasing dietary needs of the ever growing Kenyan population. Since majority of the Kenyans depend on AIVs as a source of nutrition and income, there is need for urgent intervention.

2.2. Emerging pre- and postharvest technologies for fresh vegetables

There is an increased awareness of quality attributes of vegetables including freshness, colour, texture, flavour, nutritional content, health promoting secondary compounds and food safety among consumers and traders. Modification of existing pre- and postharvest techniques and/or the adoption of novel technologies that allow for production of safe and high quality products are strategies undertaken to meet these increasing customer demands (Gonzalez and Barrett, 2010). There are evidences on the biological benefits associated with a particular novel vegetable pre- and postharvest treatment technique, for example, impact of the technology on vegetable like in this case electric current and UV-C (Figure 2.1). In this section, we focus on emerging pre- and postharvest treatment technologies, hereby exemplarily demonstrating pre-harvest and postharvest application of electric current, UV-C irradiation and their impact on morphological, physiological and biochemical changes on fresh vegetables.

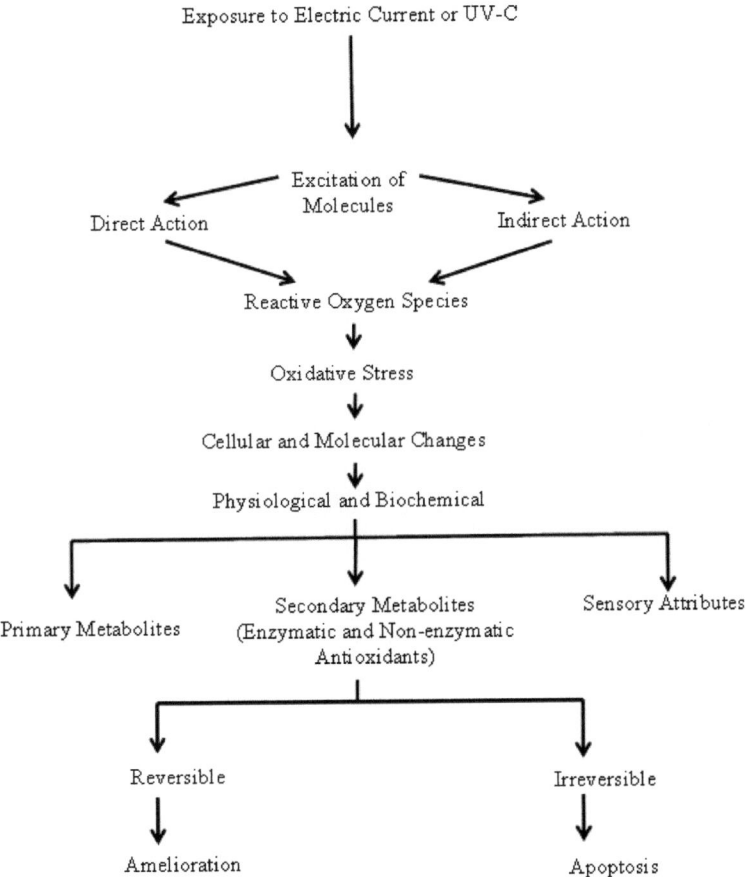

Figure 2.1: Schematic representation of the effect of electric current or UV-C on molecular, biochemical and physiological changes in vegetables.

(Adapted with slight modifications from: Kasote et al., 2015; Rohanie and Ayoub, 2012).

2.2.1. Electric Current (fields): Impact on morphology, physiology and bioactive chemical compounds in vegetables

The theory of electro hydrodynamics can be invoked to explain the physical action of ions in a substrate resulting from ionisation in an electric field. Thus, the familiar Coulomb force of the product of field strength and charge density becomes the principal driving force for physical action of the ions. When the ions are subjected to electric fields, the charged particles will accelerate. The kinetic energy gained by the particles is partly spent in ionising other molecules via the Ramsauer–Townsend effect (Bailey and Townsend, 1921) and partly in colliding with neutral molecules in the drift region of the fluid medium in which they travel. This results in collisions, while the momentum is transferred to the molecules hence frictional resistance. This produces the ion drag phenomenon with the associated electric force when the substrate mass between the electrodes moves towards the plate. The generation of vortex motions by the electric current with associated enhancement in heat transfer from metallic plates has been well documented in fluid mechanics (Jones, 1978). Therefore, the presence of an electric field affects molecular bonding of a material, including vegetable tissues. Furthermore, Sidaway (1966) showed the differences of plant response towards the negative and positive signs of electrostatic fields. It is also demonstrated that electric fields accelerate mass transfer by affecting membrane permeability properties (Rastogi et al., 1999). The application of electricity with the voltage of ≤ 2 V is reported to allow ions and molecules crossing the cell membranes (Soliva-Fortuny et al., 2009; Weaver and Chizmadzhev, 1996). This effect was also confirmed by Angesbach et al. (2000) who reported formation of pores across the cell membrane when a transmembrane potential of 1.7 V was reached in potato (*Solanum tuberosum* L.) tissue. They demonstrated that, conductive channels that occurred across the membrane resealed again shortly after electric current application and the cell membrane recovered its electrical insulating properties. Such a phenomenon offers numerous possibilities to induce targeted stress reactions in plant systems or cell cultures, whereas cells regain their vitality and metabolic activity. Therefore, the application of electric current, especially at low intensity (< 20 V) does not necessarily result in irreversible cell rupture as it is mostly perceived. In view of the urgency for increased food quality production in our century and in the future, it seems appropriate to bring this subject to the attention of researchers and others who would seek to apply the technology.

2.2.1.1. Pre-harvest application effects of electric fields on vegetables

The application of electricity can affect growth and development of plants to a great extent. This little-known technology, called electroculture, when applied to growing plants can affect growth rates, yields, and crop quality (Pohl, 1978). Studies also indicate that electroculture does not only protect plants from weeds, diseases, insect pests, and frost but also reduces the requirements for fertilizer or pesticides (Pohl, 1978). This technology has been applied to plants, seeds, soil, water, and nutrients (Diprose et al., 1984). Plants also have electric fields, which seem to be a vital part of their physiology (Scott, 1967). For example, an electrogenic proton pump helps in the regulation of cytoplasmic pH, and the active transport of mineral ions, hormones, or organic metabolites (Spanswick, 1981). Small changes in intracellular pH may act as a regulatory signal for certain critical steps in cell activity (Kurkdjian and Guern, 1989). Internal electric fields of plants may be affected by externally applied electric fields (Murr, 1965). Studies demonstrated that electric fields affected growth and development as well as physiological and biochemical compounds of vegetables (Table 2.3). Electric fields can significantly improve growth of vegetables (Costanzo, 2008; Murr, 1965, 1964; Ward, 1996). This could be attributed to the changes in the biophysical mechanisms. Studies have also demonstrated effects of electric fields on mineral element uptake and accumulation on vegetables (Dannehl et al., 2012; Murr, 1965, 1964; Ward, 1996; Zvitov et al., 2003). This may be attributed to changes in the enzymatic activities as well as electrolyte leakage as a result of membrane permeability (Gürsul et al., 2016). In electric current field studies, electrodes are used and therefore possibility of heavy metal accumulation. However, studies demonstrated that using metals as electrodes, resulted in slight increase in heavy metals but did not have toxic effects as the contents were within the legal regulations for human consumption (Dannehl et al., 2012). In other studies, physiological activities on vegetables were enhanced by electric fields (Montavon et al., 1987; Morris, 1980; Zvitov et al., 2003), attributed to stress related metabolic activities. Electric fields have effects on enzymatic and non-enzymatic composition of secondary plant compounds (Bratton and Henry, 1977; Dannehl et al., 2012; Dannehl et al., 2009; Gürsul et al., 2016; Montavon et al., 1988). The authors suggested that the physiological stress may result in changes in plant secondary metabolism.

Table 2.3: Summary of studies on pre-harvest application effects of electric fields on vegetables during production.

Vegetable	Type	Intensity	Effects	Reference
Glycine max (L.) Merr.	AC	1800-3600 V m^{-1}	Increased seedling length.	Costanzo, 2008
Zea mays L., *Phaseolus vulgaris* L.	AC	50 KV/1 mA	No effect on N and P levels and increased dry weight, Fe, Zn, and A contents.	Murr, 1964, 1965
Solanum lycopersicum L.	DC	6 V	Increased in dry weight, Mg, Ca, and N contents.	Ward, 1996
Cucumis sativus L., *Phaseolus vulgaris* L., *Commelina communis* L.	DC	5-20 V/0.5 kV cm^{-1}	Increase in stomatal opening, higher contents of K, Na, Ca and S in leaves.	Zvitov et al. 2003
Solanum lycopersicum L.	DC	3–7 µA	Increased peroxidase activity and indoleacetic acid in leaves while lower levels were observed in the roots.	Bratton and Henry, 1977
Pisum sativum L.	DC	9.0 V/15–20 µA	Inhibited accumulation of indoleacetic acid (auxin).	Morris, 1980
Spinacia oleracea L.	DC	10 V/12.5 µA	Increased glucose-6-phosphate dehydrogenase and peroxidase activity.	Montavon et al., 1987, 1988
Raphanus sativus L.	DC	200-1000 mA	Increased the phenolic compounds in tubers and roots.	Dannehl et al., 2009
Lepidium sativum L.	DC	200-1800 mA	Induced biosynthesis of chlorophyll, proteins, and phenolics, no significant accumulation of heavy metals was observed.	Dannehl et al., 2012
Solanum lycopersicum L.	DC	600-1200 V cm^{-1}	Increased phenylalanine ammonia lyase activity, phenolic compounds and cell membrane permeability.	Gürsul et al., 2016

2.2.1.2. Postharvest application effects of electric fields on fresh vegetables

Electric current has been reported to preserve or improve quality in vegetables even after harvest (Kharel et al., 1996). The studies on postharvest effects of electric field on fresh vegetables include biosynthesis of ethylene (Inaba et al., 1991), accumulation of bioactive compounds (Dannehl et al., 2011), morphological and physiological changes (Dymek et al., 2014; Kharel et al., 1996) (Table 2.4). Atungulu et al. (2004) reported that mechanism by which electric current could affect produce quality includes changes in physiological and secondary metabolism as well as inhibiting growth of microbial spores. Forney et al. (2001) reported that negatively charged air ions reduced growth rates of *Botrytis cinerea* Pers. and *Sclerotinia sclerotiorum* (Lib.) de Bary on fresh carrots (*Daucus carota* L.).

Table 2.4: Summary of studies on postharvest application effects of electric fields on fresh vegetables.

Vegetable	Type	Intensity	Effects	Reference
Cucumis sativus L.	DC	0.5-3.0 mA	Induced ethylene biosynthesis.	Inaba et al., 1991
Solanum lycopersicum L.	DC	100–500 mA	Increased lycopene, ß-carotene, total phenol and antioxidant content.	Dannehl et al., 2011
Capsicum annum L.	DC	15 A	Extended freshness/greenness, reduced respiration and fresh weight loss.	Kharel et al., 1996
Eruca sativa L.	DC	600 V cm^{-1}	Leaf viability and permeability were unpredictable.	Dymek et al., 2014

2.2.1.3. Postharvest application effects of electric fields on vegetables during processing

The application of electric field technology in food processing has attracted large interest. The technology has been applied in processed vegetables for improving freezing tolerance, salt diffusion, dry matter accumulation, drying efficiency, as well as secondary metabolites accumulation (Table 2.5). The results were mainly attributed to stress induction reactions as well as changes in electrolyte leakage.

From the above review, it is clear that electric fields can be applied during production, after harvest as well as for processing purposes to improve growth and yield as well as quality and safety of vegetables. It has been demonstrated that the effect of electric fields on vegetables dependents on intensity and species or even cultivar. Up to now, information on effects of electric current on quality attributes of fresh leafy vegetables especially AIVs are scant or even lacking.

Table 2.5: Summary of studies on postharvest application effects of electric fields on vegetables during processing.

Vegetable	Type	Intensity	Effects	Reference
Spinacia oleracea L.	DC	580 V cm^{-1}	Improved freezing tolerance.	Phoon et al., 2008
Apium graveolens L., *Agaricus bisporus* L. *Eleocharis dulcis* (Burm.f.) Trin. ex Hensch.	DC	658-1842 V m^{-1}	Increased salt diffusion.	Kusnadi and Sastry, 2012
Daucus carota L.	DC	1 kV cm^{-1}	Maintained their initial quality parameters (weight loss, texture and colour attributes) after thawing.	Shayanfar et al., 2014
Beta vulgaris L. subsp. *vulgaris*	DC	1.2–2.5 kV cm^{-1}	Enhanced disintegration of cells and increased dry matter content.	Eshtiaghi and Knorr, 2002
Chenopodium rubrum L., *Morinda citrifolia* L.	DC	1.6 kV cm^{-1}	Increased total amaranthin content from *Chenopodium rubrum* L. and of total anthraquinones from *Morinda citrifolia* L.	Dörnenburg and Knorr, 1993
Beta vulgaris L.	DC	1 kV cm^{-1}	Increased extractability of betalain (red pigment).	Fincan et al., 2004

2.2.2. UV-C Irradiation: impact on morphology, physiology and bioactive chemical compounds in fresh vegetables.

UV radiation constitutes that part of the electromagnetic spectrum between visible light (400-700 nm) and X-rays (0.01-10 nm). Typically, the wavelength for UV radiation ranges from 10-400 nm which is subdivided into UV-A (315–400 nm), UV-B (280–315 nm), UV-C (200–280 nm), and vacuum UV (10–200 nm) (Shama, 2007; Tobiska and Nusinov, 2000). In spite of UV radiation being potentially harmful, it is an important component of terrestrial radiation to which plants have been exposed since invading land. UV-C can detrimentally affect plant tissues which includes tissue structural damage, changes in cytomorphology and water permeability of inner epidermal cells (Rohanie and Ayoub, 2012). However, plants have evolved mechanisms to avoid and repair UV radiation damage. Therefore, it is not surprising that photomorphogenic responses and accumulation of secondary compounds on UV-C exposed vegetables are often associated with adaptations to protection against harmful radiations from UV-C by either filtering excess radiation or scavenging for free radicals. UV-C irradiation has been shown to affect DNA of microorganisms (Terry and Joyce, 2004). For this reason UV-C treatment has been used as a germicidal or mutagenic agent in controlling microorganisms in water, air and surface treatments as well as in fruits and vegetables. In addition to this direct germicidal activity, UV-C irradiation can modulate induced defence system in plants. Nevertheless, low dosages of UV-C irradiation (0.25–8.0 kJ m^{-2}) stimulated beneficial reactions in biological organs, a phenomenon known as hormesis (Shama, 2007). Therefore, it is important to distinguish hormetic UV-C treatment from conventional UV-C treatment. Conventional UV-C treatment is directed at microorganisms present on the surfaces of an object, whereas in hormetic UV-C treatment the object itself is the target of the incident UV-C. According to Shama (2007), hormesis involves the use of low dosages of potentially harmful agents directed against a living organism or living tissue in order to elicit a beneficial or protective response. This is manifested through the stimulation of anti-fungal chemical species such as phytoalexins (e.g. scoparone and resveratrol), degrading fungal cell wall enzymes (e.g. chitinases, glucanases), and accumulation of vitamins (vitamin C and E), carotenoids, and other phenolic compounds which exhibit antioxidant potential; improving the nutritional status of vegetables (Lado and Yousef, 2002). UV-C irradiation can induce the expression of defence response genes, and suppress the expression of genes involved in cell wall disassembly, and lipid metabolism (Liu et al., 2011). UV-C dosage is a critical parameter in the induction of hormetic effects in fresh produce and it is therefore essential to have precise knowledge of the dosage, or range of the dosage that induces the desired effects. UV-C treatment has a potential for commercial use as a surface treatment in leafy vegetables (Shama, 2007). Recent advances in the science and engineering of UV-C irradiation have demonstrated that UV-C treatment holds considerable promise for quality preservation or improvement and shelf life extension on vegetables. Although the use of UV-C is well established for water treatment, air disinfection, and surface decontamination, its study is still limited in vegetables especially leafy vegetables.

2.2.2.1. Pre-harvest application effects of UV-C on vegetables

Pre-harvest UV-C application affects morphology, physiology and bioactive compounds on vegetables. Studies have demonstrated application of UV-C on seeds, seedlings, mature plants as well as in in-vitro culture (Table 2.6). UV-C application may result to stress responsive mechanism being characterised by changes in mineral elements uptake as well as physiological and biochemical. However, increase in UV-C depending on plant species and variety may result in photo-oxidative damage, negatively affecting plants. Therefore, response of vegetables to UV-C depends on age of the plant at the time of application, plant species, and variety as well as UV-C intensity. This could be attributed to the difference in plant physiological stress tolerance.

2.2.2.2. Postharvest application effects of UV-C on vegetables

Morphological and physiological effects

Postharvest UV-C application affects morphology and physiology of vegetables (Table 2.7). Studies have demonstrated that UV-C may affect structural compounds and increase tissue brightness, attributed to UV-C photobleaching and tissue browning attributed to accumulation of phytochemical compounds (Allende and Artés, 2003). Allende et al. (2006) observed that increasing UV-C dosage resulted in induction of tissue softening and browning suggesting its negative effect to the produce. Costa et al. (2006) attributed pheophytin accumulation and delayed chlorophyll degradation to the changes in secondary metabolism as a photoprotection mechanism of photosynthetic apparatus against UV-C irradiation. UV-C can affect respiration rate and water loss in vegetables attributed to stress related and structural changes, respectively (Artés-Hernández et al., 2009; Burana and Srilaong, 2010; Escalona et al., 2010). Studies have also demonstrated that combining UV-C treatment with hot water treatment (Lemoine et al., 2008), or aqueous chlorine dioxide (Lee et al., 2012), or ozonised water (Huyskens-Keil et al., 2011) or modified atmosphere packaging (Tomás-Callejas et al., 2012) improved morphological and physiological properties of vegetables suggesting the compatibility and synergistic effects with other postharvest treatments. Application of UV-C can result in delayed chlorophyll degradation (Chairat et al., 2013; Khalili et al., 2017; Lemoine et al., 2008; Zhang et al., 2016). This could be attributed to the protection of the photosynthetic apparatus from oxidative damage associated with the reduction in the catabolic activities of chlorophyll degrading enzymes (chlorophyllase). Storage conditions (temperature and duration of storage) of UV-C treated vegetables may also have an influence on their morphological and physiological effects attributed to the changes in enzymatic metabolism.

Table 2.6: Summary of studies on pre-harvest UV-C application effects on vegetables.

Vegetable	Intensity/dosage	Effects	Reference
Pisum sativum L.	254 nm, 10 s to 8 min	Induced phenylalanine ammonia lyase gene promoters (PS PAL1 and PS PAL2).	Pluskota et al., 2005
Phaseolus vulgaris L., var. oratus and var. ellipticus, *Brassica oleracea* L., var. capitata alba and var. capitata rubra, *Beta vulgaris* L., *saccharifera* Alef. and ssp. *esculenta* (Salisb) Gurke, var. rubra	460, 494, and 760 µW cm^{-2}	Plant height, fresh weight, dry matter, chlorophylls, photosynthetic activity, and protein synthesis increased with reducing UV-C dosage. UV-C stimulated synthesis of ascorbic acid, carotenoids and anthocyanin contents depending on applied dosage, species and varieties.	Kacharava et al., 2009
Malva parviflora L., *Plantago major* L., *Rumex vesicarius* L. and *Sismbrium erysimoids* Desf	6 h for 6 days	Decreased chlorophylls (chlorophyll a, b, and total chlorophyll) contents while carotenoid content was increased. Increased protein content while proline content was reduced	Salama et al., 2011
Phaseolus vulgaris L.	60 min	Increased total phenolic compounds, anthocyanins content as well a non-enzymatic antioxidants (total ascorbate and total glutathione) and enzymatic antioxidant activities (superoxide dismutase, catalase, ascorbate peroxidase and glutathione reductase)	Younis et al., 2010

Table 2.7: Summary of studies on postharvest UV-C application effects on morphology and physiology of vegetables.

Vegetable	Dosage/storage conditions	Effects	Reference
Lactuca sativa L.	0, 0.4, 0.81, 2.44, 4.07, and 8.14 kJ m^{-2} 10 days at 5 °C	Increased tissue brightness and browning. Decreased growth of psychrotrophic bacteria, coliform, and yeast.	Allende and Artés, 2003
Lactuca sativa L.	0, 1.18, 2.37 and 7.11 kJ m^{-2} 10 days at 5 °C	Lower UV-C dosage extended shelf life while higher UV-C dosages induced tissue softening and browning.	Allende et al., 2006
Brassica oleracea L. var. *italica*	0, 4, 7, 10 and 14 kJ m^{-2} 6 days at 20 °C	Reduced pheophytin accumulation and delayed chlorophyll degradation, reduced chlorophyllase activity and increased Mg-chelatase activities. No tissue damage was observed.	Costa et al., 2006
Spinacia oleracia L.	0, 4.54, 7.94 and 11.35 kJ m^{-2} 13 days at 5 or 8 °C	No effect of chlorophyll contents, respiration rates while higher UV-C dosage resulted in higher water loss	Artés-Hernández et al., 2009
Brassica oleracea L. var. *italica*	0, 5, 8 and 10 kJ m^{-2} 5 days at 20 °C	Better green colour retention (delayed chlorophyll degradation), delayed yellowing, better protein retention, maintained organoleptic quality, reduced the level of reducing sugars but showed no effect on the total sugar contents.	Lemoine et al., 2008
Brassica oleracea var. *alboglabra*	0, 1.8, 3.6, 5.4 and 7.2 kJ m^{-2} 8 days at 20 °C	Inhibited chlorophyll degrading enzymes (chlorophyllase), reduced 1-aminocyclopropane-1-carboxylate oxidase activity (reduced ethylene production), and reduced respiration rate and water loss.	Burana and Srilaong, 2010
Spinacia oleracia L.	0, 2.4, 7.2, 12 and 24 kJ m^{-2} 13 days at 5 °C	Increased respiration rate, no tissue damage.	Escalona et al., 2010
Asparagus officinalis L.	1 kJ m^{-2} 4 days at 20 °C	Reduced respiration rates and increased spear tissue toughness while cell wall compounds (e.g. lignin, pectin) were not affected.	Huyskens-Keil et al., 2011
Lactuca sativa L. var. *longifolia* and *Brassica oleracea* L. var. *acephala*	10 kJ m^{-2} 7 days at 4 °C	Did not affect L*, a*, and b* values, had better scores on sensory evaluations (appearance, odour and acceptability)	Lee et al., 2012
Brassica rapa subsp. *narinosa* (L.H. Bailey) Hanelt	4.54 kJ m^{-2} 11 days at 5 °C	Did not affect total chlorophyll content while respiration rate was increased	Tomás-Callejas et al., 2012
Brassica oleracea var. *alboglabra*	0, 1.8, 3.6, 5.4 and 7.2 kJ m^{-2} 8 days at 5 °C	Delayed leaf yellowing, inhibited activities of chlorophyllase and Mg-chelatase, and reduced ethylene production and respiration rates.	Chairat et al., 2013
Brassica oleracea L. var. *italica*	0, 1.5, 4.5, or 10 kJ m^{-2} 12 days at 4 °C	Higher chlorophyll, sugar and protein retention.	Khalili et al., 2017
Brassica oleracea var. *capitata* f. *rubra*	0, 1, 3 and 5 kJ m^{-2} 12 days at 4 °C	Reduced L*, a* and b* values exhibited by darker leaf colour.	Zhang et al., 2016

Effects on secondary metabolites and antioxidative properties

Postharvest UV-C application influences secondary compounds and antioxidative properties of vegetables (Table 2.8). Application of UV-C influences the composition of carotenoids, flavonoids, glutathione and ascorbic acid in vegetables (Artés-Hernández et al., 2009; Duarte-Sierra et al., 2012; Tomás-Callejas et al., 2012; Zhang et al., 2016). The application of UV-C may result in stress related physiology hence accumulation of plant secondary compounds. Studies have demonstrated that UV-C affect accumulation of enzymatic plant compounds such as peroxidase, superoxide dismutase, catalase and ascorbate peroxidase (Chairat et al., 2013; Costa et al., 2006; Zhang et al., 2016). This could be attributed to their involvement in free radicle sequestration. UV-C application results in accumulation of reactive oxygen species (ROS) as result of UV-C oxidative damage (Zhang et al., 2016) which may negatively affect cell functioning, if threshold levels are exceeded, thus the need for quenching. Application of UV-C may also result in increasing antioxidant properties (Artés-Hernández et al., 2009; Costa et al., 2006; Khalili et al., 2017). Increasing oxidative properties associate with the accumulation of enzymatic and non-enzymatic plant secondary compounds, confirming their antioxidative activities. The composition of enzymatic and non-enzymatic plant secondary compounds as well as oxidative properties is also dependant on storage temperature and duration attributed to UV-C physiological adaptation changes, which varies with plant species and variety.

Microbiological effects

Postharvest UV-C application affects microbiological status of vegetables (Table 2.9). Studies have demonstrated that UV-C may help in the reduction of microbial growth in vegetables (Allende and Artés, 2003; Allende et al., 2006; Artés-Hernández et al., 2009; Escalona et al., 2010; Kang et al., 2013; Lee et al., 2012; Tomás-Callejas et al., 2012). The microbial inhibitions could be associated with the UV-C germicidal effects (Allende et al., 2006) while in other studies it was suggested that the reduction in microbial load could be attributed to UV-C induced accumulation of plant secondary compounds (e.g. phytoalexins), which have inhibitory effects in microbial growth (Escalona et al., 2010). UV-C had no effect on microbial growth and the authors concluded that microbial load and pathogen development are highly persistent, depending on vegetables (Hassenberg et al., 2012).

From the studies, it is clear that the effects of UV-C treatment on vegetables vary depending on the stage of species, variety/cultivar, maturity, plant organ/part, applied UV-C dosage, adaptation period and storage conditions, warranting the need for more studies as suggested by most of the authors.

Table 2.8: Summary of studies on postharvest UV-C application and their effects on secondary metabolites and antioxidative properties of vegetables.

Vegetable	Dosage/storage conditions	Effects	Reference
Brassica oleracea L. var. *italica*	0, 4, 7, 10 and 14 kJ m^{-2} 6 days at 20 °C	Delayed peroxidase activity and increased antioxidant capacity	Costa et al., 2006
Spinacia oleracia L.	0, 4.54, 7.94 and 11.35 kJ m^{-2} 13 days at 5 or 8 °C	Higher UV-C dosage reduced polyphenol and antioxidant capacity	Artés-Hernández et al., 2009
Brassica rapa subsp. *narinosa* (L.H. Bailey) Hanelt	4.54 kJ m^{-2} 11 days at 5 °C	No effect on phenolic compounds and antioxidant capacity	Tomás-Callejas et al., 2012
Brassica oleracea L. var. *italica*	0, 0.3, 0.6, 0.9, 1.2, 1.5, 3.0 and 6.0 kJ m^{-2} 30 days at 4 °C	Amino acid pools decreased with UV-C dosage	Duarte-Sierra et al., 2012
Brassica oleracea var. *alboglabra*	0, 1.8, 3.6, 5.4 and 7.2 kJ m^{-2} 8 days at 5 °C	Increased activities of peroxidase and superoxide dismutase enzymes	Chairat et al., 2013
Brassica oleracea L. var. *italica*	0, 1.5, 4.5, or 10 kJ m^{-2} 12 days at 4 °C	Increased total antioxidant capacity with increasing UV-C dosage	Khalili et al., 2017
Brassica oleracea var. *capitata* f. *rubra*	0, 1, 3 and 5 kJ m^{-2} 12 days at 4 °C	Increased activities of superoxide dismutase, peroxidase, catalase, and ascorbate peroxidase and also stimulated the accumulation of flavonoids, glutathione and ascorbic acids, and hydrogen peroxidase	Zhang et al., 2016

Table 2.9: Summary of studies on postharvest UV-C application effects on microbiological properties of vegetables.

Vegetable	Dosage/storage conditions	Effects	Reference
Lactuca sativa L.	0, 0.4, 0.81, 2.44, 4.07, and 8.14 kJ m^{-2} 10 days at 5 °C	Decreased growth of psychrotrophic bacteria, coliform, and yeast	Allende and Artés, 2003
Lactuca sativa L.	0, 1.18, 2.37 and 7.11 kJ m^{-2} 10 days at 5 °C	Inhibited growth of *Enterobacter, Erwinia, Escherichia, Leuconostoc, Pantoea, Pseudomonas, Rahnela, Salmonella, Serratia* and *Yersinia*	Allende et al., 2006
Spinacia oleracia L.	0, 4.54, 7.94 and 11.35 kJ m^{-2} 13 days at 5 or 8 °C	Decreased mesophilic and psychrophilic counts	Artés-Hernández et al., 2009
Spinacia oleracia L.	0, 2.4, 7.2, 12 and 24 kJ m^{-2} 13 days at 5 °C	Inhibited initial microbial load (psychrotrophic, Enterobacteria, *Salmonella enterica, Listeria monocytogenes,* and *Pseuomonas marginalis*)	Escalona et al., 2010
Lactuca sativa L. var. *longifolia* and *Brassica oleracea* L. var. *acephala*	10 kJ m^{-2} 7 days at 4 °C	Reduced the initial populations of total aerobic bacteria, yeast and mould. The inoculated *Escherichia coli* and *Salmonella enterica* were completely eliminated	Lee et al., 2012
Asparagus officinalis L.	1 kJ m^{-2} 4 days at 20 °C	Had no effects on mould, yeasts, and aerobic mesophilic counts	Hassenberg et al., 2012
Brassica rapa subsp. *narinosa* (L.H. Bailey) Hanelt	4.54 kJ m^{-2} 11 days at 5 °C	Inhibited epiphytic microbial growth	Tomás-Callejas et al., 2012
Brassica rapa subsp. *narinosa* (L.H. Bailey) Hanelt and *Beta vulgaris* subsp. *vulgaris*	5 kJ m^{-2} 11 days at 4 ± 1 °C	Reduced total aerobic bacteria, yeast and moulds population	Kang et al., 2013

3. Analysis of postharvest loss along the supply chain of African indigenous leafy vegetables

Gogo, E.O., Opiyo, A.M., Ulrichs, Ch., Huyskens-Keil, S., International Journal of Vegetable Science – submitted (Ref: WIJV-2017-0047).

Abstract

Due to high perishability, African indigenous leafy vegetables (AIVs) tend to suffer heavy postharvest losses. There is a lack of information regarding management of postharvest loss of these vegetables which contributes to food insecurity, poverty, slow economic growth in developing countries, and causes environmental problems. This study sought to identify, and assess, types and causes of postharvest loss in the AIVs supply chain. The study was done across the AIVs producing counties of Nakuru, Kisii and Kakamega, in Kenya, involving 45 AIVs farmers from each county. Parameters studied were socio-demographic profiles, harvesting, transportation and marketing in relation to postharvest loss. The AIV production is primarily by women who were mainly small-scale farmers. Major problems identified were inappropriate harvesting and handling techniques, inadequate postharvest treatment and preservation methods, poor roads, lack of cold storage facilities, unhygienic market conditions, and lack of implementation by regulatory bodies on AIV handling, quality and safety standards, and was affected by county and supply chain stage. Yellowing, wilting, presence of foreign bodies, mechanical damage and insect pest and disease damage were major postharvest problems along the supply chain. On average, farmers experienced loss between 10-50% with some experiencing >50%, and this varied with county and supply stage. Shorter AIV shelf life (1-2 d) is a major concern. Postharvest loss is unique for specific counties and supply chain stage, and attributed to AIV production, harvesting, handling, distribution and marketing dynamics.

3.1. Introduction

The diet in many developing countries is mostly cereal based, lacking vitamins, protein, micro-nutrients and phytochemicals, resulting in 'hidden hunger' phenomenon (McGuire, 2015). Consumption of leafy vegetables rich in these compounds is restricted due to availability, which is linked to seasonal variation and affordability. Reducing food loss and waste is a major global goal (Parfitt et al., 2010). Loss is waste of food that would otherwise feed malnourished populations, and represents a waste of human effort, farm inputs, livelihoods, investments, and scarce water (Kitinoja et al., 2011). Minimizing loss and waste of horticultural products can effectively reduce the area needed for production and/or increase food availability (Kader, 2005).

Food loss refers to decreases in edible food throughout the supply chain that specifically leads to edible food for human consumption. Food loss mainly occurring at the end of the food chain, i.e., retail and final consumption, is called food waste and is a product of retailer and consumer behaviours (FAO, 2011; Parfitt et al., 2010). About one-third of edible parts of food produced for human consumption is lost, or wasted, globally translating to a loss of about 1.3 billion tons annually (FAO, 2011, Kitinoja and Al Hassan, 2012). In developed countries, food is to a great extent thrown away even if it is still suitable for human consumption because of demand for high quality.

In developing countries, food is mainly lost during the early and middle stages of the supply chain with only limited amounts wasted at the consumption stage (FAO, 2011; Kitinoja et al., 2011). That food loss is caused by lack of appropriate preservation and postharvest treatment and cold storage facilities, lack of appropriate transportation facilities, poor roads, inappropriate packaging, insufficient market hygiene, lack of efficient food handling, quality and safety regulation standards, and insufficient stakeholder training (Hailu and Derbew, 2015). In the absence of reliable estimates of postharvest loss at the different stages, ways to evolve correct policies for minimizing loss is difficult. Without evidence of the current situation of loss, arguments over potential for reducing food loss as a contribution to mitigating food insecurity will remain largely rhetorical in developing countries.

In Kenya, unreliable postharvest loss data deny decision makers in government, donors, researchers and development agencies the opportunity to optimise efforts and strategize for food loss prevention (Ndaka et al., 2012). With changes in demographics, farming practices and consumer needs, it is important to have a holistic approach in postharvest studies. Addressing the whole postharvest system rather than its individual components is necessary, which may differ even within a country and a commodity (Ndaka et al., 2012). Postharvest loss along the value chain is inadequate with the majority of studies focusing on cereal based crops (Affognon et al., 2015; Ndaka et al., 2012). Studies regarding vegetables, especially African indigenous leafy vegetables (AIVs), have been poorly represented (Gogo et al., 2016).

AIVs are affected by heavy loss, especially after harvest, mainly due to their highly perishable nature (Gogo et al., 2016). The AIVs are currently referred to as 'underutilized species' (Virchow, 2003). Public awareness of these species has increased since they were first introduced by the Convention on Biological Diversity in 1992, and the Global Plan of Action for the Conservation and Sustainable Utilisation of Plant Genetic Resources for Food and Agriculture (Virchow, 2003). A number of organizations, including a German ministry funded project entitled "Horticultural Innovation and Learning for Improved Nutrition and Livelihood in East Africa" has focussed on investigating, and promoting, these crops as a strategy to improve livelihoods and nutrition of rural, peri-urban, and urban inhabitants in developing countries. Underutilized and neglected crops can be an alternative source of nutrients, vitamins and health promoting plant compounds in the human diet (Virchow, 2003). In most cases, these plants are adapted to local agro-ecological conditions, thrive well with minimum resources, have a comparative advantage in marginal lands, and may contribute to low-input sustainable production systems (Thompson et al., 2007). They play a role in improving living standards of resource limited communities (Maundu et al., 1999). In the past AIVs were found only in secondary markets, but have since become common in most supermarkets and municipal markets of major towns and cities, where they are sold in increasing quantities (Chelang'a et al., 2013; Onyango and Imungi, 2007).

The priority AIVs produced and marketed include African nightshades (*Solanum scabrum* Mill.), vegetable amaranth (*Amaranthus* spp.), spiderplant (*Cleome gynandra* L.), cowpea [*Vigna unguiculata* (L.) Walp], Ethiopian kale (*Brassica carinata* L.), slender leaf/rattle pod (*Crotalaria ochroleuca* G. Don. and *C. brevidens* L.), jute mallow (*Corchorus olitorius* L.) and pumpkin leaves (*Cucurbita maxima* L. and *C. moschata* L.) (Baldermann et al., 2016; Maundu et al., 1999). For most of these, scientific knowledge is rare or only beginning to emerge. AIVs have high metabolic activity after harvest and deteriorate quickly in storage. Spiderplant, African nightshade, cowpea and vegetable amaranth postharvest loss amounted to 3.1, 3.5, 4.2 and 5.5%, respectively, as a result of wilting (Onyango and Imungi, 2007). It is important that all postharvest handling operations from harvest through marketing should be given as much attention as production practices. The objective of the study was to identify and assess causes of postharvest loss along the AIV supply chain in Kenya.

3.2. Materials and methods

The study was carried out in the AIVs producing counties of Nakuru, Kisii and Kakamega in Kenya in peri-urban and urban areas, including Nakuru town and Njoro (Nakuru county), Kisii town and Keumbu (Kisii county) and Kakamega town and Kabras (Kakamega county). Nakuru, Kisii and Kakamega are cosmopolitan counties with populations of each over 1 million. The AIVs produced in these counties are distributed to municipal markets of other towns and cities. Major supermarkets, as well as other smaller supermarkets, are important outlets for AIVs especially for middle- and upper-class workers who have limited time to purchase at open-air markets.

The study involved primary and secondary data collection (Hox and Boeije, 2015). Qualitative data were obtained from focus group discussions and detailed interviews with farmers who are key actors in the AIV supply chain; quantitative data was obtained through use of questionnaires. Secondary data on AIV postharvest loss proved to be a challenge as very few institutions could sufficiently provide the required information. Quantitative data was generated through distribution of a semi-structured questionnaire (Williams, 2007) which was pre-tested, and adjusted, prior to being administered. The questionnaire targeted 45 randomly selected AIV producers from peri-urban, and urban areas, of each county identified by agricultural extension officers.

Variables collected through interviews, focus group discussions and questionnaires were divided into subsections. The first include: socio-demographic profiles of AIV farmers and recorded age, gender, marital status, education level, main occupation, and identification of the key family decision maker to better understand the social characteristics of AIV farmers (Koukouli et al., 2002). Second, AIV production acreage, main AIV produced, harvest stage, time and method, average yield, harvest operations, and causes of loss at harvest were determined. Third, AIV cropping seasons and seasonality, postharvest treatments and preservation, to include cropping seasons, seasonal gluts, season for high loss, main preservation methods, packaging, cold storage, and farmer satisfaction level on the available technologies. Fourth, AIV transportation and causes of transport loss to include: distance to market, targeted market, transportation time and mode, and causes of loss during transport. Fifth, AIV marketing and causes of market loss to include: market place, sale duration, AIV handling, grading and grading criteria, consumer satisfaction and reason for lack of satisfaction, and causes of market losses. Sixth, evaluation of AIV visual appearance (physical quality) along the supply chain to include: yellowing, wilting, presence of foreign bodies, mechanical damage and disease and insect pest damage. Seventh, to include: quantitative postharvest loss along the supply chain and AIV shelf life.

Data obtained were subjected to descriptive statistics. Results are presented as means ± standard deviations. Analysis was performed using Statistical Package for Social Sciences (ver. 23, SPSS Inc., Chicago, IL).

3.3. Results and discussion

The sociodemographic profiles of AIV farmers in the counties varied (Table 3.1). Young adults were the main age group of farmers cultivating AIVs. Fewer AIV farmers were over 56 years in all counties. This could imply that AIV farming is done by an economically active and productive population. Farmers who were directly involved in AIV cultivation were mainly female which agrees with Ayanwale and Amusan (2014) and Opiyo et al. (2015) who reported

Table 3.1: Sociodemographic profiles (%), as means ± standard deviations, of farmers cultivating African indigenous leafy vegetables in Kenya (n = 45 for each county).

Variable	Category	County Nakuru	Kisii	Kakamega
Age (years)	18-35	66.7±5.0	80.0±4.4	66.7±4.5
	36-55	26.7±4.1	20.0±4.2	26.7±2.4
	>56	6.6±0.0	0.0±0.0	6.6±0.0
Gender	Male	20.0±1.0	13.3±2.2	13.3±1.1
	Female	80.0±4.9	86.7±4.4	86.7±4.7
Marital status	Single	13.3±1.2	0.0±0.0	13.3±1.4
	Married	73.3±4.5	93.3±5.5	60.0±3.5
	Separated	6.7±0.0	6.7±0.0	13.3±0.8
	Divorced	0.0±0.0	0.0±0.0	6.7±0.0
	Widowed	6.7±0.0	0.0±0.0	6.7±0.0
Education	Limited	40.0±3.4	53.3±4.2	26.7±1.1
	Primary certificate	26.7±2.2	40.0±2.9	40.0±2.7
	Secondary certificate	26.7±2.4	0.0±0.0	20.0±1.5
	College/Diploma certificate	6.6±0.1	6.7±0.1	13.3±1.0
Occupation	Government employment	6.6±0.0	6.6±0.0	13.3±1.2
	Own/Family business	26.7±0.7	13.3±0.3	13.3±1.3
	Casual jobs	46.7±3.9	73.4±4.5	73.4±4.4
	Private sector employment	6.7±0.0	6.7±0.0	0.0±0.0
	None	13.3±0.6	0.0±0.0	0.0±0.0
Decision maker	Husband	80.0±4.5	80.0±5.5	60.0±3.2
	Wife	6.7±0.0	6.7±0.0	0.0±0.0
	Son(s)	13.3±0.6	0.0±0.0	20.0±1.2
	Daughter(s)	0.0±0.0	13.3±0.2	20.0±1.1
	Others (extended family)	0.0±0.0	0.0±0.0	0.0±0.0

the majority AIV producers were female. As a vulnerable part of society and most being housewives, this could help create job opportunities for women not currently involved in AIV production, given the increasing demand of AIVs (Muhanji et al., 2011). The majority of AIV farmers were married in the counties indicating the farmers had families who depended on either AIVs produced as food, or sales from the AIVs as a source of livelihood. In Kisii, a majority of AIV farmers had limited education (dropped out at primary level) or had attended only primary school. In Nakuru and Kakamega, a majority had a limited education and had a primary education, respectively. This implies most AIVs producers were either illiterate or semi-literate. The main occupation of the AIV farmers across all counties was casual jobs with that being the case for most in Kisii and Kakamega, than in Nakuru. Most AIV producers rarely had college or diploma certificates (education), had no job speciality or profession, and could only rely on jobs that did not require any speciality as a result; AIV production was the main source of household income

(Muhanji et al., 2011). Males (husbands) were the main decision makers indicating their importance in AIV value chain.

The land under AIV production, main AIV produced, harvesting stage, harvesting time and method, average yield, harvest operation and causes of loss at harvest varied (Table 3.2). Most AIV producers were small-scale farmers who are resource limited (Masinde et al., 2007; Muhanji et al., 2011). This has implications for the type of technologies to recommend for adoption as some may not be affordable. African nightshade was the major AIV produced across all counties, followed by vegetable amaranth. The remainder grew spider plant, cowpea, Ethiopian kale and slender leaf, jute mallow or pumpkin leaves. This could be attributed to consumer demand and preferences, especially in peri-urban and urban areas (Chelang'a et al., 2013; Muhanji et al., 2011). AIVs were mainly harvested between 4-8 weeks after sowing as previously reported by Onyango et al. (2009). This is important because it affects nutritional qualities of AIVs. Studies demonstrated varying nutritional and phytochemicals (responsible for bitterness) contents with maturity stage of AIVs (Abugre et al., 2011; Flyman and Afolayan, 2008). This indicates market demand depends on harvest stage, which also affects harvest method. Most farmers from Kisii and Kakamega preferred to harvest in the evening (between 3-6 pm), but a majority of farmers from Nakuru harvested AIVs in the morning (6 am-noon). Generally, AIVs are highly perishable and suffer wilting following harvest. Harvesting early in the morning could result in disease problems because of the presence of dew, especially during the AIV distribution. The main harvesting method across all counties was by sequential harvest. Onyango et al. (2009) reported higher yield per unit area from multiple harvests (sequential) on a single plant. This could be why most farmers preferred this method. Average yield was similar in all counties which agree with Onyango et al. (2009). Abukutsa-Onyango (2003) reported most AIV farmers used traditional production technologies, limiting production potential. A large majority of Kakamega AIV farmers preferred to sort, and tie, the produce in bundles for distribution. A majority of farmers from Kisii and Nakuru preferred to harvest, immediately take the produce to the market, and carry out postharvest operations while in the market.

The major postharvest loss at harvest was insect pests and diseases, which were highest in Kisii, followed by Kakamega and Nakuru, followed by unfavourable weather conditions, however, not different with insect pest and diseases in Kisii. Other causes of loss at harvest were lack of appropriate variety and harvest method and time. Harvest method affects yield and quality of AIVs (Wangolo et al., 2015). This could be attributed to lack of resistant varieties which are less prone to insect pest and disease attacks. Loss at harvest worsened by inadequate farmer knowledge in dealing with problems associated with climate change and harvest intensity and frequency (Shiundu and Oniang'o, 2007). AIV farmers rely on traditional seed banking from previous harvests which do not provide adequate yield, are susceptible to insect pest and disease attack and have higher loss at harvest (Adebooye et al., 2005; Gogo et al., 2016; Ojiewo et al., 2013).

Table 3.2: Production, harvest operations and causes of losses at harvest (%), as means ± standard deviations, of the main African indigenous leafy vegetables cultivated in Kenya (n = 45 for each county).

Variable	Category	County Nakuru	Kisii	Kakamega
Production area (ha)	<0.4	40.0±4.5	26.7±3.1	20.0±2.1
	0.4-0.8	46.7±4.0	60.0±6.5	53.3±4.0
	>0.8	13.3±3.5	13.3±2.0	26.7±3.6
Main AIV	Vegetable Amaranth	20.0±3.5	20.0±2.0	20.0±5.9
	African Nightshade	46.7±5.2	53.3±4.7	46.7±4.8
	Spider Plant	6.7±0.3	0.0±0.0	6.7±0.0
	Cowpea	6.7±0.0	13.3±2.4	6.7±0.2
	Ethiopian Kale	6.6±0.1	6.7±0.2	6.6±0.0
	Others (slender leaf, jute mallow, pumpkin leaves)	13.3±2.1	6.7±0.3	13.3±3.5
Harvesting stage (weeks from sowing)	<4	13.3±2.1	13.3±2.4	13.3±2.6
	4-8	86.7±4.4	86.7±4.5	80.0±6.3
	>8	0.0±0.0	0.0±0.0	6.7±1.1
Harvesting time	Morning (6 am-noon)	66.7±4.5	33.3±6.0	20.0±3.4
	Afternoon (noon-3 pm)	0.0±0.0	0.0±0.0	13.3±1.4
	Evening (3-6 pm)	33.3±4.0	66.7±4.6	66.7±9.2
Harvesting method	Uprooting[a]	20.0±2.2	13.3±0.7	13.3±0.9
	Sequential[b]	80.0±4.4	86.7±4.6	86.7±4.4
Average yield (Mt·ha^{-1})	<40	13.3±1.0	6.7±0.2	13.3±1.1
	40-60	73.3±5.6	80.0±4.9	80.0±8.2
	>60	13.3±1.4	13.3±1.0	6.7±0.5
Harvest operation	Transfer to the shade and later (>2 hours after harvest) to the market	60.0±4.3	73.3±4.7	13.3±2.1
	Transport to the market immediately	40.0±3.2	26.7±2.3	86.7±4.8
Cause of loss at harvest	Variety	0.0±0.0	0.0±0.0	6.7±1.6
	Weather, i.e., temperature, rain	46.7±3.4	0.0±0.0	13.3±0.3
	Insect pest and diseases	40.0±2.9	100.0±4.4	73.3±4.9
	Harvesting method/time	13.3±2.8	0.0±0.0	6.7±0.2

[a] harvest stage <4 weeks from sowing.
[b] harvest 4-8 weeks from sowing.

The AIV cropping seasons and seasonality, season for high loss, main postharvest treatment and preservation methods, and farmer satisfaction on available technologies varied (Table 3.3). Most AIV farmers in Kisii and Nakuru produced 3 crops a year; a majority from Kakamega produced their AIVs twice a year. Those producing 2 or 3 times were not different in Nakuru.

Table 3.3: Seasonality, postharvest treatments, and preservation (%), as means ± standard deviations, of African indigenous leafy vegetables in Kenya (n = 45 for each county).

		County		
Variable	Category	Nakuru	Kisii	Kakamega
Cropping season for AIVs	Once a year	6.7±0.2	6.6±0.8	20.0±0.2
	Twice a year	40.0±6.2	26.7±2.1	53.3±4.6
	Three times a year	53.3±7.4	66.7±3.4	26.7±0.7
Season for gluts in the market	Rainy season	86.7±4.9	93.3±7.4	86.7±6.3
	Dry season	13.3±2.1	6.7±0.9	13.3±2.1
Season for high losses	Rainy season	80.0±3.4	80.0±5.5	80.0±3.3
	Dry season	20.0±2.5	20.0±1.1	20.0±0.5
Main preservation methods	Blanching	40.0±2.8	26.7±1.3	26.7±1.6
	Sun drying (directly in the sun)	60.0±3.4	60.0±2.4	53.3±4.5
	Solar drying (using solar dryers)	0.0±0.0	13.3±3.6	13.3±2.1
	Freeze drying	0.0±0.0	0.0±0.0	6.7±0.6
Use of special packaging material	Yes	20.0±2.1	46.7±2.1	40.0±2.7
	No	80.0±3.4	53.3±2.4	60.0±3.8
Packaging type	None	0.0±0.0	6.6±0.3	0.0±0.0
	Gunny bags	73.3±2.2	66.7±4.5	60.0±2.9
	Normal polythene bags	26.7±2.4	26.7±3.2	33.3±1.8
	Special polythene bags, i.e., modified atmosphere bags	0.0±0.0	0.0±0.0	6.7±2.1
Electricity available on-farm	Yes	73.3±2.4	26.7±1.4	66.7±3.3
	No	26.7±2.3	73.3±2.1	33.3±2.4
Awareness of cold storage of leafy vegetables	Yes	93.3±8.5	86.7±2.4	86.7±4.8
	No	6.7±2.5	13.3±2.5	13.3±1.2
Satisfaction on available postharvest preservation and treatments methods	Very satisfied	20.0±0.2	0.0±0.0	26.7±1.9
	Moderately satisfied	46.7±2.6	20.0±2.3	66.7±2.9
	Not satisfied	33.3±2.4	80.0±3.5	6.6±0.2
Comments	More research	73.3±2.5	73.3±3.9	66.7±3.4
	Government support	26.7±0.3	26.7±3.4	33.3±2.1

The main cropping seasons in Kenya is during the long and short rains, between April to June and October to November, respectively (Gogo et al., 2016). Cropping under rain-fed conditions, although occasionally supplemented by irrigation, especially during short rains, is only possible for 2 seasons. Due to high demand for AIVs throughout the year, supplementary irrigation is important to ensure a supply of AIVs year round. Most AIV farmers are resource limited and cannot afford such facilities.

The majority of AIV farmers indicated that they did not use special packaging materials. This could be attributed to high cost. Farmers resorted to using gunny bags. Some farmers used conventional polyethylene bags (non-perforated) for packaging AIVs. Non-perforated polyethylene bags increases respiration resulting in heat and water accumulation. This contributes to favourable conditions for pathogen development resulting in loss of AIV quality. Nutritional quality of AIVs are better maintained using modified atmosphere packaging materials compared with non-perforated packaging and non-packaged AIVs (Mampholo et al., 2015).

The majority of AIV farmers from Nakuru and Kakamega had access to electricity, fewer from Kisii had electricity. This could be attributed to the majority of the respondents growing in the environs of peri-urban and urban centres. The Kenyan Government supports rural electrification and most citizens can afford the cost of electricity installation (Yadoo, 2012). Most AIV farmers indicated they were aware of AIV cold storage. However, they were not applying the technology due to lack of cold storage facilities and high cost of electricity. Farmers do not know the appropriate cold storage conditions for specific AIVs (Gogo et al., 2016). The number of AIV farmers satisfied with currently available postharvest treatment and preservation methods varied (Table 3.3). A majority of farmers from Kakamega and Nakuru were moderately satisfied, while most farmers from Kisii were not satisfied. Most farmers indicated there is need to conduct more research on the appropriate preservation and postharvest treatment methods. The remaining group of farmers requested government support. This could be attributed to the available methods of postharvest treatment, such as sun drying (directly in the sun), solar drying (using solar dryers) and blanching were probably ineffective, expensive, unsustainable, or farmers were not aware of how to appropriately use them.

The distance to the market, target market, transportation mode and time, and causes of loss during transportation varied (Table 3.4). The distance from the farm to the market was generally over 2 km. Farmers from Kakamega and Kisii mainly targeted major towns and cities; farmers from Nakuru targeted the surrounding community and main supermarkets. This indicates a diverse market for AIVs (Muhanji et al., 2011). The main transportation time by farmers from Kisii and Kakamega was evening (after 6 pm); the majority of farmers from Nakuru transported their produce in the morning or evening. Differences in transportation time could be due to consumer demand and targeted markets. The main mode of transport from Kisii was by vehicle (pick-ups), from Nakuru, the main transport mode was motorcycle or bicycle, while Kakamega farmers preferred bicycle, motorcycles or vehicles. Differences in mode of transport could be attributed to distance to the market and the target market. Causes of postharvest loss in Nakuru and Kisii were mainly poor roads, while in Kakamega, unfavourable weather conditions and poor roads were the main cause of postharvest loss. Other causes of loss were poor handling and insect pest and diseases which agree with Onyango and Imungi (2007).

Table 3.4: Transportation and causes of losses during transportation (%), as means ± standard deviations, of African indigenous leafy vegetable in Kenya (n = 45 for each county).

Variable	Category	County Nakuru	Kisii	Kakamega
Market distance (km)	<1	33.3±2.3	20.0±2.1	13.3±0.4
	1-2	20.0±2.9	20.0±2.2	20.0±1.2
	>2	46.7±3.4	60.0±2.5	66.7±2.3
Target market	Surrounding community	40.0±2.9	13.3±1.1	13.3±0.6
	Main supermarkets	33.3±1.4	33.3±1.5	20.0±1.1
	Major towns/cities	26.7±1.0	53.3±2.4	66.7±2.4
Transport time	Morning (6-11 am)	53.3±2.3	13.3±3.0	6.7±0.2
	Afternoon (noon-6 pm)	0.0±0.0	0.0±0.0	6.6±0.3
	Evening (>6.00 pm)	46.7±2.1	86.7±4.3	86.7±5.7
Transport mode	Pedestrian	20.0±2.3	0.0±0.0	6.7±0.6
	Bicycle	33.3±1.4	6.6±0.3	26.7±2.3
	Motorcycle	40.0±2.6	26.7±2.1	33.3±1.4
	Vehicle	6.7±0.4	66.7±5.2	33.3±1.8
Cause of loss during transport	Poor roads	73.3±3.2	80.0±3.7	33.3±0.2
	Weather, i.e., sun/heat	20.0±1.1	20.0±1.5	40.0±2.1
	Poor handling	0.0±0.0	0.0±0.0	26.7±1.3
	Insect pest and diseases	6.7±0.8	0.0±0.0	0.0±0.0

Poor AIV transportation and handling results in mechanical injuries such as bruising, surface abrasions, and cuts resulting in significant postharvest loss especially vitamin C (Lee and Kader, 2000; Mampholo et al., 2015).

The results for variables of market place, sale duration, postharvest handling during sale, grading and grading criteria, consumer satisfaction and causes of market loss varied (Table 3.5). The majority of farmers across counties indicated they directly supplied AIVs to supermarkets, hotels, schools or hospitals. Other farmers sold their vegetables at open (no shade) and closed (with temporary or permanent shade) municipal or county markets, indicating there is availability and accessibility of diversified AIV markets (Chelang'a et al., 2013). Most AIVs traded in markets were sold within a day, followed by farmers who could sale all their AIVs within 2 d. This indicates the availability of a ready market and high demand of AIVs. During sale, a majority of farmers tied their AIVs in bundles, or bunches, equivalent to 1 kg. The bunches allowed for frequent handling by consumers which could provide avenues for contamination as well as mechanical damage.

The majority of farmers indicated grading was demanded by consumers in Kisii followed by farmers in Kakamega and Nakuru who indicated similar numbers of customers did and did not require grading. The main grading criterion was external appearance, with the remainder of farmers indicating leaf size as the grading criterion. Customers mainly look at external appearance, i.e., fresh and dark green leaves, as quality indicators for AIVs (Gogo et al., 2016).

Table 3.5: Marketing and causes of market losses (%), as means ± standard deviations, of African indigenous leafy vegetables in Kenya (n = 45 for each county).

Variable	Category	County		
		Nakuru	Kisii	Kakamega
Market place	Direct supply, i.e., supermarkets, hotels, schools and hospitals	66.7±4.2	60.0±2.1	53.3±4.0
	Open market	26.7±3.1	33.3±1.0	26.7±2.2
	Closed market/Temporary shade	6.6±0.6	6.7±0.1	20.0±2.8
Sale duration	Within a day	86.7±7.2	73.3±4.5	53.3±3.6
	2 days	13.3±2.3	20.0±2.2	33.3±2.1
	>2 days	0.0±0.0	6.7±0.6	13.3±1.8
Handling at sale	Tie in small bunches (1 kg)	73.3±4.5	93.3±4.8	73.3±4.2
	Package in normal polythene bags	26.7±2.1	6.7±0.4	20.0±2.1
	Package in special polythene bags[a]	0.0±0.0	0.0±0.0	6.7±0.6
Grading demand by customer	Yes	53.3±1.6	73.3±4.1	46.7±2.2
	No	46.7±2.3	26.7±2.2	53.3±3.5
Grading criteria	General appearance	93.3±6.2	66.7±4.7	86.7±4.5
	Leaf size	6.7±0.3	33.3±2.2	13.3±0.4
Consumer satisfaction	Very satisfied	0.0±0.0	13.3±1.1	20.0±1.1
	Moderately satisfied	66.7±4.5	46.7±2.2	80.0±6.5
	Not satisfied	33.3±2.1	40.0±1.4	0.0±0.0
Reason for lack of satisfaction	Yellowing/discolouration	40.0±2.3	26.7±2.1	60.0±3.1
	Wilting	60.0±3.5	66.7±4.5	40.0±1.4
	Dirt/hygiene	0.0±0.0	6.7±0.2	0.0±0.0
Remaining AIVs	Sell the following day	40.0±2.1	46.7±2.3	33.3±2.1
	Family consumption	53.3±3.4	40.0±3.3	53.3±3.8
	Feed to livestock	0.0±0.0	6.7±0.6	6.7±0.4
	Throw away	6.7±0.4	6.7±0.4	6.7±0.2
Cause of market loss	Poor handling	6.7±0.1	6.6±0.6	0.0±0.0
	Market hygiene	0.0±0.0	26.7±2.2	6.7±0.6
	Poor Packaging	20.0±1.1	26.7±2.5	26.7±2.1
	Lack of cold storage facilities	40.0±2.1	13.3±1.5	13.3±1.2
	Lack of buyers/consumers	33.3±1.4	26.7±1.7	53.3±2.3

[a] with perforation.

The majority of farmers indicated their customers were moderately satisfied with the grading criteria and the overall quality of the AIVs. There is a need to improve, or maintain, the quality of AIVs to meet consumer demands along the supply chain (Onyango and Imungi, 2007). The main reason for lack of consumer satisfaction was wilting in Kisii and Nakuru, while the majority of farmers from Kakamega indicated yellowing (discoloured AIVs) was the main reason for lack of consumer satisfaction. Some farmers from Kisii indicated hygiene to be a concern. This could be attributed to lack of cold storage facilities, inappropriate packaging, and handling in the market. In case of the remaining AIVs, the majority of farmers across all counties indicated that they would use it for family consumption, while in Kisii; a similar majority indicated they would sell it the following day. Others indicated they used remaining AIVs to feed livestock; some indicated they discarded the remaining AIVs. The main cause of postharvest market loss in Nakuru were lack of cold storage facilities, lack of buyers, and poor packaging. In Kisii, farmers indicated that most market loss was due to market hygiene, poor packaging and lack of buyers, and lack of cold storage facilities. Lack of buyers could be attributed to seasonal gluts of AIVs during which buyers have a lot to choose from, and some sellers supply AIVs to consumers at their door steps. Improving distribution and preservation could help reduce postharvest loss (Wafula et al., 2016). Major postharvest issues that occurred were: yellowing, wilting, presence of foreign bodies, mechanical damage, disease and insect pest damage (Figure 3.1). In all counties, the majority of farmers indicated that problems of leaf quality were based on visual appearance which increased along the supply chain. The majority of farmers from Kisii and Nakuru, and a large minority from Kakamega, indicated there were no signs of leaf yellowing at harvest (Figure 3.1A). Some farmers reported that <10% of their AIVs were yellow at harvest. Before the AIVs were transported, most farmers indicated no vegetables were yellow. In Kakamega, some farmers indicated that <10% of their AIVs were yellow before transportation. The problem of AIV leaf yellowing increased during transport. Similarly, AIV leaf yellowing was a problem at the market as the majority of farmers indicated that <10% of their AIVs were yellow in markets. Problems of leaf yellowing could be attributed to poor packaging along the supply chain.

Leaf wilting was a major problem (Figure 3.1B). At harvest, and before transport, the majority of farmers from all counties indicated that <10% of their vegetables were wilted. Wilting became a major problem during transportation, and at the market, with the majority of farmers indicating between 10-50% of their AIVs wilting at these stages. In Nakuru, a majority reported wilting after transportation and at market; in Kisii most reported wilting after transportation and at market, and in Kakamega most reported wilting after transport and at the market; some indicated most AIVs to be wilted at these advanced stages in the supply chain. Leaf wilting could be attributed to exposure of AIVs to wind during transport in open vehicles causing them to dry out, or lack of cold storage facilities along the AIV supply chain. With the absence of cold storage, poor handling and lack of appropriate packaging these vegetables tend to have high water loss resulting in wilting symptoms.

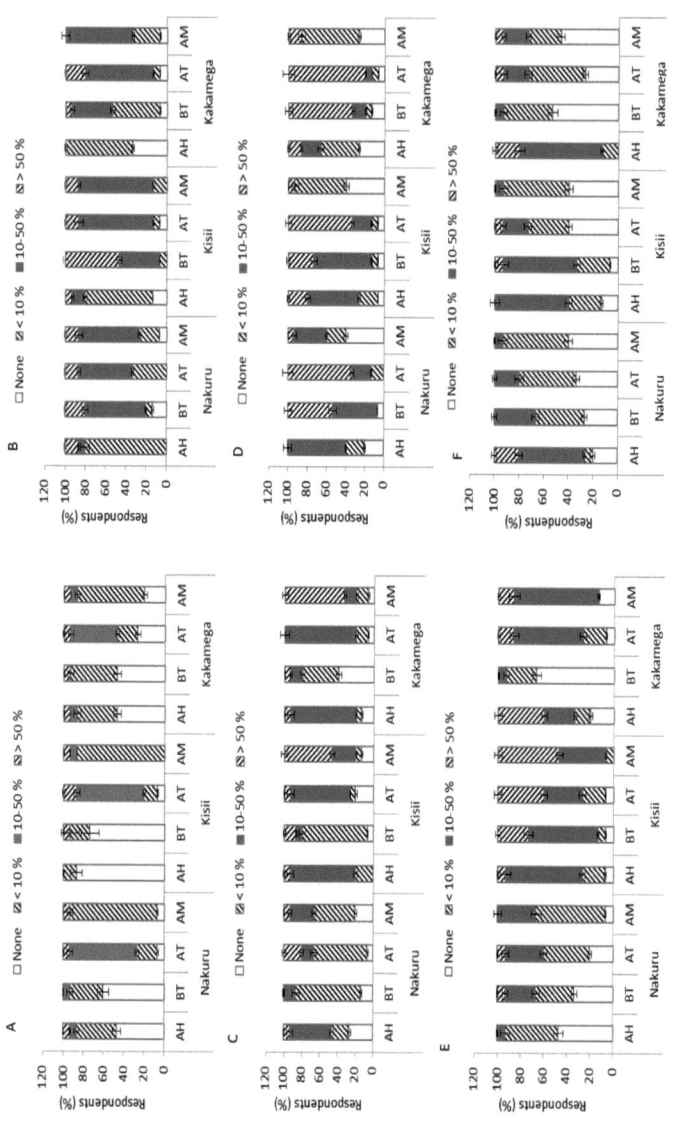

Figure 3.1: Postharvest evaluation on the visual appearance (A = Yellowing, B = Wilting, C = Foreign bodies, D = Mechanical damage, E = Disease damage, and F = Insect pest damage) of African indigenous leafy vegetables along the supply chain in Kenya. AH = At harvest, BT = Before transport, AT = After transport and AM = At the market. Values represent means±standard deviations, (n =45 for each county).

Presence of foreign bodies was another issue in the AIVs supply chain (Figure 3.1C). At harvest, the majority of farmers indicated a significant amount of foreign bodies in the AIVs. Before transport, the majority of farmers indicated <10% presence of foreign bodies in their AIVs. This reduction is probably due to sorting and grading done based on physical appearance. During transport, and at the market, foreign bodies were mainly dust and dirt. This could be attributed to poor handling, poor packaging and poor roads during transportation as well as unhygienic conditions in the market. At the market, many farmers indicated that selling their AIVs tied in bundles exposed vegetables to dust and this is worsened by customers frequently handling vegetables with bare hands.

AIV farmers indicated that mechanical damage was a problem in the AIV supply chain. Mechanical damage was a problem throughout the supply chain with various levels of damage reported. During transport, and at the market, AIVs had mechanical damage problems as indicated by a majority of farmers (Figure 3.1D). Mechanical damage along the supply chain could be attributed to poor roads and poor handling throughout the supply chain. Mechanical damage has been reported to accelerate senescence, breakage and bruising providing entry points to pathogen attack (Hodges et al., 2011; Kitinoja et al., 2011).

Disease and insect pest damage were problems in the AIV supply chain. The majority of disease problems were due to bacterial soft rot (*Erwinia* spp.) and grey mould (*Botrytis cinerea*), while most insect pest problems were due to aphids (*Aphis* spp.), white flies (*Trialeurodes vaporariorum*), flea beetles (*Phyllotreta* spp.), and red spider mites (*Tetranychus urticae*). The disease problem advanced along the supply chain and is attributed to inadequate handling and improper packaging. Disease problems may be present at harvest but not visible until later stages in the supply chain due to high temperature and relative humidity, enhancing their development (Bhat et al., 2010). At harvest, and before transport, the majority of farmers indicated that their vegetables were not affected by diseases and insect pests with some indicating disease and insect damage of <10% in all counties. During transport, and at market, disease problems increased (Figure 3.1F), while insect pest damage remained relatively constant for the majority of farmers (Figure 3.1E). This could be due to higher incidences of mechanical damage as a result of poor handling providing avenues for disease as well as poor hygienic conditions and packaging. Farmers tend to sprinkle water on their AIVs, especially in markets, to maintain leaf freshness (turgidity). This treatment increases relative humidity, and coupled with high temperatures, may encourage disease development (Gogo et al., 2016). Banach et al. (2015) stated that using water to wash vegetables, without considering its quality, is an entry point for contamination resulting in postharvest loss.

The majority of farmers from Nakuru and Kisii indicated that they experienced <10% of loss at harvest; farmers from Kakamega indicated higher loss at harvest (Figure 3.2). This could be attributed to differences in harvest time and methods. During transport, the majority of farmers

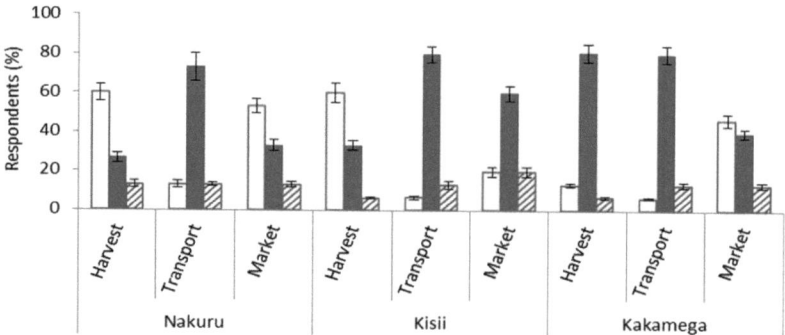

Figure 3.2: Assessment of postharvest loss of African indigenous leafy vegetables along the supply chain in Kenya. Values represent means ± standard deviations, (n = 45 for each county).

indicated they experienced a higher rate of loss (10-50%). Most farmers from Nakuru and Kakamega indicated they experienced <10% of loss at the market; Kisii farmers indicated higher losses. Less than 10% of loss occurring at the market was reported by most farmers from Nakuru and Kakamega, followed by Kisii farmers. Generally, farmers indicated loss in the entire supply chain to be over 50%. Most farmers indicated their AIVs had a shelf life of between 1-2 d (Figure 3.3). Postharvest loss, and shorter shelf life of AIVs along the supply chain, is attributed to lack of improved varieties, insect pest and diseases, poor harvesting techniques, poor handling, inappropriate packaging, lack of cold storage facilities, poor roads, and unhygienic market conditions.

AIVs contribute to nutritional and economic issues in sub-Saharan Africa. The study evaluated AIV postharvest loss and causes of loss along the supply chain. Postharvest loss was unique for specific counties and supply chain stage, and due to AIV production, harvest, handling, distribution and marketing dynamics.

Acknowledgment

The study was made possible by support of the German Government from the Federal Ministry of Education and Research and the Federal Ministry of Economic Cooperation and Development within the framework of the program GlobE (Global Food Security). This study was completed under the project "Horticultural Innovations and Learning for Improved Nutrition and Livelihood in East Africa". We thank Egerton University, Kenya for supporting the survey.

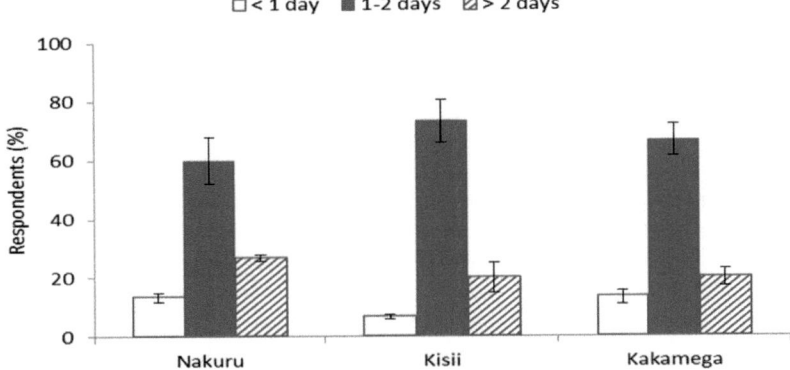

Figure 3.3: Shelf life of African indigenous leafy vegetables under farmers' ambient conditions in Kenya. Values represent means ± standard deviations, (n = 45 for each county).

4. Nutritional and economic postharvest loss analysis of African indigenous leafy vegetables along the supply chain in Kenya

Gogo, E.O., Opiyo, A.M., Ulrichs, Ch., Huyskens-Keil, S., 2017. Postharvest Biology and Technology 130, 39-47. http://dx.doi.org/10.1016/j.postharvbio.2017.04.007.

Abstract

Over the last decade, African indigenous leafy vegetables (AIVs) such as African nightshade (*Solanum scabrum* Mill.*)* have featured increasingly in both formal and informal markets in the peri-urban and urban centres of Africa, due to the increasing awareness of their nutritive and medicinal as well as expanding economic value. AIVs are rich in nutritional and health promoting plant compounds such as vitamins, minerals, proteins, dietary fibre and antioxidant compounds. However, the crop is highly perishable and more than half of it is lost before it reaches the consumer. In Kenya, appropriate postharvest handling and treatments, storage or refrigeration facilities are lacking. More so, the information on postharvest losses of the AIVs is limited, making the management of such losses along the supply chain very difficult. The objective of the study was to determine nutritional and economic losses of African nightshade plants along the supply chain, i.e. from producer until marketing. The study was conducted in the three main commercial AIVs producing counties in Kenya, i.e. Nakuru, Kisii and Kakamega, where three farmers from each county were randomly selected. The farmers were allowed to carry out their normal routine AIVs handling procedure right from harvesting to selling; and samples were collected at each supply chain stage (at harvest, before transport, after transport and at the market). Dry matter, selected macro-nutrients (N, P, K, Ca and Mg) and micro-nutrients (Fe and Zn), protein, carotenoids and chlorophyll content, cumulative produce and economic losses as well as the causes of losses were evaluated. The results obtained revealed significant quantitative, nutritive, and economic losses of African nightshade along the supply chain. The dry matter content was reduced by between 32.8-45.5%, depending on the county, along the supply chain. The mineral elements and protein were reduced by between 3.2-29.4%, while chlorophylls and carotenoids were reduced by between 70.9-90.9% and 70.4-91.9%, respectively. Cumulative produce loss was between 71.8-292.4% while the economic loss was between 12.6-34.4%. The findings indicate the immense losses of nutritional, quantitative and economic values of African nightshade along the supply chain. Lack of certified seed varieties, unfavourable weather, inadequate postharvest handling practices and technologies as well as insect pest and diseases are the main causes of losses during the supply chain. Therefore, maintaining quality attributes and managing postharvest losses in AIVs could be among the key issues to improving food security in developing countries.

4.1. Introduction

The main global challenge is how to feed over 9.1 billion people with qualitative valuable and safe food by the year 2050 (Parfitt et al., 2010). While considerable attention is geared towards increasing food production by 70% to meet this target, one important and complementary factor that is often forgotten is reducing food loss and waste (Hodges et al., 2011). More alarmingly, evidence suggests that postharvest losses tend to be highest in developing countries like Kenya who is highly dependent on a sufficient food access (Onyango et al., 2009). Under these circumstances, in a malnutrition and increasingly competitive world, reducing postharvest food losses is a major agricultural goal. In fact, investments made to manage food loss after harvest are usually less costly for the grower and the consumer and less harmful to the environment than efforts to increase production (Kitinoja and AlHassan, 2012). Even a partial reduction in postharvest losses can significantly reduce the overall cost of production and lessen dependence on marginal land and other scarce resources (Kader, 2005).

Estimation of postharvest loss is by tracking or indirect estimates via surveys by actors in the supply chain who experienced the losses (Hodges et al., 2011). While the direct measurement by tracking approach may focus only on discarded quantitative losses, the estimate by survey approach may not give true representative values because of the possibility of either underestimating or overestimating actual losses. Currently, an up to date database on postharvest handling and loss management practices is a major problem in small-scale farming systems of developing countries like Kenya, who form the majority of producers (Gogo et al., 2016). Postharvest losses consist of quantitative, qualitative and economic losses. Qualitative losses occur as a result of either altered physical condition, perceived substandard value, deterioration in texture, wilting, flavour, change in colour, and or nutritional value, whereas quantitative losses refers to physical losses of food as unacceptable for human consumption and hence readily discarded; while economic loss is the loss in monetary value (Hailu and Derbew, 2015; Hodges et al., 2011).

It has been reported that the food insecurity situation has worsened in Sub-Saharan Africa since 1970, where the percentages of malnourished people remains high, at around 35 % with absolute numbers increasing annually due to population growth (Rosegrant et al., 2005). The situation is not different in Kenya with both poverty and, in particular, food insecurity being major developmental problems. About 56% of Kenyans live below the poverty line and about 50.6% of the population lack access to adequate food; moreover, even the little they get is of poor nutritional value and quality, resulting to serious micronutrient deficiency problems (especially vitamins, Fe and Zn), the so called 'hidden hunger' (Irungu et al., 2007; McGuire, 2015). Accordingly, this translates to socioeconomic consequences which lead to the enactment of the Kenyan food security policy. The main aim of the Kenyan food security policy, as stated in vision 2030, is to ensure that an adequate supply of nutritionally balanced food is available in all parts of the country at all times (Abukutsa-Onyango, 2003; FAO, 2011). As acknowledged in this policy, indigenous foods including African indigenous leafy vegetables

(AIVs) and reduction in postharvest losses would contribute immensely to the alleviation of these problems without necessarily increasing production, both as a source of income and as a nutritional food component (Habwe et al., 2008; Kitinoja et al., 2011).

For many years, the use and hence the commercialisation of AIVs have remained low despite their nutritive value and potential economic use. Their commercialisation has only begun to gain prominence recently in the Kenyan markets and especially in the urban and peri-urban centres (Brückner and Caglar, 2016; Chelang'a et al., 2013). However, available AIVs cannot meet the consumption demand being attributed to their seasonality and heavy postharvest losses (Gogo et al., 2016). Hence, promoted marketing, consumption and most importantly improved postharvest handling of AIVs that are well adapted to the agro-ecological conditions would go a long way in ensuring food security (Shiundu and Oniang'o, 2007). Minimizing postharvest losses of horticultural perishables is a very effective way of reducing the area needed for production and increasing food availability (Kader, 2005). AIVs domesticated in Africa, including African nightshade (*Solanum scabrum* Mill.) have been known to be rich in micronutrients such as iron and carotenoids (vitamin A) (Mampholo et al., 2016), possess antibiotic, probiotic and prebiotic properties (Chege et al., 2014; Kinyuru et al., 2012), and contain antioxidants and phytochemicals that contribute to protect people against carcinogenic diseases, high blood pressure and diabetes (Kimiywe et al., 2007). However, after harvest, AIVs are prone to deterioration due to their high perishability nature and high surface area to volume ratio. Faster rate of physical and biochemical changes resulting in loss of weight, colour, texture and nutritional value have been reported to be the most critical bottleneck that hampers this lucrative industry (Gogo et al., 2016). Therefore, reducing such losses after harvest is important for sustainable agricultural development and increasing food availability (Karki et al., 2016; Mampholo et al., 2016). Onyango and Imungi (2007) reported a loss of 3.1%, 3.5%, 4.2% and 5.5% for spider plant (*Cleome gynandra* L.), African nightshade, cowpea (*Vigna unguiculata* (L.) Walp) and vegetable amaranth (*Amaranthus* spp.), respectively as a result of excessive wilting alone, in Nairobi (Kenya) groceries. In a study done in Kenya on potato value chain, losses were reported to be 12.0% during harvest, 0.8% during storage, 8.8% during handling and transportation, 15.6% during sorting, 12.0% during processing and 25.0% as a result of quality loss (Kaguongo et al., 2014). Based on these results, it was concluded that there is a pressing need for more quantitative evidence of the actual level and nature of postharvest loss on such commodities (Onyango and Imungi, 2007). The present study sought to evaluate quantitative and qualitative postharvest losses, i.e. cumulative produce loss, nutritive loss (selected mineral elements and protein), carotenoids and chlorophyll losses as well as economic loss of African nightshade plants along the supply chain.

4.2. Material and methods

4.2.1. Study site and plant material

The study was conducted in the three main commercial AIVs producing counties in Kenya (Nakuru, Kisii and Kakamega) between March and April, 2016. The sites were selected due to their distinct characteristics in the distribution of African nightshade plants to the peri-urban and urban centres of Kenyan cities. African nightshade plant was chosen based on the initial survey that revealed the vegetable to be the most commonly produced and traded in all the studied counties (Gogo et al., 2016). With the support of agricultural extension officers and farmers, African nightshade used for the study was of the same variety (*Solanum scabrum* Mill. cv. Olevolosi) and same harvesting stage (42 d from sowing). Moreover, this was the most preferred variety by the consumers in peri-urban and urban dwellers due to its sweet taste (and lack of bitter taste).

4.2.2. Characteristics of farmers and experimental design

The farmers selected from Nakuru were mainly supplying their AIVs to a major supermarket (Ukwala) in Nakuru town that had cold storage facilities for vegetables. Distance from farmer's field to the supermarket was approximately 10 km. AIVs for this market were tied in bundles, packaged in baskets and transported on a motorbike. AIVs farmers from Kisii mainly sold their produce to Nakuru county closed market under ambient conditions. Distance from farmer's field to the market was approximately 210 km. AIVs were packed in gunny bags and transported in a pick-up vehicle. AIVs farmers from Kakamega county sold their vegetables at Kakamega county open market under ambient conditions. Distance from farmer's field to the market was approximately 5 km. AIVs were tied in bundles, packaged in 10 kg polythene bags and transported on a bicycle. Three farmers from each county were randomly selected. Each of these farmers served as a replicate.

4.2.3. Sample collection and preparation

At each stage of the supply chain (at harvest, before transport, after transport and at the market), samples were collected for analysis (nutritive and qualitative analysis). At every stage, 0.5 kg samples were collected and immediately deep frozen in liquid nitrogen to stop further biochemical reactions, then packed and transported in ice boxes and stored in a deep freezer (-20 °C) for later compound analysis. An aliquot of 1 g fresh weigh sample from each replicate was used for the analysis of carotenoids and chlorophylls while another 50 g was used for the dry matter determination. The remaining samples were lyophilized, ground, mixed to a fine homogenized powder, and stored in a desiccator for mineral and protein analysis.

4.2.4. Data collection

Data (or samples) were collected at harvest, before transport, after transport and in the market of each county site. Owing to the large quantity of harvestable yield, approximately 50 kg samples were used for the evaluation and were treated similarly with the remaining vegetables throughout the supply chain. From each farmer, data were collected three times at one day interval for each weekly harvesting period, for two weeks.

4.2.4.1. Microclimate characteristics

Temperature (°C) and relative air humidity (%) was monitored during the AIV supply chain. Data loggers (WatchDog 2475; Spectrum Technologies Inc., USA) were used to collect climatic data (temperature and relative humidity) which was recorded at 10 min interval during AIV handling along the supply chain.

4.2.4.2. Causes of postharvest losses

The causes of postharvest losses of the AIV were determined through semi-structured questionnaires, interviews, focused group discussions and observations. This involved mainly farmers who were the key actors in the supply chain.

4.2.4.3. Determination of cumulative produce loss

At each stage of supply chain, cumulative produce loss was computed based on the total weight after harvest and subsequently weighing only those leaves considered sellable by farmers at each supply chain stage. Cumulative produce loss was computed to the ratio of loss and total harvested weight and expressed as percentage.

4.2.4.4. Dry matter determination

To determine the DM, fresh samples were placed in a drying oven at 105 °C for 24 h until constant weight was achieved. The dry matter percentage was calculated by the ratio of the dry matter to the fresh weight and expressed as percentage. Dry matter was determined for both fresh and lyophilized samples.

4.2.4.5. Analysis of mineral elements by inductively coupled plasma-atomic emission spectroscopy (ICP-AES)

The analysis of mineral composition (P, K, Ca, Mg, Fe and Zn) of African nightshade leaves was performed using the modified method of Babalola and Akinwande (2014) by ICP-AES on wet digested samples. Duplicate aliquots of approximately 1 g of the previously homogenised samples were digested with 10 mL of 65% HNO_3 in a tightly closed screw cap glass tubes for 16 h at room temperature, and then for a further 4 h at 90 °C. For the analysis of K and P, 1 mL of the mineralised solution was added to 8 mL of deionised water and 1 mL of 1 g L^{-1} scandium solution as internal standard. In order to determine the levels of Ca, Mg, Fe, and Zn, 3 mL of the digested solution was added to 6 mL of deionised water and 1 mL of 1 g L^{-1} scandium solution. The instrumental analysis was performed using atomic emission spectrometer (Optima 2000™ DV ICP, PerkinElmer Inc., USA). Instrument operating conditions were: radiofrequency power, 1400 W; plasma gas flow, 15.0 L min^{-1}; auxiliary gas flow, 0.2 L min^{-1}; nebulizer gas flow 0.75 L min^{-1}, crossed flow; standard axial torch with 2.0 mm injector of silica; peristaltic pump flow, 1 mL min^{-1}; no. of replicates, 2. The spectrometer was calibrated for Ca, Mg, Fe, and Zn determinations (at 393.4, 279.6, 238.2 and 213.9 nm, respectively) with nitric acid/water (1:1, v:v) standard solutions of 2, 5 and 10 mg L^{-1} of each element, and for P and K (at 213.6 and 766.5 nm, respectively) with nitric acid/water (1:9, v:v) standard solutions of 30, 50 and 100 mg L^{-1}. Results obtained were expressed as g kg^{-1} for macro-elements and mg kg^{-1} for micro-elements, on dry matter basis of the lyophilized samples.

4.2.4.6. Analysis of total N and protein

Total N was determined by Kjeldahl method (Persson et al., 2008), where plant samples were digested using a wet oxidation process in 96% H_2SO_4 which was later subsequently distilled and received in boric acid indicator. This was achieved by digesting approximately 1 g of the lyophilized finely grounded plant samples in a 10 mL 96% H_2SO_4 for 3 h. Selenium salt mixture (selenium prodder, $CuSO_4$ and K_2SO_4) was added to bring the digestion temperature to 400 °C. The digest was allowed to cool and then transferred to 100 mL volumetric flask and filled with distilled water. A 10 mL of the digested plant material was then distilled after adding 46% NaOH solution and received in a mixture of 1% H_3BO_3 and mixed indicator (methylred and bromocresol green). Subsequently, the distillate was titrated in a 0.1 N H_2SO_4. Total N was calculated using the formulae:

$$Total\ N\ (\%) = \left(\frac{V \times N \times 14 \times 100}{a \times b}\right) \times 100$$

Where V is the volume of the acid used in titration, N is the normality of the acid, and a and b are mL of the digest and weight of the sample used for the analysis, respectively. Protein was then determined by multiplying N by the factor 6.25. The results were expressed as g kg^{-1}, on dry matter basis of the lyophilized samples.

4.2.4.7. Analysis of chlorophylls and carotenoids

Extraction and determination of the chlorophylls and carotenoids was conducted according to the method described by Goodwin and Britton (1988). An aliquot of 0.5 g fresh frozen material was homogenized with acetone/hexane (4:5, v:v) for 1 min and centrifuged for 10 min (1789 ×g). The procedure was repeated twice. The supernatants were collected in a 25 mL volumetric flask and brought to volume with the same acetone/hexane mixture. Three replications of the sample were measured twice with a UV-Vis spectrophotometer (UV-Mini-1240, Shimadzu, Japan) at the following wavelengths: 450 nm (total carotenoids), as well as

663 nm and 645 nm for chlorophyll a and b which was subsequently summed up to get total chlorophyll content, respectively. Total carotenoids and chlorophylls were calculated by the formula described by Goodwin and Britton (1988). Results were expressed as g kg^{-1}, on dry matter basis of the fresh samples.

$$Total\ carotenoids = (450 \times V \times 4)/FW$$

Where E450 is the absorbance at 450 nm, V is the volume of the solution (25 ml), 4 is a constant and FW is the fresh weight of the sample

$$Chlorophyll\ a = \{(10.1 \times E663) - (10.1 \times E665) \times V\}/FW$$

$$Chlorophyll\ b = \{(16.4 \times E665) - (1.01 \times E663) \times V\}/FW$$

Where E663 and E645 is the absorbance of chlorophyll a and b respectively, V is the volume of the solution and FW is the fresh weight of the sample

4.2.4.8. Economic loss determination

Since cumulative produce loss affects profitability, it was projected on per hectare basis and used to calculate economic loss. In the computation average yield of African nightshade plants (50 t ha^{-1}) and unit cost of African nightshade plants (KES 25.00 per kg/Euro 0.23 per kg) were taken into account. Economic loss was then computed using the formula:

$$Economic\ loss\ per\ ha\ (KES/€) = Loss\ per\ ha\ (kg) \times Price\ per\ kg\ (KES/€)$$

4.2.5. Data Analysis

The univariate procedure of SAS (version 9.1; SAS Institute, Cary, NC, USA) was used to check for normality of the data before analysis. Data were then subjected to analysis of variance (ANOVA) using the GLM at $p < 0.05$. Means for significant treatments, at the F test, were separated using Tukey's honestly significant difference (Tukey's HSD) test at $p < 0.05$. Data are presented in graphs and tables as means ± standard deviations. Data on causes of losses was analysed for descriptive statistics where frequency distributions were determined and presented as a percentage.

4.3. Results

4.3.1. Microclimate conditions along the supply chain of African nightshade plants

Throughout the supply chain, data on temperature and relative air humidity were recorded (Table 4.1). Both temperature and relative air humidity did not differ markedly along the supply chain and in all the counties except at Nakuru market where temperature was lower and relative humidity higher. In Nakuru, temperature and relative humidity varied between 10.6-23.7 °C and 60.2-79.3%, depending on supply chain stage with highest temperature and lowest relative air humidity being recorded during transportation while lowest temperature and highest relative air humidity were observed at the market. Temperature and relative humidity in Kisii African nightshade supply chain had a slight variation of between 21.7-24.6 °C and 60.6-64.2%, respectively. A similar slight variation was recorded in Kakamega supply chain with temperature and relative humidity varying between 22.9-24.2 °C and 62.9-64.8%, respectively.

4.3.2. Causes of postharvest losses of African nightshade leaves along the supply chain

The major causes of postharvest losses at harvest were reported to be the insect pest and diseases at 100.0, 73.3, and 40.0% from Kisii, Kakamega and Nakuru, respectively. This was closely followed by unfavourable weather conditions. Other causes of losses at harvest reported were lack of appropriate variety and harvesting method and time. All respondents indicated weather to be the main cause of losses before transport. However, it was also observed that farmers took a long time after harvest before transporting their vegetables to the market while being left at ambient conditions. Main causes of postharvest losses during transportation were mainly poor roads as indicated by 80.0% and 73.3% of the farmers from Kisii and Nakuru, respectively followed by unfavourable weather conditions (20.0 %).

Table 4.1: Weather conditions during the supply chain evaluation of African nightshade leaves from the main producing counties in Kenya.

	Nakuru**		Kisii***		Kakamega****	
	Temperature (°C)	Relative Humidity (%)	Temperature (°C)	Relative Humidity (%)	Temperature (°C)	Relative Humidity (%)
At harvest	23.3±2.1*	62.7±4.1	24.6±1.9	60.6±3.1	23.2±2.1	64.8±2.7
Before Transport	22.5±1.5	61.3±2.4	23.2±1.8	64.2±2.7	24.1±1.6	63.5±1.9
During Transport	23.7±2.6	60.2±3.5	23.8±3.8	60.7±4.9	22.9±3.1	62.9±2.4
In the Market	10.6±1.5	79.3±3.6	21.7±1.1	62.8±2.2	24.2±2.7	63.9±2.8

*Means ± standard deviations.
**AIVs from Nakuru were sold at supermarket under cold storage conditions. Distance from farmer's field to the supermarket was approximately 10 km (30 min). AIVs were tied in bundles, packaged in baskets and transported in a motorbike.
***AIVs from Kisii were sold in the Nakuru county closed market under ambient conditions. Distance from farmer's field to the market was approximately 210 km (3 h). AIVs were package in gunny bags and transported in a pick-up vehicle.
****AIVs from Kakamega were sold at Kakamega county open market under ambient conditions. Distance from farmer's field to the market was approximately 5 km (30 min). AIVs were tied in bundles (1 kg), packaged in 10 kg polythene bags and transported in a bicycle.

However, in Kakamega, unfavourable weather conditions (40.0%) were reported to be the main cause of postharvest losses followed by poor roads (33.3%). Other causes of losses were poor handling and insect pest and diseases. The main cause of postharvest market losses in Nakuru were lack of cold storage facilities (40.0%), followed by lack of buyers (33.3%) and poor packaging (20.0%), while 26.7%, of farmers from Kisii indicated that majority of market losses were due to market hygiene, poor packaging and lack of buyers (consumers), followed by lack of cold storage. Majority of the farmers from Kakamega (53.3%) indicated lack of buyers to be the main cause of market losses which occurred mainly during the rainy season resulting in market gluts, while the remaining farmers indicated poor handling and packaging as causes of market losses (Table 4.2).

4.3.3. Cumulative produce loss and dry matter of African nightshade leaves along the supply chain

Dry matter content and cumulative produce loss of African nightshade plants were significantly influenced along the supply chain. Generally, dry matter was reduced by 32.8, 38.4, and 45.5% from Nakuru, Kisii and Kakamega; respectively while cumulative produce loss increased by 292.4, 174.1, and 73.8% from Kisii, Nakuru and Kakamega, respectively along the supply chain.

Table 4.2: Causes of postharvest losses (%) of African nightshade leaves during supply from the main producing counties in Kenya (n = 45).

Supply chain stage	Causes of losses	County		
		Nakuru	Kisii	Kakamega
Harvest	Variety	40.0	100.0	73.3
	Weather (temperature, rain.....)	46.7	0.0	13.3
	Insect pest and diseases	0.0	0.0	6.7
	Harvesting method/time	13.3	0.0	6.7
Transportation	Poor roads	73.3	80.0	33.3
	Weather i.e. sun/heat	20.0	20.0	40.0
	Poor handling	0.0	0.0	26.7
	Insect pest and diseases	6.7	0.0	0.0
Market	Poor handling	6.7	6.6	0.0
	Market hygiene	0.0	26.7	6.7
	Poor packaging	20.0	26.7	26.7
	Lack of cold storage facilities	40.0	13.3	13.3
	Lack of buyers/consumers	33.3	26.7	53.3

Cumulative produce loss of African nightshade plants was reduced significantly along the supply chain in all the studied counties except from Kakamega where no statistical differences in cumulative produce loss were observed during transportation until marketing (Figure 4.1A).

Among the counties, there were no significant differences in cumulative produce losses at harvest of African nightshade. During transportation, cumulative produce loss of African nightshade plants from Kisii was significantly higher than those from Kakamega, though not significantly different with those from Nakuru. Similarly at the market, cumulative produce loss was significantly lower in Kakamega compared with Nakuru and Kisii which were not significantly different from each other.

There was a significant reduction in dry matter content along the supply chain of the counties (Figure 4.1B). However, there were no significant differences in dry matter content of African nightshade plants after transportation until marketing in Nakuru and Kisii while in Kakamega, no significant differences were observed at harvest and before transport, thus main losses occurred from harvest until transport in Nakuru and Kisii and main losses in Kakamega occurred after transportation. The dry matter content of African vegetable in all the counties did not vary significantly at each supply chain stage except after transport where dry matter content of African nightshade plants from Kakamega was significantly higher than that of Kisii and at the market where African nightshade plants from Nakuru had significantly higher dry matter content than Kakamega.

4.3.4. Mineral element and protein contents of African nightshade leaves along the supply chain

Mineral elements (N, P, K, Ca, Mg, Fe, and Zn) (Figure 4.2A-G) and protein (Figure 4.3) content of African nightshade leaves were significantly influenced along the supply chain in all the studied counties. In general, mineral elements and protein content of African nightshade plants were reduced along the supply chain; however there was no significant difference observed after transport until marketing in most of the mineral elements (N, P, K, Ca, and Mg) and protein content. N and protein contents were reduced by 29.4, 18.6, and 14.8% from Kakamega, Nakuru and Kisii, respectively. P content was reduced by 10.9, 10.5, and 7.8% from Nakuru, Kakamega and Kisii, respectively along the supply chain. Similarly, K content of African nightshade leaves from Nakuru, Kakamega and Kisii was reduced by 20.9, 15.5, and 10.7%, respectively. Ca content of African nightshade plants was reduced by 18.2% (Kakamega), 12.6% (Kisii) and 10.2% (Nakuru) along the supply chain. Mg content was reduced by 28.0, 19.5, and 15.1% from Nakuru, Kisii and Kakamega, respectively along the supply chain. The content of Fe in African nightshade plants was reduced by 10.1, 5.4, and 4.2% from Nakuru, Kisii and Kakamega, respectively, while Zn content was reduced by 9.9, 5.9, and 3.2% from Nakuru, Kakamega and Kisii, respectively. Kakamega had the highest loss in N, protein and Ca while Nakuru had the highest loss in P, K, Mg, and Zn. The content of P, K, Fe and Zn contents were significantly lower along the supply chain of African nightshade from Kisii compared to Nakuru and Kakamega while N content had similar high losses in Kakamega and Nakuru.

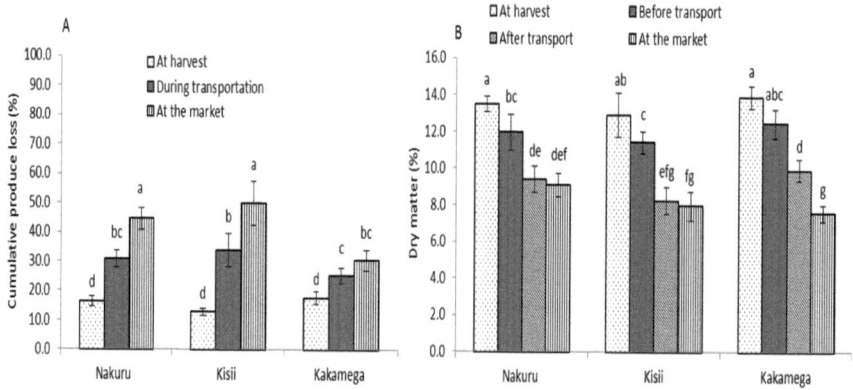

Figure 4.1: Cumulative fresh produce loss (A) and dry matter content (B) of African nightshade leaves during postharvest supply chain analysis in different counties of Kenya. Means ± standard deviations across the counties and along the supply chain followed by the same letter are not significantly different ($p < 0.05$) according to Tukey's HSD test.

4.3.5. Total chlorophyll contents of African nightshade leaves along the supply chain

Total chlorophyll contents of African nightshade leaves were significantly influenced along the supply chain. There was a general reduction of leaf chlorophyll content along the supply chain in all the studied counties. Significantly highest total chlorophylls loss was observed in African nightshade leaves from Kakamega followed by Nakuru and lastly Kisii. Total chlorophyll content was reduced by 90.9, 87.1, and 72.5% from Kakamega, Nakuru and Kisii, respectively (Figure 4.4). When compared at each supply chain stage, chlorophylls content were significantly higher on African nightshade plants from Kakamega followed by Kisii and lastly Nakuru.

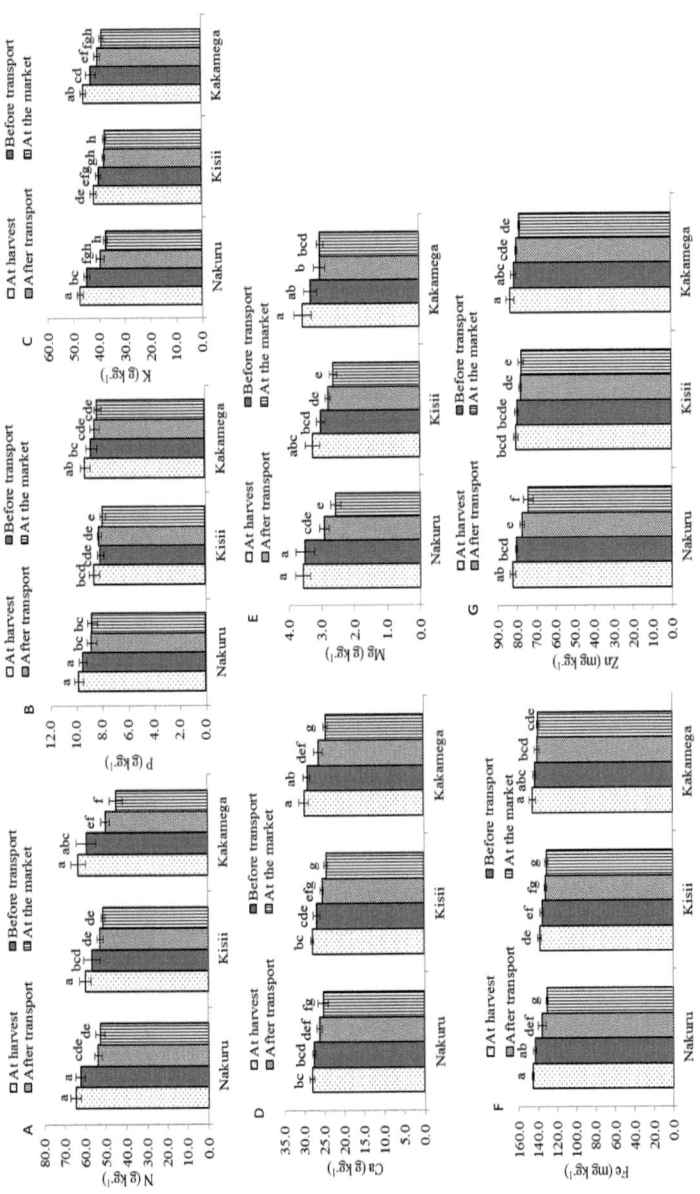

Figure 4.2: Mineral element contents of African nightshade leaves during postharvest supply chain from the main producing counties in Kenya. Dry matter content corresponding to specific mineral element measurements from harvest to market was 95.6, 95.2, 95.7, 94.8 % from Nakuru; 94.3, 94.9, 95.1, 94.7% from Kisii; and 94.6, 94.9, 95.3, 95.0% from Kakamega. Means ± standard deviations across the counties and along the supply chain followed by the same letter within an element are not significantly different ($p < 0.05$) according to Tukey's HSD test.

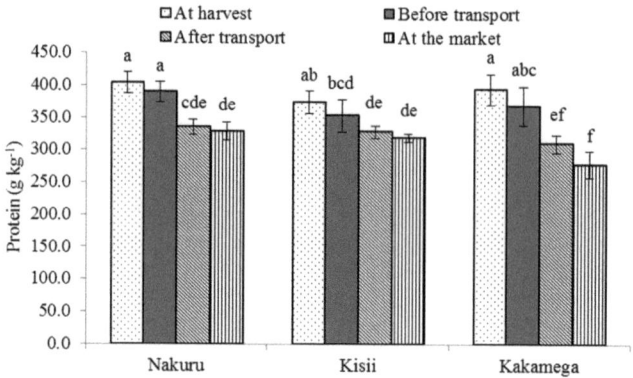

Figure 4.3: Protein contents of African nightshade leaves during postharvest supply chain analysis from the main producing counties in Kenya. Dry matter content corresponding to the specific measurements from harvest to market was 95.6, 95.2, 95.7, 94.8% from Nakuru; 94.3, 94.9, 95.1, 94.7% from Kisii; and 94.6, 94.9, 95.3, 95.0% from Kakamega. Means ± standard deviations across the counties and along the supply chain followed by the same letter are not significantly different ($p < 0.05$) according to Tukey's HSD test.

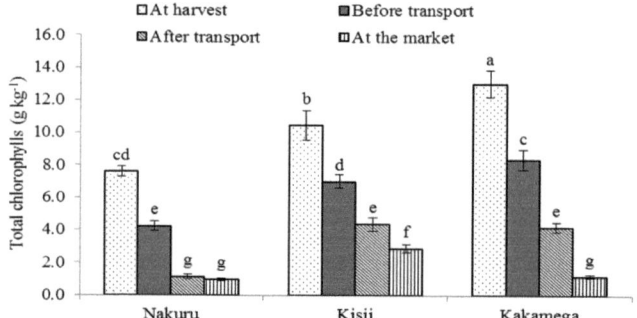

Figure 4.4: Total chlorophylls contents of African nightshade leaves during postharvest supply chain analysis from the main producing counties in Kenya. Dry matter content corresponding to the specific measurements from harvest to market was 13.5, 12.0, 9.4, 9.1% from Nakuru; 12.9, 11.4, 8.2, 8.0% from Kisii; and 13.9, 12.4, 9.9, 7.6% from Kakamega. Means ± standard deviations across the counties and along the supply followed by the same letter are not significantly different ($p < 0.05$) according to Tukey's HSD test.

4.3.6. Carotenoid contents of African nightshade leaves along the supply chain

Total carotenoid contents of African nightshade leaves were significantly influenced along the supply chain. Total carotenoid contents were significantly reduced along the supply chain in all the studied counties but no differences were observed in total carotenoid contents of African nightshade between transportation and marketing from Nakuru and Kisii. Overall total carotenoid content reduction along the supply chain from Kakamega, Nakuru and Kisii was 91.3, 85.9, and 70.4%, respectively. Just like other carotenoids, significantly the highest total carotenoids content was on African nightshade plants from Kakamega, Kisii and Nakuru, in decreasing order (Figure 4.5). However, no significant differences were observed on total carotenoid contents of African nightshade after transportation between Kisii and Kakamega and at the market from Nakuru and Kakamega.

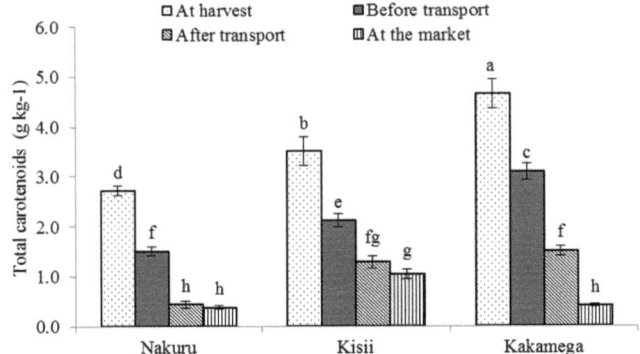

Figure 4.5: Total carotenoid contents of African nightshade leaves during postharvest supply chain analysis from the main producing counties in Kenya. Dry matter content corresponding to the specific measurements from harvest to market was 13.5, 12.0, 9.4, 9.1% from Nakuru; 12.9, 11.4, 8.2, 8.0% from Kisii; and 13.9, 12.4, 9.9, 7.6% from Kakamega. Means ± standard deviations across the counties and along the supply chain followed by the same letter are not significantly different ($p < 0.05$) according to Tukey's HSD test.

4.3.7. Economic loss during postharvest supply chain of African nightshade leaves

There was an influence on the quantitative economic loss along the supply chain of African nightshade in all the studied counties (Table 4.3). At harvest, the highest economic loss was obtained from African nightshade plants coming from Kakamega followed by Nakuru and lastly Kisii. However, during transportation until marketing, the highest economic loss of African nightshade plants came from Kisii, followed by Nakuru and lastly Kakamega.

Table 4.3: Economic loss during postharvest supply chain of African nightshade plants in Kenya.

Value chain	Final fresh weight (kg)	Loss (kg)	Cumulative produce loss (%)	Loss per ha (kg)	Economic loss per ha (KES)*
A. Nakuru					
At harvest	41.8	7.1	14.5	7259.7	181,492.80
After transport	34.5	14.4	29.4	14723.9	368,098.20
In the market	27.7	21.2	43.4	21676.9	541,922.30
B. Kisii					
At harvest	51.5	7.4	12.6	6281.8	157,045.80
After transport	39.1	19.8	33.6	16808.2	420,203.70
In the market	39.7	29.2	49.6	24787.8	619,694.40
C. Kakamega					
At harvest	39.2	8.3	17.5	8736.8	218,421.10
After transport	35.6	11.9	25.1	12526.3	313,157.90
In the market	33.1	14.4	30.3	15157.9	378,947.40

Average yield = 50 t/ha, Price = KES 25.00/kg, Weight at harvest = 41.8 kg (Nakuru), 51.5 kg (Kisii) and 39.2 kg (Kakamega)

$Loss\ (kg) = Fresh\ weight\ at\ harvest\ (kg) - Final\ fresh\ weight\ (kg)$

$Loss\ (kg)\ per\ ha = \dfrac{Average\ yield\ (kg) \times Loss\ (kg)}{Weight\ at\ harvest\ (kg)}$

$Loss\ (\%) = \left(\dfrac{Fresh\ weight\ at\ harvest\ (kg) - Final\ fresh\ weight\ (kg)}{Fresh\ weight\ at\ harvest\ (Kg)}\right) \times 100$

$Economic\ loss\ per\ ha\ (KES) = Loss\ per\ ha\ (kg) \times Price\ per\ kg\ (KES)$

*KES 100 = $ 0.99 = € 0.88

4.4. Discussion

The present study sought to analyse nutritional and economic losses and their causes during the supply chain of African nightshade leaves. There was little variation in microclimate conditions during the supply chain in all the counties except for Nakuru where temperature and relative air humidity were higher at the market. The African nightshade plants at Nakuru were mainly supplied to supermarkets that normally have cold storage facility associated with the low temperature and higher relative humidity conditions observed at the market. Studies have demonstrated that low temperature storage help to maintain storability and retain the quality characteristics of AIVs during storage (Nyaura et al., 2014). However in this study, it became obvious not to be the solely cause of produce losses, concluding that postharvest loss is a combination of various factors which need to be identified in more detail.

There was a significant loss in cumulative produce weight and dry matter content of African nightshade plants along the supply chain in all the studied counties. Higher losses of dry matter were observed in Kakamega compared with other counties. However, higher cumulative produce loss was observed in Nakuru and Kisii compared with Kakamega, being attributed to the shortest distance to market in Kakamega. The losses in dry matter and cumulative produce loss could also be associated with differences in pre-harvest and harvest factors (e.g. lack of certified seeds, insect pest and diseases, harvesting time/methods), postharvest handling (e.g. poor packaging such as non-perforated polythene bags), transportation (e.g. road conditions, sun/heat), and market conditions (e.g. unhygienic conditions leading to contamination) in the studied counties. For instance, the AIVs from Kakamega were sold at Kakamega county open market under ambient conditions where the distance from farmer's field to the market was approximately 5 km (30 min) and were tied in bundles (1 kg), packaged in 10 kg polythene bags and transported in a bicycle. African indigenous leafy vegetables are highly perishable; hence, the significant loss in dry matter content and increase in cumulative produce loss could be attributed to the faster rate of metabolic activities of such vegetables after harvest (Page et al., 2001). Furthermore, it was observed that farmers constantly sprinkled cold water on their vegetables to maintain freshness, contributing to the loss of dry matter content along the supply chain. The dry matter loss was also comparatively low in Nakuru, once the vegetables were refrigerated. Poor handling and storage conditions may also accelerate physiological characteristics resulting in higher water loss, hence fresh weight and changes in physical appearance (texture, colour, size, and shape) and thereby affecting AIV marketability (Onyango and Imungi, 2007), thus explaining the significant increase in cumulative produce loss. Similar results were observed by Koraddi and Devendrappa (2011) during vegetable storage under household and laboratory refrigerated conditions. However, the variation in cumulative produce loss among the studied counties could be attributed to differences in distance to the market and transportation mode as observed in the study (i.e. Nakuru county; market distance: 10 km, transportation mode: motorbike. Kisii county; market distance: 210 km, transportation mode: pick-up vehicle. Kakamega county; market distance: 5 km, transportation mode: bicycle). Longer market distance in addition to poor road and transportation conditions, hence faster water loss or wilting and tissue damage was reported to be a major problem during transportation or marketing (Mampholo et al., 2016). Macro-nutrients (N, P, K, Ca, and Mg), micro-nutrients (Fe and Zn) and protein content of African nightshade leaves were significantly reduced along the supply chain in the studied counties. Nutrient loss ranged from 3.2% (Zn) to as high as 29.4% (N and proteins). There was also significant differences in mineral elements (P, K, Ca, Fe, and Zn) being lower in Kisii compared to other counties. This could be attributed to pre-harvest factors such as cultural practices. For instance, farmers in Kisii reported that they could not access certified seed varieties, and therefore, they were using traditional seed banking which could affect mineral composition. The overall nutrient loss in the counties varied depending on the specific nutrient elements of African nightshade from Kakamega, higher loss of N, Ca, and protein, whereas vegetables from Nakuru revealed higher losses of K, Mg, Fe, and Zn. This could be attributed to differences in African nightshade handling conditions in the studied counties as there are no clear guidelines on the AIV handling, quality and safety standards (Gogo et al., 2016). The loss in nutrients along the supply chain could be presumably due to their involvement in enzymatic metabolic reactions during senescence. The differences in nutrient content among the counties such as higher losses of N, Ca and protein in Kakamega, and K, Mg, Fe in Nakuru could be due to a combination of factors such as different cultivation regimes, growing conditions, climatic conditions and postharvest handling (Page et al., 2001; Shiundu and Oniang'o, 2007; Mampholo et al., 2015). For instance, even though Kakamega had the shortest distance to the market, it had the greatest loss in N, Ca and protein contents. The results are consistent with that of Okpalamma et al. (2013) who observed losses in K, Ca, Mg, Zn, Fe and vitamins during storage of fluted pumpkin (*Telfairia occidentalis* Hook F.) attributed to the effects of oxidative reactions as a result of heat and light. Similarly, Page et al. (2001) observed more than 70% reduction in protein content of broccoli (*Brassica oleracea* L. var. italica Plenck.) stored at room temperature after 6 d of storage. They suggested that the expression patterns of several protease genes are senescence enhanced due to their involvement in converting vacuolar proteins to their more mature forms. The contents and loss of total chlorophylls and total carotenoids varied depending on the county and supply chain stage. Even though African nightshade from Kakamega had the highest total chlorophyll and total carotenoid contents, they had the highest loss of similar compounds during supply chain, attributed to different climatic conditions, and production systems in the studied counties (Motsa et al., 2015; Opiyo et al., 2015). For instance, temperature, light and plant nutrition affects photosynthesis and hence chlorophyll and total carotenoids synthesis and degradation processes. Differences in chlorophyll and carotenoid contents along the supply chain could be associated with differences postharvest handling and market conditions. In addition, postharvest handling conditions such as harvesting, storage, transportation, packaging and market conditions have an effect on the bioactive compounds of vegetables (Mampholo et al., 2016). Temperature and relative humidity are also reported to affect quality characteristics of fresh produce. For example, temperature has a pronounced effect on respiration thus loss of reserve substances, i.e. carbohydrates, proteins while relative humidity is a driving force of transpiration mediated water loss. Leafy vegetables are very prone to damage when exposed to high temperatures, delays between harvests and cooling, can increase water loss, resulting in the loss of nutritional attributes. Kader (2005) reported that it is essential to keep leafy vegetables at their optimum temperature and relative humidity ranges in order to maintain good quality and minimize postharvest losses in market chains. Rapid decline in chlorophylls and carotenoids could be attributed to inappropriate postharvest handling practices i.e. poor harvesting, mechanical damage, poor storage and poor packaging resulting in their enzymatic degradation (Finger et al., 1999) along the supply chain. Mampholo et al. (2015) observed significant losses in ascorbic acid, chlorophylls, carotenoids, flavonoids, and total phenols of vegetable amaranth and African nightshade (*Solanum retroflexum* Dunal.) during postharvest life and this was associated with the peroxidation of cell membrane. Moreover, mechanical injuries such as bruising, surface abrasions and cuts can result in the loss of chlorophylls and carotenoids also as a result of a cell membrane breakdown followed by an accelerated senescence.

The economic loss of African indigenous leafy vegetables increased along the supply chain and varied with counties depending on the supply chain stage with the highest economic loss observed in Kisii county, associated with the produce loss as well as qualitative loss. Product quality such as size, shape, and colour, absence of defects and decay, texture and nutritional attributes is a critical aspect for AIVs farmers as it determines the price as well as consumer acceptance (Chelang'a et al., 2013). In addition, postharvest losses translate to quantitative losses and hence affecting amount of AIVs sold (Kader, 2005).

4.5. Conclusion and recommendation

African indigenous leafy vegetables are no doubt important for not only nutritional and health security but also job creation, especially in the developing countries. However, from the study, it is evident that African nightshade plants, one of the important AIVs in Kenya suffer significant quantitative, nutritional and economic losses along the supply chain. Quantitative, nutritional and economic losses differed among the counties, i.e. higher losses in cumulative produce, dry matter, N, Ca, protein, total chlorophylls, and total carotenoids were observed in Kakamega while Nakuru revealed higher losses of K, Mg, Fe, and Zn associated with differences market distance, transportation and market conditions. Thus, losses of African nightshade plants are attributed to a combination of many factors with some unique to specific supply chain stage. At harvest, losses were due to lack of certified seeds, weather conditions, insect pest and diseases as well as inappropriate harvesting method or time. During transportation losses were due to poor road conditions, poor handling as well as disease contamination. At the market, the losses were attributed to poor handling, unhygienic market conditions, inappropriate packaging, lack of cold storage facilities, and season gluts. Sprinkling of cold water on the vegetables along the supply chain to maintain freshness under unhygienic conditions was also noted to be a potential source of contamination leading to postharvest losses. This study provides highly valuable information on postharvest losses to farmers, researchers, policy makers, and all the actors in the AIV supply chain for the intervention purposes. In order to encourage and sustain AIV commercial farming, there is need for more studies on affordable, safe and easy to apply postharvest treatments combined with training of farmers on appropriate postharvest handling practices, i.e. appropriate harvest technologies, issues of optimised transportation and postharvest preservation and postharvest treatments ensuring the maintenance of high quality AIVs during distribution and marketing. This will help in increasing food access of the high nutritive value of AIVs as well as reducing postharvest losses which could be a viable strategy to solve food insecurity problems in developing countries.

Acknowledgement

The study was funded by the German Government from the Federal Ministry of Education and Research (BMBF) and the Federal Ministry of Economic Cooperation and Development (BMZ) within the GlobE (Global Food Security) under the Horticultural Innovations and Learning for Improved Nutrition and Livelihood in East Africa (HORTINLEA) project. We are grateful to Egerton University, Kenya for supporting the study.

5. Impact of direct-electric-current on growth and bioactive compounds of African nightshade (*Solanum scabrum* Mill.) plants

Gogo, E.O., Huyskens-Keil, S., Krimlowski, A., Ulrichs, Ch., Schmidt, U., Opiyo, A., Dannehl, D., 2016. Journal of Applied Botany and Food Quality 89, 60-67. http://dx.doi.org/10.5073/JABFQ.2016.089.007.

Abstract

Production of indigenous African leafy vegetables such as African nightshade (*Solanum scabrum* Mill.), whose high nutritional and medicinal value is well documented is still limited due to insufficient pre-harvest techniques. Electric current is known to improve quality in food crops. Therefore, in the present study, the effects of direct-electric-current (DC) on growth and characteristic bioactive and health promoting compounds were evaluated in different morphological sections, i.e., leaves and stems of African nightshade cv. Olevolosi. Six weeks old plants were exposed to different DC applied with a voltage of 8 and 16 V, 10 h/day for 12 days. Non-treated plants served as control. Plant growth, primary and secondary plant compounds were evaluated. Applying DC increased leaf fresh (11.5-14.4%) and dry (12.1-24.2%) weight as well as marketable leaves (29.1-55.3%). Biosynthesis of chlorophylls and carotenoids was enhanced by increased DC. Furthermore, dietary fibre fractions such as hemicellulose was promoted (23.3-45.3%) by DC applications, while cellulose and lignin remained unaffected. Minerals accumulated with increasing DC. Alteration of cell membrane permeability due to DC may enhance physiological processes leading to the improved growth and acceleration of bioactive compounds in African nightshade leaves.

5.1. Introduction

African leafy vegetables such as African nightshade (*Solanum scabrum* Mill.) have the potential to contribute to poverty alleviation and nutritional security because of their ease to grow, minimum production input requirement, and being highly rich in minerals, vitamins, fibre and bioactive compounds (Kamga et al., 2013). Recently, attention is being directed to these vegetables because of their high contents in bioactive phytochemicals (Mibei et al., 2012). These chemicals possess strong antioxidant properties and have been implicated in prevention of diseases such as cancer, arteriosclerosis, diabetes and aging (Voutilainen et al., 2006). Furthermore, diets rich in micronutrients and antioxidants are strongly recommended as supplements in medicinal therapy for fighting HIV/AIDS (Friis et al., 2002). As a result of changing lifestyle and eating habits, the protection against diseases such as cancer and diabetes are on the rise. Consequently, these circumstances are leading to increasing demands for high quality and healthy food products (Oniang'o et al., 2008).

During postharvest processes, high electric fields were used to destroy plant cells in order to increase the bioavailability of consumed secondary plant compounds in processed food products (Gonzalez and Barrett, 2010). Moreover, the application of electricity is also known to stimulate plant growth (Black et al., 1971; Costanzo, 2008), and has been used to protect plants from insect pests and diseases and in weed management (Diprose et al., 1984). However, information in terms of the effect of weak direct-electric-current (DC) treatments on growth, yield and quality of leafy vegetables are scarce or just currently being investigated. Internal electric fields of plants are affected by the externally applied electric fields, already early being reported (Scott, 1967), influencing crop physiology. It is assumed that electric fields accelerate mass transfer by affecting cell membrane permeability properties (Ade-Omowaye et al., 2002; Black et al., 1971).

Recently, different intensities of DC in the range of 200 to 1800 mA were applied to roots of radish plants (*Raphanus sativus* L.) and garden cress (*Lepidium sativum* L.) during growth, whereby primary and secondary bioactive compounds (phenols, carotenoids), without visible damages to the plants were increased (Dannehl et al., 2012; Dannehl et al., 2009). Previous studies during postharvest processes also noted that DC intensities between 100 and 500 mA with varied application times between 15 and 60 min resulted in the accumulation of carotenoids, phenolic compounds and an increase in antioxidant activity in tomatoes (*Solanum lycopersicum* L.) (Dannehl et al., 2011). However, plant tissue is characterized by a heterogeneous structure and the uptake, as well as the availability of nutrients into plant cells are determined by the direction of the current flow (Ben-Ammar et al., 2011). Cell size, cell size distribution, and cell orientation may have an impact on the effectiveness of the applied electric current (Ben-Ammar et al., 2011). Therefore, the present study focused on the investigation of effects of DC on growth parameters, as well as primary (structural carbohydrates) and secondary bioactive (chlorophyll, carotenoid pattern) compounds, as well as mineral composition in different morphological sections, i.e. leaves and stems of African nightshade (*Solanum scabrum* Mill.) cv. Olevolosi during plant growth. Additionally, the content of heavy metals in African nightshade was determined, in order to examine a possible accumulation of toxic elements by DC, which might be caused by electrolysis of the metal electrodes used.

5.2. Materials and methods

5.2.1. Experimental site and plant material

Seeds of African nightshade (*Solanum scabrum* Mill.) cv. Olevolosi were procured from AVRDC (The World Vegetable Centre, Eastern and Southern Africa Arusha, Tanzania). The African nightshade plants were grown in the experimental station under greenhouse conditions at Humboldt-Universität zu Berlin (Dahlem, Berlin, Germany). The experiment was conducted from 30.06.2014 until 19.08.2014. The weekly mean values of the microclimatic conditions are presented in figure 5.1. Average air temperature ranged between 15 °C to 27 °C (night and day), while the average relative humidity was recorded ranging between 60% and 85%. Daily light quantity ranged from 150 Wm^{-2} to 300 Wm^{-2}.

5.2.2. Experimental set up and DC treatments

All plant boxes were equipped with stainless steel plates (EN-Standard: X5CrNi18-10; ThyssenKrupp Nirosta GmbH; Krefeld, Germany) with the dimensions of 90 cm × 8 cm × 0.1 cm (length × width × thickness), which were used as electrodes. To minimize the surface area of the box acting as conducting surfaces and thus altering the electric field pattern and distribution of current, the electrodes were centrally placed within each box. A part of the horticultural substrate (Profi-Substrate + Ton + Fe, Gramoflor GmbH & Co., Vechta, Germany) was first added to about 2 cm before the plate was placed into each box and more substrate was added to about 10 cm mark. Five seedlings were transplanted (3 weeks after sowing) in each box at a spacing of 20 cm apart. A power supply (Voltcraft, VLP 1303 pro, Hirschau, Germany) with an output of 0-30 V was integrated in this system. To close the electric circuit, wires were fixed at the stainless steel plate and at the top of each plant. As such, the DC flow was directed from the horticultural substrate to the top of the plant. The experiment was carried out in a completely randomized design with 3 replications. Excluding non-treated plants, the established plants were exposed to an electrical voltage of 8 and 16 V applied ten hours a day for 12 days. Output DC was monitored and recorded three times a day (8 am, noon and 6 pm) on a one-day interval from the start of the experiment until harvesting. Irrigation was done manually early in the morning on a daily basis ensuring an equal amount of water was applied to each treatment.

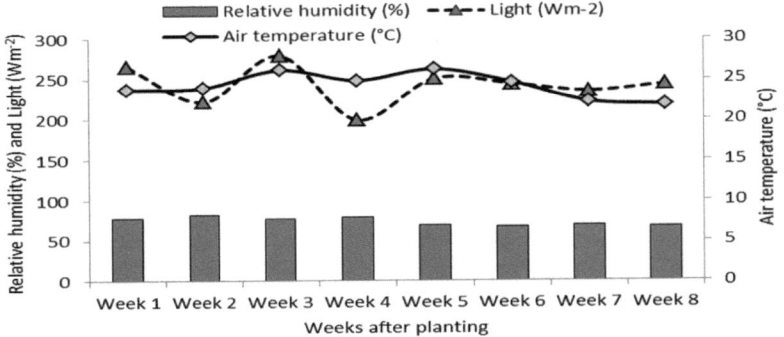

Figure 5.1: Microclimate condition during greenhouse production of African nightshade plants

5.2.3. Determination of growth parameters

Plant height, total leaf number, stem diameter and number of primary shoots were determined on three central plants from each box at a 3-days interval from the beginning of the treatments until harvesting (12 days). After harvest, the leaves and stems of each plant per treatment were separated. Leaves per plant were used to determine leaf area (Leaf area meter-3100, Bachofer, Germany) of all plants, fresh weight, and amount of marketable and non-marketable leaves. Non-marketable leaves in this context were leaves which were considered not sellable due to discolouration. The plant compartments (stems and leaves) were used for further chemical analysis as described below.

5.2.4. Bioactive primary and secondary plant compound analysis

Three replicates of leaves and stems from freshly harvested plants of the control and each DC treatment were used for analysis of each of the phytochemical compound. One part of the harvested plants was immediately used for the determination of the dry matter. The other part of the harvested plant material was shock-frozen with liquid nitrogen and kept at -20 °C for subsequent analysis of chlorophylls and carotenoids. The remaining samples were freeze-dried for 48 h (Christ Alpha 1-4, Christ; Osterode, Germany), ground and mixed to a fine homogenized powder and stored in a desiccator for further analysis such as structural carbohydrates, minerals elements and heavy metals.

5.2.5. Determination of dry matter, chlorophylls and carotenoids

To determine the dry matter, approximately 30 g fresh material per sample was placed in a drying oven at 105 °C for 24 h until constant weight was achieved. Subsequently, the dry weight of each sample was measured in order to calculate the dry matter by the ratio of the dry weight to the fresh weight of the samples. The results were expressed as % dry matter. The dry matter of each sample was further used to calculate all phytochemicals on a dry weight basis.

The extraction and determination of the chlorophylls and carotenoids content in African nightshade was conducted according to the method described by Goodwin and Britton (1988). An aliquot of 0.5 g fresh material was homogenized with acetone/hexane (4:5, v:v) (Ultra-Turrax T 25, Jahnke & Kunkel, IKA-Labortechnik, Staufen, Germany) for 1 min at 18,000 rpm, and afterwards centrifuged for 10 min (4000 rpm). This procedure was carried out twice. The resulting supernatants were collected in a 25 ml volumetric flask and filled up with acetone/hexane (4:5, v:v). Three replications of the representative sample were measured twice with a spectrophotometer (UV-Vis spectrophotometer, UV-Mini-1240, Shimadzu, Japan) at wavelengths of 450 nm (total carotenoids), 453 nm (β-carotene), 505 nm (lycopene), 445 nm (lutein), as well as 663 nm and 645 nm for chlorophyll a and b, respectively. Carotenoids and chlorophylls were calculated as described by Nagata and Yamashita (1992) and expressed as mg/g DM.

5.2.6. Inductively coupled plasma-optical emission spectrometry (ICP-OES) analysis

For the determination of mineral elements (N, P, C, K, Ca, Mg, Na, Zn, Fe) and heavy metals (Cr, Cd, Pb and Ni), the ICP-OES analysis was applied for leaves and stems from each treatment in duplicates of three replications. For the microwave digestion, 0.2 g of each freeze dried sample was weighed into deionized containers. An aliquot of 5 ml HNO_3 (65%) and 3 ml H_2O_2 (30%) were added. The containers were then packed and placed into a microwave (MARS Xpress, CEM; North Carolina, USA) and digested according to the following program: step 1, 20 min to reach 200 °C; step 2, 5 min at 200 °C; step 3, 1 min to reach 210 °C; step 4, 5 min at 210 °C; step 5, 1 min to reach 220 °C; step 6, 5 min at 220 °C; and step 7, 30 min to cool down to room temperature. The resultant solution was transferred to 50 ml volumetric flasks using distilled water and finally filtrated into plastic flasks. Thereafter, the analysis of the elements in the digestion solution was conducted via ICP-OES with an ICP Emission Spectrometer (iCAP 6300 Duo MFC, Thermo; Waltham, USA). The operating conditions employed for ICP-OES were 1150W RF power, 0.55 l/min nebulizer gas flow with argon employed as plasmogen as well as carrier gas and performed with a cross-flow nebulizer (MIRA MIST, Thermo Scientific; Cambridge England), in addition to radial (Ca, Mg) and axial (Fe, Zn, Cu, Al, Cd, Cr, Ni, Pb) view. For each element, a single-element standard solution (Roth, Karlsruhe, Germany) of 1000 mg/l was used to prepare the reference analytic solutions in 1.4 mol/l HNO_3. The calibration curves were established with the following reference solutions: blank 1.4 mol/l HNO_3; 1–200 mg/l of Ca; 0.5–50 mg/l of Mg; 0.5–10 mg/l of Al; 0.5–5 mg/l of Cu, Zn, and Fe; 0.01–1 mg/l of Cd, Cr, Ni, and Pb. The elements in the solutions were analyzed in duplicate at wavelength as follows: Ca at 317.9 nm, Mg at 279.0 nm, Fe at 259.9 nm, Zn at 213.8 nm, Cu at 324.7 nm, Al at 369.1 nm, Cd at 214.4 nm, Cr at 267.7 nm, Ni at 231.6 nm and Pb at 220.3 nm. The contents of macro- and micronutrients, as well as heavy metals in leaves and stems of African nightshade were expressed as g/kg DM.

5.2.7. Determination of carbon and nitrogen content

Carbon and nitrogen analysis were determined using three replicates of freeze-dried leaves and stems per treatment using an elemental analyzer (vario MAX, Elementar Analysensysteme GmbH; Hanau, Germany) according to DIN-ISO-10694 (1995) and DIN-ISO-13878 (1998). As such, an aliquot of 0.3 g of sample material was weighed into individual crucibles and catalytically combusted at 900 °C with pure oxygen. The combustion products and helium (as the carrier gas) passed through specific adsorption columns at a temperature of 830 °C to separate carbon and nitrogen. Based on the differences in thermal conductivity of these elements, carbon and nitrogen were determined successively with a thermal conductivity detector. Each analysis was performed twice and the results were calculated using glutamic acid as the standard reference. The results obtained were expressed as g/kg DM.

5.2.8. Determination of structural carbohydrates content

Cellulose, hemicellulose and lignin were analyzed according to Goering and Van Soest (1972), Van Soest et al. (1991) and AOAC (1999). One gram freeze-dried sample was extracted with 100 ml acid detergent fibre (ADF) reagent (N-cetyl-N,N,N-trimethyl-ammoniumbromid dissolved with 96% H_2SO_4) using a Fibertec System (M 1020, Tecator, Sweden). Thereafter, the solution was vacuum-filtered, washed with boiled, double-distilled water until removal of the acidity and again washed with 90% acetone. The residue was dried at 105 °C for 24 h, weighed, ash-dried at 500 °C for 24 h and weighed again to calculate ADF (acid detergent fibre). The dried ADF residue was used for acid detergent lignin (ADL) determination. Cellulose content was calculated as the difference between ADF and ADL. The contents of lignin and cellulose were expressed as mg/g DM.

Using the neutral detergent fibre (NDF) approach (Van Soest and Goering 1963), one gram of freeze-dried material was cooked in 100 ml of NDF mixture (Titriplex III, di-sodium borate, dodecylhydrogensulfate-Na, ethylene-glycol-monoethylester) to determine the hemicellulosic cell wall fraction. The solution was subsequently vacuum-filtered, and washed with demineralized water and with 90% acetone. The insoluble residue was dried at 105 °C for 24 h, weighed, ash-dried at 500 °C for 24 h and weighed again to calculate NDF. The hemicellulose content was obtained by subtracting ADF from NDF and expressed as mg/g DM.

5.2.9. Statistical analysis

The impact of different DC treatments on plant growth and bioactive compounds, minerals and heavy metals in African nightshade were evaluated using analysis of variance (ANOVA) with the statistical program SAS (version 10). Proc-Univariate procedure was used to check for normality of data and all comparisons of the mentioned parameters were calculated using Tukey-tests at a significance level of $p < 0.05$. The same significance level was used for the calculation of differences between the electric current flows when a voltage of 8 and 16 V was applied using Fisher's t-test. Mean values labeled with different small letters indicate significant differences. The mean variability is shown as standard deviation.

5.3. Results

5.3.1. Changes in electrical current flow during African nightshade production

Results obtained from the voltmeter readings indicated that different voltage applications led to significant differences in DC flows during the experiment (Figure 5.2). Doubling the voltage resulted in a maximum DC flow of 172 µA through plants, whereas a maximum flow of 73 µA was found at 8 V. There was a periodic fluctuation of the current flow up to 56 µA from one day to another at a higher electrical voltage (16 V) while the current flow at a lower voltage intensity (8 V) remained relatively constant after 6 days of electrical treatments.

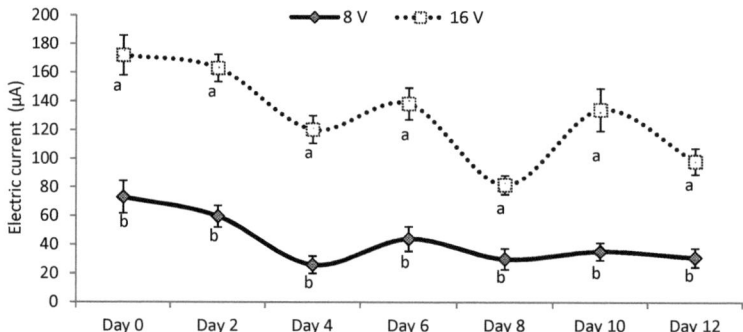

Figure 5.2: Changes in current flow on African nightshade plants during production as influenced by DC intensity. Means (± standard deviation) followed by the same letter are not significantly different according to t-test ($p < 0.05$).

5.3.2. Effect of different electrical voltages on growth of African nightshade plants

As expected, growth of African nightshade plants increased with time. However, different electrical voltages did not influence plant height (Table 5.1A), leaf number (Table 5.1B), stem diameter (Table 5.1C), and primary shoots (Table 5.1D). Furthermore in terms of leaf area (LA), both DC treatments did not differ significantly from non-treated plants (Figure 5.3). However, lower voltage (8 V) reduced LA by 12.4% compared to the higher voltage (16 V).

5.3.3. Effect of different electrical voltages on fresh and dry weight of African nightshade plants

Different electrical voltages had a significant influence on fresh weight of leaves, but not on stems (Figure 5.4A). In terms of leaf fresh weight, the values indicated that the results were significantly increased by 11.5% and 14.4% at 8 V and 16 V treatments, respectively, when compared to the control plants. However, the reverse effect was found in the case of stem fresh weight, where this parameter decreased with increasing voltages. The control stems had the highest fresh weight with 58.2 g followed by those treated with a voltage of 8 V (53.9 g) and 16 V (49 g).

In terms of leaves, similar results were found on a dry weight basis (Figure 5.4B). Thus, the same increase pattern was observed, where only the voltage treatment with 16 V caused a significant increase in leaf dry weight by 24.2% compared to the control leaves. On the other hand, a lower electrical voltage (8 V) tendentiously increased stem dry weight by 5.8% while doubling voltage tended to reduce stem dry weight by 2.9% compared to the control.

Different voltage applications significantly influenced both marketable and non-marketable leaves harvested (Figure 5.4C). A lower voltage application (8 V) increased marketable leaves by 55.3% while a higher voltage (16 V) increased marketable leaves by 29.1% compared to plants grown under non-treated conditions. Regarding non-marketable leaves, the control had the highest amount with 5.7 leaves/plant, whereas number of leaves of DC at 8 V and 16 V was significantly reduced by 77.2% and 64.9%, respectively. No significant differences were observed between 8 V and 16 V.

5.3.4. Effect of different electrical voltages on chlorophyll and carotenoid contents of African nightshade plants

Varying responses of leaves and stems of African nightshade plants were noted due to different voltage treatments. Generally, a voltage of 16 V resulted in higher chlorophyll and carotenoid contents in African nightshade leaves, while a lower voltage treatment reduced both chlorophyll and carotenoids content. Leaves had higher chlorophyll and carotenoid contents compared with stems. Compared to the control, a voltage of 8 V significantly reduced the contents of lutein

Table 5.1: Effect of different electrical voltages on growth of African nightshade plants.

DC	Days after treatment application			
	0	4	8	12
	A. Plant height (cm)			
Control	41.4 ± 3.4 g	49.3 ± 3.6 f	58.4 ± 2.3 bcd	65.2 ± 3.0 ab
8 V	41.0 ± 3.5 g	52.1 ± 5.1 def	60.9 ± 5.6 bc	68.8 ± 5.5 a
16 V	40.6 ± 1.2 g	50.7 ± 1.8 ef	56.9 ± 3.2 cde	64.2 ± 4.2 ab
	B. Leaf number (no./plant)			
Control	10.3 ± 0.3 e	12.3 ± 0.9 d	13.4 ± 0.7 bc	14.9 ± 0.7 a
8 V	10.2 ± 0.2 e	12.4 ± 0.5 cd	13.6 ± 0.4 b	14.8 ± 0.8 a
16 V	10.4 ± 0.8 e	12.8 ± 0.5 bcd	13.7 ± 0.7 b	14.8 ± 0.8 a
	C. Stem diameter (mm)			
Control	9.6 ± 0.7 cd	10.0 ± 0.4 abcd	10.6 ± 0.7 abc	10.9 ± 1.0 a
8 V	9.2 ± 0.3 d	9.8 ± 0.4 bcd	10.4 ± 0.8 abcd	10.5 ± 0.7 abc
16 V	9.3 ± 0.6 d	9.8 ± 0.4 bcd	10.1 ± 0.5 abcd	10.1 ± 0.4 abc
	D. Primary shoots (no./plant)			
Control	4.9 ± 0.8 de	5.4 ± 0.8 bcde	6.1 ± 0.4 abcd	6.9 ± 0.4 ab
8 V	4.1 ± 1.0 e	5.1 ± 1.3 de	6.7 ± 0.9 abc	7.6 ± 0.9 a
16 V	4.2 ± 1.0 e	5.3 ± 1.0 cde	6.8 ± 0.8 abc	7.6 ± 0.8 a

Mean values (± standard deviation) within a growth variable followed by the same letter are not significantly different according to Tukey-test ($p < 0.05$).

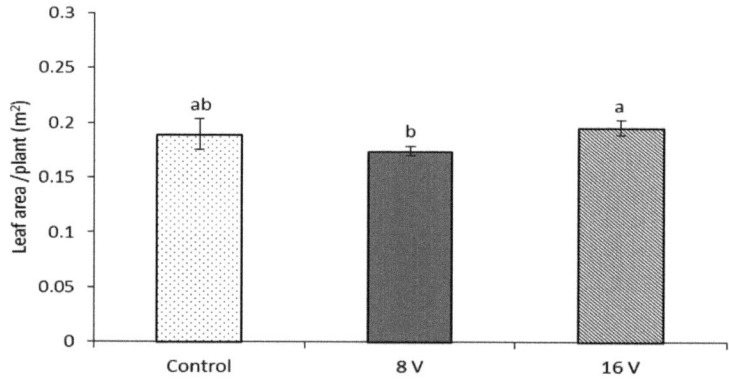

Figure 5.3: Effect of different voltage applications on leaf area of African nightshade plants. Mean values (± standard deviation) followed by the same letter are not significantly different according to Tukey-test ($p < 0.05$).

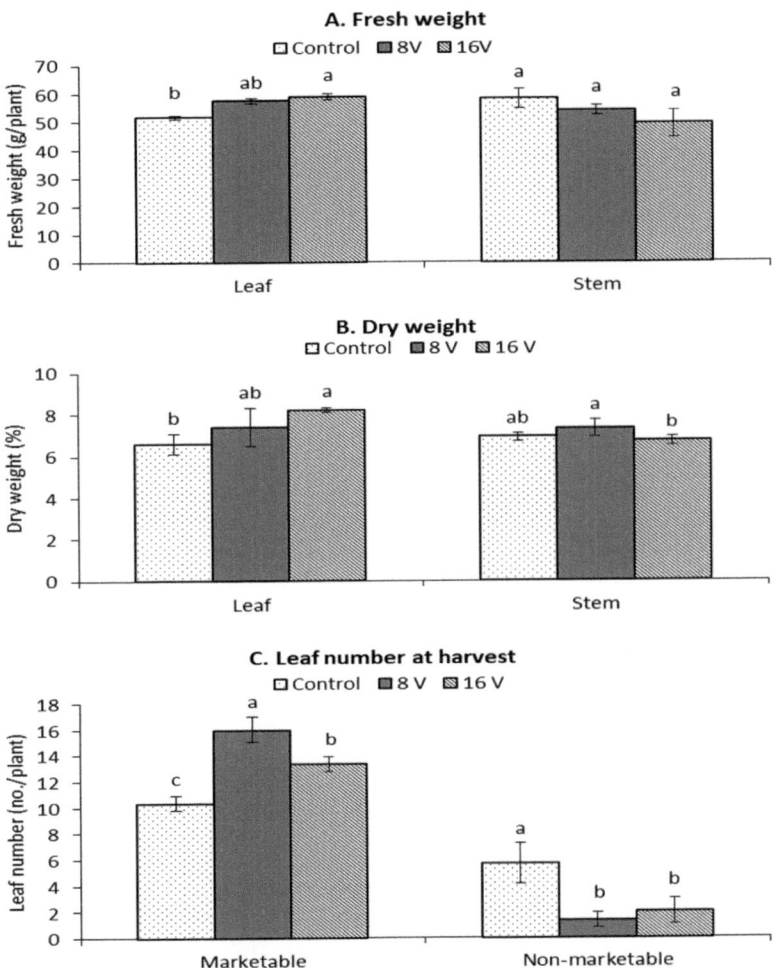

Figure 5.4: Effect of different voltage applications on fresh (A) and dry (B) weight and marketable and non-marketable leaves (C) of African nightshade plants. Mean values (± standard deviation) within a specific variable followed by the same letter are not significantly different according to Tukey-test ($p < 0.05$).

(15.6%), β-carotene (16.2%), total carotenoids (16.0%) and chlorophyll a (15.5%) in African nightshade leaves, whereas lycopene and chlorophyll b were not statistically different from control and a higher voltage treatment (Table 5.2A). On the other hand, compared to the control, a higher voltage of 16 V increased lutein (4.6%), β-carotene (4.4%), total carotenoids (4.5%) and chlorophyll a (4.0%) contents of African nightshade leaves, however, only tendentiously. Regarding African nightshade stems, an increase in voltage treatments resulted in a significant increase in almost all carotenoids and chlorophylls (Table 5.2B). When compared with the control plants, mainly the highest voltage treatment (16 V) increased lutein, β-carotene, total carotenoids, chlorophyll a and b contents in stems by 20.0%, 30.0%, 22.0%, 21.8%, 22.0%, respectively, whereas lycopene was affected to a smaller extent (10.0%). Plants treated with a voltage of 8 and 16 V did not differ significantly from each other when bioactive compounds such as lutein, lycopene and chlorophylls were considered. However, doubling the voltage led to an increase in ß-carotene by 18.2% and total carotenoids by 13.6% in stems compared with the lower voltage (8 V) applied on African nightshade plants.

5.3.5. Effect of different electrical voltages on structural carbohydrates of African nightshade plants

There was a similar response to different voltage in terms of structural carbohydrates in leaves and stems of African nightshade plants. A higher content of structural carbohydrates was obtained in stems compared to leaves. In leaves, only the treatment of 16 V resulted in a significant increase in hemicellulose (40.0%) content compared to the non-treated plants. In consideration of both DC treatments, no significant differences were found (Figure 5.5A). However, neither 8 V nor 16 V influenced cellulose and lignin content in leaves significantly. Similar results were obtained in stems. The hemicellulose content was significantly increased by 52% and 38.7% when 8 V and 16 V were applied, respectively, compared to the control (Figure 5.5B). Cellulose and lignin contents in stems were not significantly affected by different voltages.

5.3.6. Effect of different electrical voltages on mineral compounds and heavy metals in African nightshade plants

Voltage treatments differently affected minerals and heavy metals of African nightshade plants, in both leaves and stems. A general increase in voltage resulted in an increase in most of the mineral elements and heavy metals analyzed. Generally, a higher content of N, C, Ca, Mg, Fe, Zn, Ni, and Cd was observed in leaves while stems had higher K, Na, Pb and Cr contents. In leaves, a voltage of 8 V significantly influenced the contents of Ca, Pb and Cr which were increased by 20.2%, 42.1%, and 52.7%, respectively, compared to the contents observed in control leaves (Table 5.3A). A voltage of 16 V evoked nearly the same accumulations, except for the content of Ca which was increased by 27.5% when compared to the non-treated plants.

Table 5.2: Effect of voltage applications on chlorophylls and carotenoids content (mg/g DM) of African nightshade plants.

DC	Lutein	β-carotene	Lycopene	Total carotenoids	Chlorophyll a	Chlorophyll b
A. Leaves						
Control	2.0 ± 0.15 a	2.1 ± 0.16 a	1.5×10^{-1} ± 0.01 a	8.2 ± 0.62 a	16.9 ± 1.52 a	7.5 ± 0.74 a
8 V	1.7 ± 0.24 b	1.7 ± 0.24 b	1.5×10^{-1} ± 0.02 a	6.9 ± 0.97 b	14.3 ± 1.58 b	6.9 ± 0.54 a
16 V	2.1 ± 0.10 a	2.2 ± 0.10 a	1.6×10^{-1} ± 0.01 a	8.6 ± 0.40 a	17.6 ± 0.70 a	7.6 ± 1.01 a
B. Stems						
Control	1.0×10^{-1} ± 0.01 b	1.0×10^{-1} ± 0.01 b	7.9×10^{-3} ± 0.00 a	4.1×10^{-1} ± 0.03 b	7.8×10^{-1} ± 0.07 b	4.1×10^{-1} ± 0.02 b
8 V	1.1×10^{-1} ± 0.01 ab	1.1×10^{-1} ± 0.01 b	8.4×10^{-3} ± 0.00 a	4.4×10^{-1} ± 0.04 b	8.6×10^{-1} ± 0.09 ab	4.8×10^{-1} ± 0.01 ab
16 V	1.2×10^{-1} ± 0.01 a	1.3×10^{-1} ± 0.00 a	8.7×10^{-3} ± 0.00 a	5.0×10^{-1} ± 0.02 a	9.5×10^{-1} ± 0.05 a	5.0×10^{-1} ± 0.02 a

Mean values (± standard deviation) within a specific variable and plant part followed by the same letter are not significantly different according to Tukey-test ($p < 0.05$).

Table 5.3: Effect of voltage applications on mineral element and heavy metal content (g/kg DM) of African nightshade plants.

Element	A. Leaves			B. Stems		
	Control	8 V	16 V	Control	8 V	16 V
N	29.60 ± 3.20 a	27.10 ± 3.40 a	28.60 ± 4.30 a	7.40 ± 0.80 a	6.79 ± 0.60 a	8.34 ± 1.30 a
C	425.50 ± 2.30 a	421.00 ± 3.80 a	424.40 ± 3.10 a	410.70 ± 5.80 a	413.10 ± 5.30 a	409.00 ± 4.80 a
P	6.13 ± 0.39 a	5.73 ± 0.54 a	6.02 ± 0.37 a	3.46 ± 0.18 a	3.6 ± 0.22 a	3.86 ± 0.22 a
K	33.35 ± 0.82 a	32.20 ± 3.17 a	32.56 ± 4.68 a	40.72 ± 2.68 a	39.37 ± 3.26 a	41.42 ± 3.64 a
Ca	21.56 ± 0.16 c	25.91 ± 0.77 b	27.49 ± 3.28 a	12.38 ± 1.02 a	12.90 ± 0.57 a	14.10 ± 1.18 a
Mg	3.12 ± 0.39 a	3.25 ± 0.39 a	3.07 ± 0.41 a	1.60 ± 0.05 b	1.76 ± 0.26 ab	1.85 ± 0.11 a
Na	1.10×10^{-1} ± 0.00 a	0.90×10^{-1} ± 0.00 a	0.97×10^{-1} ± 0.00 a	2.38×10^{-1} ± 0.03 ab	2.10×10^{-1} ± 0.02 b	2.76×10^{-1} ± 0.03 a
Fe	9.04×10^{-2} ± 0.00 a	8.83×10^{-2} ± 0.00 a	9.05×10^{-2} ± 0.00 a	3.75×10^{-2} ± 0.00 a	4.14×10^{-2} ± 0.00 a	4.26×10^{-2} ± 0.00 a
Zn	3.53×10^{-2} ± 0.00 a	3.73×10^{-2} ± 0.00 a	3.98×10^{-2} ± 0.00 a	2.35×10^{-2} ± 0.00 b	3.03×10^{-2} ± 0.00 b	8.09×10^{-2} ± 0.00 a
Ni	0.00 ± 0.00 a	1.19×10^{-6} ± 0.00 a	1.15×10^{-6} ± 0.00 a	0.53×10^{-6} ± 0.00 b	0.55×10^{-6} ± 0.00 b	1.13×10^{-6} ± 0.00 a
Pb	3.40×10^{-4} ± 0.00 b	4.83×10^{-4} ± 0.00 a	4.57×10^{-4} ± 0.00 ab	3.63×10^{-4} ± 0.00 a	4.10×10^{-4} ± 0.00 a	4.79×10^{-4} ± 0.00 a
Cd	4.87×10^{-4} ± 0.00 a	5.47×10^{-4} ± 0.00 a	5.43×10^{-4} ± 0.00 a	2.34×10^{-4} ± 0.00 b	2.58×10^{-4} ± 0.00 ab	3.20×10^{-4} ± 00.00 a
Cr	3.47×10^{-4} ± 0.00 b	5.30×10^{-4} ± 0.00 a	5.10×10^{-4} ± 0.00 a	5.2×10^{-4} ± 0.00 b	9.90×10^{-4} ± 0.00 ab	20.2×10^{-4} ± 0.00 a

Mean values (± standard deviation) within a row and plant part followed by the same letter are not significantly different according to Tukey-test ($p < 0.05$).

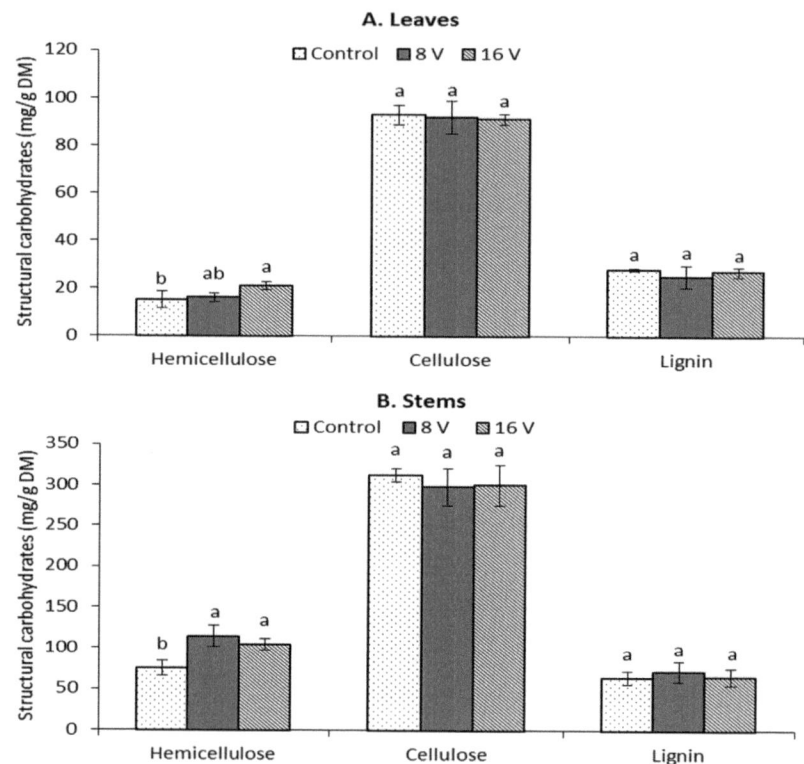

Figure 5.5: Effect of different voltage applications on different structural carbohydrates on leaves (A) and Stems (B) of African nightshade plants. Mean values (± standard deviation) within a specific variable followed by the same letter are not significantly different according to Tukey-test ($p < 0.05$).

A significant difference between lower and higher voltages occurred only when the content of Ca was considered. This was significantly increased by 6.1% when leaves were exposed to 16 V. In stems, however, a voltage of 16 V significantly increased the contents of Mg (15.6%), Zn (244.4%), Ni (113.2%), Cd (36.8%) and Cr (288.5%) compared to the control. No significant difference between elements was achieved when control plants and plants exposed to 8 V were considered (Table 5.3B). Significant differences between both voltage treatments were only demonstrated in terms of Na, Zn and Ni. The content of these elements in stems grown under 16 V conditions was increased by 31.4%, 167.0% and 105.5%, respectively. However, different voltages were not able to influence the contents of N, C, P, K, Ca, Mg, Fe and Pb in stems of African nightshade plants significantly.

5.4. Discussion

Results from the present study have demonstrated that weak voltages may be used to improve growth and bioactive compounds in African nightshade plants. The different voltages had a significant influence on current flow through African nightshade plants. This was increased with increasing voltage. This circumstance could be attributed to varying resistance caused by African nightshade plants as a result of changes in growth and development with time. On the other hand, changes in water supply could result in variation in electrical conductivity followed by changes in electrical current flows.

Even though different voltages did not affect the plant growth (leaf number, plant height, stem diameter and number of primary shoots) of nightshade plants, LA was tendentiously enhanced when a voltage of 16 V was applied compared to the control. However, Kareem (1999) successfully demonstrated that a higher electric current (110 to 220 V) at varying time (10 to 30 s) was able to improve leaf length, leaf width and stem length of cowpea (*Vigna unguiculata* (L.) Walp.), guinea corn (*Sorghum bicolor* (L.) Moench) and groundnut (*Arachis hypogaea* L.), when seeds were treated using wet (seeds soaked in water inside aluminum cup connected to live wire) and dry (seeds with empty aluminum cup connected to live wire) application methods. Kotaka and Krueger (1968) found that varying ion densities improved growth of barley (Hordeum vulgare L.), oats (*Avena sativa* L.) and lettuce (*Lactuca sativa* L.). These studies suggest that increases in ion density as a result of voltage effects may enhance the availability of nutrients in plant cells as observed in the current study. This phenomenon may result in improved physiological processes such as photosynthesis, whereby more photosynthates can be accumulated in leaves leading to a higher LA as tendentiously observed in the present study at the 16 V treatments. Okamura et al. (2011) showed that growth of radish and thale cress (*Arabidopsis thaliana* (L.) Heynh.) was more promoted when seeds were treated with 10.0 kV/m DC than with 2.5 kV/m DC. It is also important to note that plant tissue is characterized by a heterogeneous structure with a high degree of anisotropy (Ben-Ammar et al., 2011). Cell size, cell size distribution, and cell orientation have an impact on the effectiveness of electric currents on crops (Ben-Ammar et al., 2011). These influencing factors could be taken into consideration to explain the reason why some growth parameters were not affected by different electric voltages as observed in the present study.

In the current study, the use of DC increased leaf fresh and dry weight of African nightshade plants. DC was considered to affect visual damage (yellowing) of plants, therefore, marketable and non-marketable leaves were recorded. It was found that DC reduced the amount of non-marketable leaves. Murr (1963) observed tip burn to orchard grass seedlings (*Dactylis glomerata* L.) due to electric fields (40 kV/m) effect manifested by dark brown spots. Further, microscopic examination revealed chloroplast damage. However, the strength of electric field has an influence on the extent of plant damage. The results in terms of dry weight were corroborated by Ward (1996) who found that weak direct electric current (6 V) using wires as electrodes increased this parameter in greenhouse produced tomatoes. Electrical fields are reported to play a vital part in crop physiology (Scott, 1967). For example, an electrogenic proton pump helps in the regulation of cytoplasmic pH, active transport of mineral ions, hormones or organic metabolites (Spanswick, 1981). In this context, the externally applied voltages in the present study resulted in an increase in contents of mineral elements (e.g. Mg, Ca and Zn) and structural carbohydrates (hemicellulose) in a bid to cope with electric stress (Gall et al., 2015). This circumstance can promote physiological processes of African nightshade plants. For instance, Ca plays a major role in root system development associated with a better water and nutrient uptake (Picchioni et al., 2001) while Mg and Zn is involved in chlorophyll synthesis, which is important for photosynthesis (Hu and Sparks, 1991). The latter evidence could be the reason for a higher accumulation of carbohydrates as caused by increasing voltages in the present study, especially observed for hemicellulose content in leaves and stems. Hemicellulose facilitates cell wall thickening by reinforcement of secondary wall and hence reduction in water loss through transpiration (Gall et al., 2015). These plant responses were jointly responsible and sufficient, in order to increase fresh and dry weight in leaves as well as marketable leaves as observed on DC treated plants. Furthermore, the increase in mineral elements (e.g. Mg and Zn) in DC treated plants enhanced chlorophyll formation (green pigment), thus preventing yellowing (chlorosis) leading to reduced non-marketable leaves as reported in the present study.

As indicated earlier, a shift in consumer eating habits has led to increasing demand for high quality food products. In the present study, application of a voltage of 16 V through the whole plant significantly increased contents of chlorophyll a and b, as well as lutein, β-carotene and total carotenoids in stems and tendentiously in leaves of African nightshade plants. These plant bioactive compounds have antioxidant potential and are therefore very important in maintaining human health. For instance, carotenoids have been reported to possess provitamin A activity (Tang, 2010); a precursor of vitamin A, essential for the promotion of general growth, maintenance of visual function, regulation of differentiation of epithelial tissues and embryonic development (Underwood and Arthur, 1996). In addition, carotenoids have been reported to be necessary for the prevention of cardiovascular diseases and also have anticarcinogenic effects (Voutilainen et al., 2006). Just like carotenoids, chlorophylls are important for health promotion such as enhancing oxygen uptake in the blood, which can increase energy, relieve fatigue and improve many blood disorders (Ferruzzi et al., 2001). Regarding electrophysiology, studies involving the use of intermittent-direct-electric-current (IDC) between 200 and 1800 mA applied to plant roots increased phytochemical compounds in one week old garden cress sprouts compared to the control (Dannehl et al., 2012). Previously, the same group of researchers demonstrated that different intensities of IDC (100 to 500 mA) with varied application times (15 to 60 min) during postharvest resulted in accumulation of carotenoids, phenolic compounds and an increase in antioxidant activity in tomatoes (Dannehl et al., 2011). Similarly, they also reported that application of IDC

(200 to 1000 mA) to roots of radish plants during growth resulted in an increase in phenolic compounds in radish tubers as well as in roots without visible damages to the plants (Dannehl et al., 2009). Another report indicates that the application of DC (10 V/12.5 µA) resulted in an increase in peroxidase activity; an indicator of stress in spinach leaves (*Spinacia oleracea* L.) (Montavon et al., 1988). This stress response could be initiated when the plant recognizes a stimulus at the cellular level, as a result of the activity of specific ion channels such as voltage-gated ion channels embedded in a cell plasma membrane (Gaspar et al., 2002). Thus, perturbation of internal electric field as a result of applied DC could induce stress mediated changes in the electrochemical proton gradient or the cytoplasmic and vacuolar pH, among others. This in turn could result in an increase in biosynthesis of primary and secondary metabolites in order to rectify this plant state. In the present study, the higher contents of chlorophylls and carotenoids as a result of applied DC confirm this assumption.

In addition, DC improved content of hemicellulose, an important structural carbohydrate necessary in food digestion. However, DC did not significantly influence cellulose and lignin content. Stress induction by DC may result in various enzymatic activities, e.g., cell-wall bound peroxidases (Dymek et al., 2014). This could lead to biosynthesis of structural carbohydrates such as hemicellulose in African nightshade plants as observed in the present study, in order to enhance plant resistance to stress. However, the enzymatic signaling pathways of various structural carbohydrates are compartment-specific or even cell-specific (Dymek et al., 2014). This would explain why some structural carbohydrates were affected (hemicellulose) while others were not (cellulose and lignin).

Majority of the world population currently suffer from 'hidden hunger' (e.g., lacking various mineral elements, vitamin A and fibre content) in the diet (Biesalski, 2013). This is exacerbated by frequent consumption of food either lacking or having low content of such key mineral elements or phytochemicals. The present study revealed that DC treatments through the whole plant result in an increase in certain mineral elements such as Mg, Ca and Zn in African nightshade plants. However, other elements, for example, N, C, P, K and Fe were not significantly affected. An increased nutrient uptake of Mg and Ca was also found in greenhouse produced tomato treated with 6 V DC (Ward, 1996) while Black et al. (1971) reported an significant increase in K, Ca and P content in tomato when a much lower DC of 15 to 30 µA was applied. As such, additional potential induced from external electric field in plants is reported to raise pressure on the membrane due to attraction between opposite charges on both sides of the membrane, whereby a faster transport of ions is induced simultaneously (Zimmerman et al., 1974). This could cause an accumulation of elements, as this hypothesis is supported by increased contents of minerals as observed in the present study. This rapid influx of mineral ions through cation channels imbedded in the plant membrane can induce stress in plants, which can promote the synthesis of secondary metabolites as well (Dannehl et al., 2012). In order to ensure reversible membrane permeabilisation and associated plant vitality, critical electric field strength must be taken into consideration, which is dependent on plant species, as well as cell geometry and size (Heinz et al., 2002).

DC also increased the content of heavy metals, i.e. Cr, Ni, Cd and Pb of African nightshade plants, assumingly due to an electron transport between both electrodes used in the present study. Similar results were reported by Dannehl et al. (2012) when DC (200 to 1800 mA) was applied to garden cress. However, the observed results are still within acceptable thresholds regulated by law for human consumption according to European Food Safety Authority (EFSA, 2008).

5.5. Conclusion and recommendation

In general, the findings of this study have demonstrated that the application of weak dosages of DC (8 and 16 V) can improve growth, and quality in terms of health protecting plant compounds of African nightshade plants. Plant specific carotenoids (ß-carotene and lutein), chlorophyll a and b, as well as characteristic mineral elements such as Mg, Ca and Zn and structural carbohydrates (hemicellulose) in African nightshade were promoted by DC. The results showed that DC induced a defence response of plant cells and may have altered the cell membrane properties and hence physiological processes. Farmers of African leafy vegetables in Kenya commonly practice small-scale farming or kitchen gardening, where they cultivate vegetables in small plots or in pots, especially for home consumption. Therefore, the findings of the study may be beneficial to such farmers. Furthermore, this technology is also applicable in areas where electricity is absent or unstable which in most cases are the situation in rural areas as farmers can use alternative power sources, e.g. batteries, solar cells, or dynamos. Furthermore, emerging technologies such as DC could be used either as stand-alone or in synergistic combination with other technologies, in order to satisfy the increased consumer demand for high quality and healthy food products. As such, DC applications provide an alternative to enhance food security. However, it remains a need to adjust the intensity of DC and duration of exposure to various crop species and varieties for optimization of yield and quality. Furthermore, it has to be investigated in detail if such technologies are worthwhile in terms of economic aspects.

Acknowledgement

This study is part of the project Horticultural Innovations and Learning for Improved Nutrition and Livelihood in East Africa (HORTINLEA) being funded by the German Federal Ministry of Education and Research (BMBF) and the German Federal Ministry of Economic Cooperation and Development (BMZ) within the framework of the program GlobE – Global Food Security. We gratefully acknowledge the financial support of BMBF and BMZ.

The authors thank Susanne Meier and Sigrun Witt for conducting an excellent job in the laboratories.

6. Postharvest UV-C treatment for extending shelf life and improving nutritional quality of African indigenous leafy vegetables

Gogo E.O., Opiyo, A.M., Hassenberg, K., Ulrichs, Ch., Huyskens-Keil, S., 2017. Postharvest Biology and Technology 129, 107-117. http://dx.doi.org/10.1016/j.postharvbio.2017.03.019.

Abstract

Currently, consumer eating habits have shifted to an increasing demand for high quality, safe and healthy food products worldwide. In many African countries, specifically African indigenous leafy vegetables (AIVs) gained importance in this respect contributing to human diet by providing minerals, proteins, vitamins and health-promoting antioxidant compounds. Moreover, these vegetables have an immense potential in creating job opportunities in rural as well as peri-urban areas. However, AIVs tend to suffer severe quantitative and qualitative postharvest losses because of their high perishability. UV-C has been mainly applied in sanitation and food safety for its germicidal effect but also has an impact on preventing nutritional losses. To address this, studies were conducted to evaluate the effect of postharvest application of hormic UV-C dosages on bioactive plant compounds of two AIVs, i.e. African nightshade (*Solanum scabrum* Mill.) cv. Olevolosi and vegetable amaranth (*Amaranthus cruentus* L.) cv. Madiira. Eight weeks after planting, the leaves were harvested and treated with UV-C (254 nm) at either 1.7 kJ m^{-2} or 3.4 kJ m^{-2} while untreated leaves served as control. The leaves were kept for 4 and 14 d at 20 °C (65% RH) and 5 °C (85% RH), respectively. The quality parameters studied were fresh weight loss, mineral elements (N, P, K, Ca, Mg, Fe, and Zn), protein, and structural carbohydrates determining dietary fibre content and microbial counts. In addition, antioxidative, health promoting plant compounds, i.e. carotenoid, and chlorophyll contents were evaluated. The results showed that fresh weight loss of both AIVs was significantly reduced with application of lower UV-C dosage (1.7 kJ m^{-2}). Mineral elements and proteins were variedly affected with a general decline in the initial stages followed by an increase compared to the untreated leaves. Hemicellulose and cellulose was significantly increased in vegetable amaranth and lignin content was significantly increased in African nightshade following UV-C treatment. Chlorophyll and carotenoid contents declined within 2-4 d during storage, depending on storage conditions; but thereafter increased again significantly compared to the control. Aerobic mesophylic and yeast counts were significantly reduced by UV-C treatment, while mould counts were not affected. The findings demonstrate the potential of using hormic UV-C for maintaining the nutritional quality of AIVs during their supply chain as an easy to apply and effective tool, hence contributing to improved food accessibility and food safety in Sub-Saharan areas such as Kenya.

6.1. Introduction

Food insecurity, malnutrition and life style diseases such as obesity, high blood pressure, carcinogenic diseases and diabetes are a major global issue including Sub-Saharan Africa (SSA). In SSA, more than 60% of people in rural areas live below the poverty line, hence being affected by malnutrition, poor health ('hidden hunger') and have inadequate accessibility to basic necessities (Kader, 2005). Consequently, there is an increasing demand for high quality and healthy food products especially fruits and vegetables (Brückner and Caglar, 2016; Onyango and Imungi, 2007). African indigenous leafy vegetables (AIVs) have potential to address poverty and nutritional security problems because they grow easily, they require minimum production input, and they are rich in minerals, vitamins, fibre and antioxidant compounds, and moreover provide employment opportunities (Onyango et al., 2009; Shiundu and Oniang'o, 2007). However, they exhibit a high metabolic activity after harvest, high water content and hence are highly perishable with a shelf life of less than one day at ambient tropical temperature conditions (Gogo et al., 2016). A study conducted in Kenya indicated that between 2-6% of AIVs traded in Nairobi are lost within a day due to wilting alone (Onyango and Imungi, 2007). Moreover, improper packaging during AIV distribution as well as some farmers sprinkling water on them in unhygienic conditions in an attempt to maintain freshness, results in microbiological decay problems (Gogo et al., 2016). Unfortunately, limited information on postharvest handling and technologies on their loss reduction and quality management has even worsened the situation (Kader, 2005). Generally, exposure of plants to UV irradiation stress is known to have deleterious effects on tissues (Ribeiro et al., 2012). However, low dosages of UV-C are reported to stimulate defence responses of plants, a phenomenon known as hormesis (Shama, 2007). UV radiation wavelength is between 100-400 nm and is subdivided into UV-A (315-400 nm), UV-B (280-315 nm), UV-C (200-280 nm) and the vacuum UV (100-200 nm) (Ribeiro et al., 2012). The use of UV-C in water, air and surface treatment (decontamination) is well established (Fonseca and Rushing, 2008). The ability of UV-C irradiation to disinfect and delay microbial growth on the fresh produce without affecting quality has been demonstrated (Hinojosa et al., 2015; Lu et al., 2016). Furthermore, recent studies have demonstrated that UV-C treatment may be an effective tool to extend the shelf life and increase human health promoting compounds in fresh produce (Huyskens-Keil et al., 2011; Kang et al., 2013; Katerova et al., 2012; Lu et al., 2016; Stevens et al., 2004). Currently, reviews on UV-C application as a postharvest technology have been demonstrated for various vegetables including broccoli (*Brassica oleracea* L. var. italica Plenck), tomato (*Solanum lycopersicum* L.), mushroom (*Agaricus bisporus* J.E. Lange), sweet pepper (*Capsicum annuum* L.), baby spinach (*Spinacia oleracea* L.), and white asparagus (*Asparagus officinalis* L.) (Pataro et al., 2015; Ribeiro et al., 2012; Shama, 2007; Turtoi, 2013). From these studies, it is concluded that the UV-C irradiation efficacy in extending vegetable shelf life depends on the produce (species and variety, intact or minimally processed fruit and vegetables), the surface of the plant exposed to the irradiation, the initial microbial load, and on the method of application (time and duration of application and treatment dosage). Low dosages of UV-C (0.25–8.0 kJ m^{-2}) stimulate the ability of the plant to scavenge and/or control the level of cellular reactive oxygen species (ROS) that consequently activate primary and secondary compounds (Cetin, 2014; Salama et al., 2011) which may contribute to improved shelf life and enhanced nutritional quality and health benefits (Huyskens-Keil et al., 2011; Ramakrishna and Ravishankar, 2011; Tarek et al., 2016). In addition, treatments with UV-C have several advantages as it does not require complex equipment, hence easy to use, no chemical residue on the treated produce, no legal restrictions as they are generally recognized as safe (GRAS status), cheap and relatively affordable (Hassenberg et al., 2012). Therefore, the present study investigate the effects of postharvest UV-C treatments on characteristic primary (protein, macro- and micro-nutrients, dietary fibre) and antioxidative compounds (carotenoids and chlorophylls) and microbial population of vegetable amaranth and African nightshade leaves to improve shelf life and nutritional quality.

6.2. Material and methods

6.2.1. Plant material

Vegetable amaranth cv. Madiira and African nightshade cv. Olevolosi seeds were sourced from AVRDC (Arusha, Tanzania). The AIVs were grown under greenhouse conditions in 2014 and 2015 (each year in June to July) at the experimental station of Humboldt-Universität zu Berlin, Germany. Sowing was done in small tray cells and after 14 d; the seedlings were transplanted in to 6-L pots. Growing medium (Profi-Substrate + Ton + Fe, Gramoflor GmbH and Co., Vechta, Germany) was used for planting. Watering was done daily, using an automatic drip irrigation system. All other good agricultural practices were conducted uniformly when deemed necessary. In 2014, average weekly temperature, relative humidity and photosynthetically active radiation (PAR) during production was between 15.2 to 26.1 °C, 67.6-82.4% and 715.3 to 1500.2 mmol m^{-2} s^{-1}, whereas in 2015, average weekly temperature, relative humidity and photosynthetically active radiation (PAR) was between 16.9 to 26.7 °C, 66.8-83.2% and 664.9 to 1255.1 mmol m^{-2} s^{-1}, respectively (Figure 6.1).

6.2.2. Experimental set-up and treatment application

Eight weeks after sowing, the vegetable leaves were harvested and immediately treated with UV-C in an UV-C chamber (ABOX® UV Technology, UMEX GmbH, Germany), where temperature and relative air humidity were kept constant at 5 °C and 85%, respectively. UV-C dosage was achieved with medium pressure mercury vapour discharge lamps with a peak emission at 254 nm (VL-6C, 6 W-254 nm Tube, Power: 11 W, Vilber Lourmat GmbH, Germany). The lamps were placed at a distance of 0.4 m to leaves. The dosage was calculated from the product of exposure time and irradiance, as measured by a portable handheld digital radiometer (UVPAD-E, Opsytec Dr. Gröbel GmbH, Germany). Based on this, two different dosages were applied, i.e. 1.7 kJ m^{-2} and 3.4 kJ m^{-2}. The dosages were chosen based on

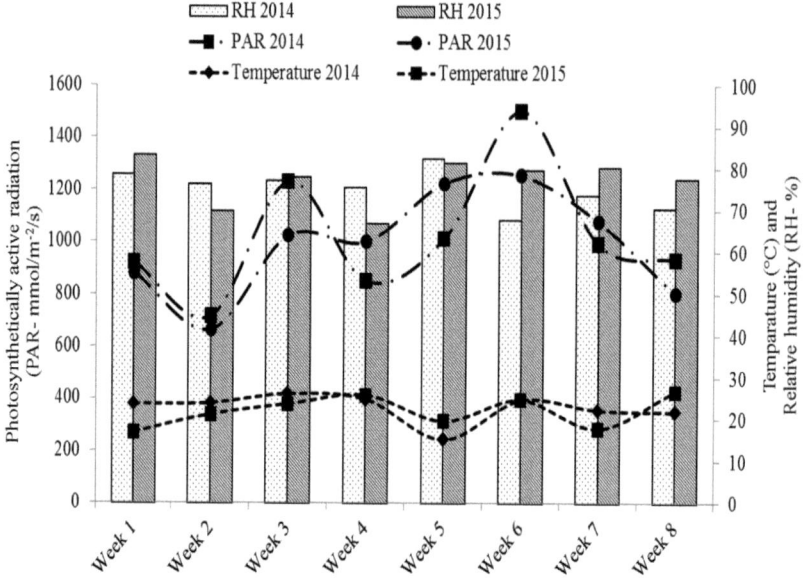

Figure 6.1: Greenhouse microclimate conditions during production of vegetable amaranth and African nightshade plants in 2014 and 2015 (June to July).

preliminary experiments and the most commonly applied UV-C dosages on leafy vegetables and were found not to have a negative effect on their visual quality (Chairat et al., 2013). Untreated leaves served as control. The treatments were applied in three replications with each containing 30 leaves arranged in a completely randomized design. During UV-C treatment, the leaves were carefully arranged one after the other and facing upwards to eliminate possible shadow effects and ensure each leaf received equal dosage. The leaves were stored at 20 °C and 5 °C for a possible maximum shelf life of 4 and 14 d, respectively. After UV-C treatment application, the leaves were stored on trays under controlled temperature and in water vapour saturated atmosphere conditions to simulate retailing condition. Samples were evaluated at harvest, 2 and 4 d after storage at 20 °C, while those stored at 5 °C samples were evaluated at harvest, 2, 4, 10 and 14 d after storage.

6.2.3. Sample preparation

At each data collection period, samples were immediately shock frozen in liquid nitrogen and kept at -20 °C for further analysis of all compounds. Fresh weight loss, dry matter content, carotenoids and chlorophylls and microbial counts were determined using shock frozen material. The remaining samples were freeze-dried for 48 h (Alpha 1-4, Martin Christ Gefriertrocknungsanlagen

GmbH, Germany), ground, mixed to a fine homogenized powder, and stored in a desiccator for further analyses of selected minerals, structural carbohydrates and protein.

6.2.4. Determination of fresh weight loss and dry matter content

Fresh weight loss was determined by dividing the difference between the initial and final weight after storage by the initial weight of the treatments and expressed as percentage. To determine the dry matter, 30 g fresh material per treatment sample was placed in a drying oven (T6060, Heraeus Instruments GmbH, Germany) at 105 °C until constant weight was achieved. The percentage of dry matter was calculated by the ratio of the dry weight to the fresh weight.

6.2.5. Determination of macro- and micro-nutrients

Macro- and micro-nutrients (P, K, Ca, Mg, Zn, and Fe) were determined using the method of inductively coupled plasma-optical emission spectrometry (ICP-OES) analysis. Analysis was done in duplicate for each replication from each treatment. For the digestion, 0.2 g of each freeze dried sample was weighed into deionized containers where 5 mL of 65% HNO_3, and 3 mL of 30% H_2O_2 were added. The contents were then digested into a microwave (MARS Xpress, CEM; USA) according to the following program: step 1, 20 min to reach 200 °C; step 2, 5 min at 200 °C; step 3, 1 min to reach 210 °C; step 4, 5 min at 210 °C; step 5, 1 min to reach 220 °C; step 6, 5 min at 220 °C; and lastly step 7, 30 min to cool down to room temperature. The solution was then transferred into 50 mL volumetric flasks and eventually filtered into plastic flasks. The elements were analysed using ICP emission spectrometer (iCAP 6300 Duo MFC, Thermo Scientific; USA). The analysis was performed with the following operating conditions: 1150W RF power, 0.55 L min^{-1} nebulizer gas flow with argon used as plasmogen as well as carrier gas, and performed with a cross flow nebulizer (MIRA MIST, Thermo Scientific; England), in addition to radial (Ca and Mg) and axial (Fe and Zn) view. A single element standard solution (Carl Roth GmbH & Co. KG, Germany) of 1000 mg L^{-1} was used in 1.4 mol L^{-1} HNO_3 as reference analytic solutions, for each element. Calibration curves were performed with the following reference solutions: blank 1.4 mol L^{-1} HNO_3; 1–200 mg L^{-1} of P, K and Ca; 0.5–50 mg L^{-1} of Mg; 0.5–5 mg L^{-1} of Zn and Fe. The elements in the solutions were analysed in duplicate using the following wavelength: P at 213.6 nm, K at 766.5 nm, Ca at 317.9 nm, Mg at 279.0 nm, Fe at 259.9 nm, Zn at 213.8 nm. All elements were expressed on a dry matter basis in g kg^{-1} for macro-nutrients and in mg kg^{-1} for micro-nutrients.

6.2.6. Determination of N and protein content

N and protein analyses were determined using an element analyzer (Vario Max CN, Elementar Analysensysteme GmbH, Germany) according to DIN-ISO-10694 (1995) and DIN-ISO-13878

(1998). In brief, 0.3 g of sample material was weighed into crucibles and catalytically combusted at 900 °C with pure oxygen. The combustion products including helium (as the carrier gas) passed through specific adsorption columns at 830 °C to separate N from C using selective sorption and quantified with a thermal conductivity detector (CONTHOS 3 – TCD, LFE GmbH & Co. KG, Germany). Each analysis was performed twice and the results were calculated using glutamic acid as the standard reference. N content was determined from the quantities of NO_x detected in the sample. Protein was calculated using N to protein conversion factor of 6.25 (Sosulski and Imafidon, 1990). The results were expressed on a dry matter basis in g kg^{-1}.

6.2.7. Determination of structural carbohydrates

Structural carbohydrates (lignin, cellulose and hemicellulose) were analysed according to Van Soest and Goering (1963) and Van Soest et al. (1991). Briefly, 1 g of freeze dried sample was extracted using 100 mL acid detergent fibre (ADF) reagent (N-Cetyl-N, N,N-trimethyl-ammoniumbromid dissolved in 96% H_2SO_4) in a fibertec system apparatus (Fibertec M 1020, Tecator, FOSS GmbH, Germany). The solution was then vacuum filtered, washed with boiled, double distilled water until all the acids were removed and finally washed with 90% acetone. The residue was oven-dried at 105 °C for 24 h, weighed, ash dried at 500 °C for 24 h and reweighed to determine ADF. The dried ADF residue was then used to determine acid detergent lignin (ADL). The difference between ADF and ADL was used to determine cellulose content. For the hemicellulose content determination, neutral detergent fibre (NDF) approach was employed where 1.0 g of freeze dried material was cooked in 100 mL NDF mixture (Titriplex III, di-sodium borate, dodecyl hydrogen sulphate sodium, and ethylene-glycol-monoethyl ester). The solution was filtered in a vacuum, and washed with demineralized water and 90% acetone. The residue was oven-dried at 105 °C for 24 h, weighed, ash dried at 500 °C for 24 h and reweighed for the determination of NDF. Hemicellulose content was obtained by the difference between NDF and ADF. The results were expressed on a dry matter basis in g kg^{-1}.

6.2.8. Determination of carotenoid and chlorophyll contents

Extraction and determination of the carotenoids (carotenes, xanthophylls, and total carotenoids) and chlorophylls a and b was conducted according to Goodwin and Britton (1988). An aliquot of 0.5 g fresh material was homogenized using a digital homogenizer (Ultra-Turrax® T 25, IKA®-Werke GmbH and Co. KG, Germany) in acetone/hexane (4:5, v:v) for 1 min at 18,000 rpm, and centrifuged (Multifuge X1R, Thermo Fisher Scientific, Heraeus Holding GmbH, Germany) for 10 min (4000 rpm) twice. The supernatants were collected in a 25 mL volumetric flask and brought to volume using the acetone/hexane mixture. Three replications of the sample per treatment were measured in duplicate using a UV-Vis spectrophotometer (UV-Mini-1240, Shimadzu, Japan). The results were expressed on a dry matter basis in g kg^{-1}.

6.2.9. Microbial analysis

To determine aerobic mesophilic, yeast and mould counts, 10 g of the sample was placed in a stomacher bag under sterile conditions. After adding 90 mL of Ringer solution, the mixture was homogenized in a stomacher (Bagmixer 400, Interscience Laboratories Inc., France) for 2 min and aliquot diluted. To determine aerobic mesophilic count, 100 µL of the diluted sample was spread on plate count agar (PCA, plates, Merck, Darmstadt, Germany) and incubated at 30 °C for 3 d. In order to determine yeast and mould counts, 100 µL of the diluted sample was spread on rose-bengal chloramphenicol plate count agar (RBC plates, Merck, Darmstadt, Germany) and incubated at 25 °C for 7 d. The analysis was repeated two times for each replication and results expressed on fresh weight basis as log CFU g^{-1}.

6.3.0. Data analysis

The univariate procedure of SAS (version 9.4; SAS Institute, USA) was used to check for normality of the data before analysis. Since there was negligible variation between treatments across the seasons, data for 2014 and 2015 were pooled and subjected to analysis of variance (ANOVA) using the proc GLM at $p < 0.05$. Means were separated using Tukey's honestly significant difference (THSD) test at $p < 0.05$. Data are presented as mean ± standard deviation.

6.3. Results

6.3.1. Effect of postharvest UV-C application on fresh weight loss

Postharvest UV-C application on vegetable amaranth and African nightshade leaves revealed an impact on fresh weight loss. At 20 °C, application of lower UV-C dosage (1.7 kJ m^{-2}) to vegetable amaranth resulted in significantly lower fresh weight loss at both 2 and 4 d of storage (Figure 6.2A). However, there was no significant difference of fresh weight loss between the control leaves and those treated with 3.4 kJ m^{-2} UV-C. Similarly, application of 1.7 kJ m^{-2} to African nightshade leaves resulted in significantly lower fresh weight loss, however only for 2 d of storage, while the 3.4 kJ m^{-2} UV-C treatment resulted in a higher fresh weight loss throughout the storage period compared to the control (Figure 6.2B). After 2 d of storage, fresh weight loss of African nightshade significantly increased with the increase in UV-C application dosage, with the control leaves having significantly lower weight loss.

At 5 °C, vegetable amaranth and African nightshade leaves showed a similar response to UV-C treatment, however only for 4 d of storage. Low UV-C application did not significantly influence fresh weight loss of both AIVs, whereas higher UV-C dosages of 3.4 kJ m^{-2} resulted in a higher fresh weight loss compared to the control. After 10 d of storage, low UV-C resulted in a

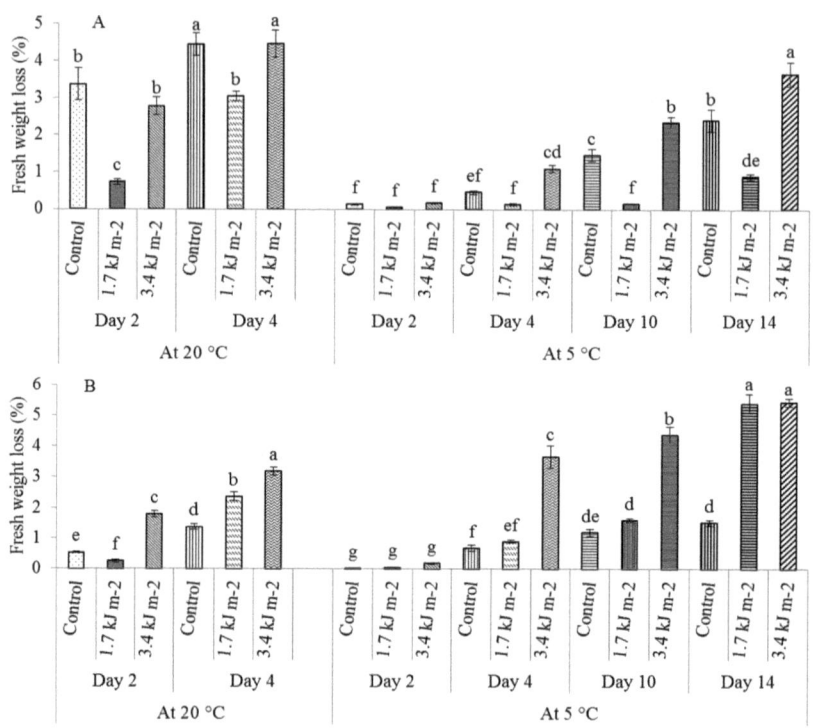

Figure 6.2: Effect of postharvest UV-C treatments on fresh weight loss of vegetable amaranth (A) and African nightshade (B) leaves during storage at different temperature regime. Means ± standard deviations followed by the same letter within a storage temperature regime and a vegetable are not significantly different according to Tukey's test ($p < 0.05$).

significant inhibition of fresh weight loss in vegetable amaranth throughout the storage period. In contrast, UV-C did not significantly reduce fresh weight losses in African nightshade leaves.

6.3.2. Effect of postharvest UV-C application on macro- and micro-nutrients and protein content

Mineral element and protein contents of the studied AIVs were variedly affected by postharvest UV-C application. At 20 °C, there was no significant difference in all minerals in vegetable amaranth except for nitrogen and protein which experienced an increase after 4 d at 3.4 kJ m^{-2} UV-C, whereas Mg experienced a slight decline after 2 d at 1.7 kJ m^{-2} in comparison to the control (Table 6.1A and Figure 6.3A). Similarly, African nightshade leaves stored at 20 °C showed no significant difference in all mineral compounds after 2 d of storage except for Zn, where a significantly higher content was found at 3.4 kJ m^{-2} compared to 1.7 kJ m^{-2} and the control. However, after 4 d of storage, UV-C dosage of 1.7 kJ m^{-2} resulted in significantly higher N, K, Ca, and protein contents and at 3.4 kJ m^{-2} UV-C revealed significantly higher P and Mg contents, whereas Fe and Zn contents were higher at both UV-C treatments compared to the control (Table 6.2A and Figure 6.3B).

At 5 °C, there were no significant differences in all the mineral elements studied on vegetable amaranth except after 2 d, where P, K and Mg at 1.7 kJ m^{-2} UV-C and after 10 d, where N and protein contents at 3.4 kJ m^{-2} UV-C were significantly lower compared to the control., while Mg content was significantly higher after 10 d at 1.7 kJ m^{-2} in comparison to the control (Table 6.1B and Figure 6.3A). After 14 d of storage, Zn content at 3.4 kJ m^{-2} and P and K contents for both UV-C treatments were significantly higher compared to the control. In African nightshade leaves, there was no significant difference in mineral element contents at 5 °C except after 10 and 14 d of storage, where both UV-C treatments resulted in a higher N, Fe, and protein contents while Zn content was higher at 3.4 kJ m^{-2} in comparison to the control (Table 6.2B and Figure 6.3B).

6.3.3. Effect of postharvest UV-C application on structural carbohydrates contents

Postharvest UV-C application had an influence on structural carbohydrates contents. At 20 °C, cellulose content of vegetable amaranth leaves was significantly higher at both UV-C dosages while hemicellulose content of UV-C treated leaves remained constant throughout the storage period compared to the control which declined after 4 d storage. Lignin content was however, significantly reduced by UV-C dosage of 1.7 kJ m^{-2} throughout the study compare with the control and higher UV-C treatments. For African nightshade leaves, no significant difference was observed in all the structural carbohydrates studied at 20 °C except for cellulose where 3.4 kJ m^{-2} UV-C resulted in significantly higher contents after 4 d compared to the control (Table 6.3A).

At 5 °C, UV-C treated vegetable amaranth leaves had significantly higher hemicellulose contents, however only for 2 d of storage compared to the control. Cellulose content was significantly lower at 3.4 kJ m^{-2} after 2 d which significantly increased after 10 d of storage compared to the control, while after 14 d; both UV-C treatments had significantly higher contents compared to the control. Within 4 d, lignin content declined first at 1.7 kJ m^{-2} and later under both UV-C treatments, while after 10 d lignin at 3.4 kJ m^{-2} was significantly lower compared to the control. For African nightshade leaves, there was no significant difference of structural carbohydrates except after 14 d of storage, where hemicellulose content was

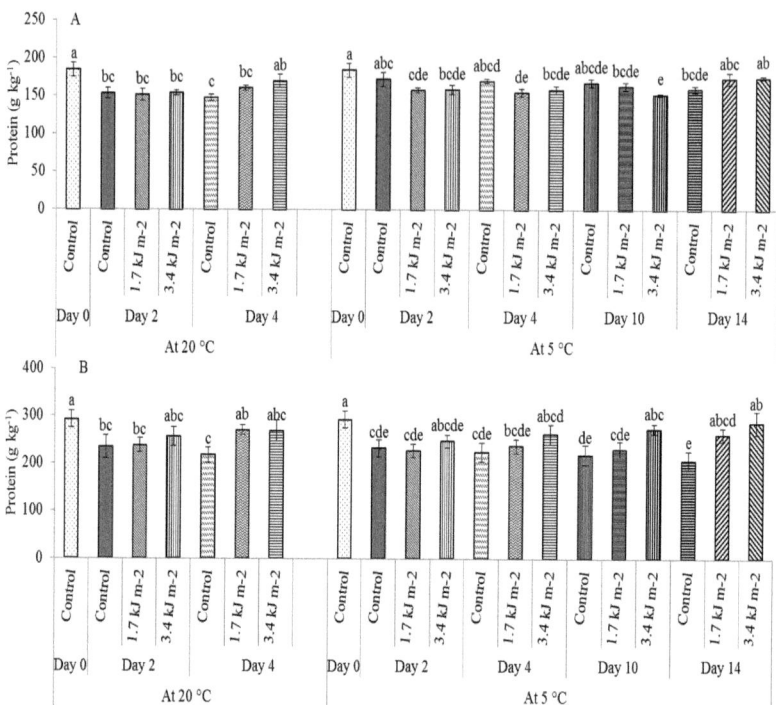

Figure 6.3: Effect of postharvest UV-C treatments on protein content of vegetable amaranth (A) and African nightshade (B) leaves during storage at different temperature regime. Means ± standard deviations followed by the same letter within a storage temperature regime and a vegetable are not significantly different according to Tukey's test ($p < 0.05$).

significantly lower at 3.4 kJ m^{-2} compared to the control. Cellulose remained almost constant and was not affected by the UV-C treatments. Lignin experienced a significant increase with both UV-C treatments in comparison to the control (Table 6.3B).

6.3.4. Effect of postharvest UV-C application on chlorophylls and carotenoids

Chlorophyll and carotenoid contents of vegetable amaranth and African nightshade leaves were influenced by postharvest UV-C applications differently. Vegetable amaranth leaves stored at 20 °C showed a strong decline in chlorophyll and carotenoid contents during storage. However,

Table 6.1: Effect of postharvest UV-C treatments on macro- and micro nutrient contents of vegetable amaranth leaves during storage at different temperature regime.

Storage days	UV-C dosage	Macro-nutrients (g kg^{-1})					Micro-nutrients (mg kg^{-1})	
		N	P	K	Ca	Mg	Fe	Zn
A. At 20 °C (retailer's simulation condition)								
Day 0	Control	29.5±1.5^a	6.0±0.1^a	59.8±1.7^a	17.3±0.8^a	3.7±0.2^a	85.2±0.7^a	61.3±1.8^a
Day 2	Control	24.6±1.1^{bc}	5.8±0.3^a	59.0±0.9^a	17.1±1.5^a	3.4±0.2^{ab}	83.8±3.0^a	60.9±4.6^a
	1.7 kJ m^{-2}	24.3±1.3^{bc}	5.6±0.2^a	58.7±1.3^a	15.6±0.6^a	2.7±0.2^c	82.6±5.1^a	60.6±0.9^a
	3.4 kJ m^{-2}	24.7±0.5^{bc}	5.6±0.1^a	58.5±1.4^a	16.1±1.0^a	3.0±0.2^{bc}	79.3±3.2^a	56.6±2.1^a
Day 4	Control	23.7±0.7^c	5.6±0.2^a	57.4±1.0^a	15.0±1.0^a	2.7±0.3^c	78.9±2.9^a	56.6±2.9^a
	1.7 kJ m^{-2}	25.8±0.5^{bc}	5.7±0.1^a	58.3±2.1^a	16.2±1.6^a	3.3±0.2^{abc}	83.1±2.4^a	55.5±4.7^a
	3.4 kJ m^{-2}	27.2±1.4^{ab}	6.3±0.4^a	58.5±2.2^a	16.8±0.9^a	3.1±0.2^{abc}	85.0±2.7^a	61.1±2.4^a
B. At 5 °C (cold storage)								
Day 0	Control	29.5±1.5^a	6.0±0.1^a	59.8±1.7^a	17.3±0.8^a	3.7±0.2^a	85.2±0.7^a	61.3±1.8^a
Day 2	Control	27.6±1.5^{abc}	5.9±0.3^a	57.8±0.5^{abc}	16.1±0.7^{ab}	3.3±0.2^{abc}	83.8±2.1^a	57.9±3.1^{ab}
	1.7 kJ m^{-2}	25.3±0.5^{cde}	4.8±0.2^c	53.1±1.2^{de}	14.0±0.2^{bc}	2.6±0.0^d	75.4±2.8^{ab}	53.4±2.5^{ab}
	3.4 kJ m^{-2}	25.5±0.9^{bcde}	5.5±0.2^{abc}	57.3±1.5^{ab}	16.4±0.7^a	3.1±0.1^{abcd}	80.3±6.0^{ab}	61.2±1.1^a
Day 4	Control	27.2±0.5^{abcd}	5.6±0.1^{abc}	55.4±0.9^{bcd}	15.5±0.8^{abc}	3.1±0.4^{abcd}	81.1±3.3^{ab}	57.8±4.8^{ab}
	1.7 kJ m^{-2}	24.9±0.8^{de}	5.3±0.2^{abc}	55.0±1.2^{bcd}	15.5±0.3^{abc}	3.1±0.1^{abcd}	71.1±2.8^a	59.1±1.8^{ab}
	3.4 kJ m^{-2}	25.5±0.8^{bcde}	5.4±0.4^{abc}	55.7±1.4^{bcd}	15.8±1.0^{abc}	3.0±0.2^{cd}	75.4±3.0^{ab}	57.8±3.7^{ab}
Day 10	Control	26.9±0.8^{abcd}	5.6±0.1^{abc}	55.2±1.7^{bcd}	14.8±0.5^{abc}	3.0±0.2^{cd}	77.5±6.3^{ab}	56.2±1.8^{ab}
	1.7 kJ m^{-2}	26.2±0.8^{bcde}	5.5±0.2^{abc}	54.4±0.9^{cde}	16.6±0.3^{ab}	3.7±0.1^a	79.4±3.1^{ab}	54.0±2.1^{ab}
	3.4 kJ m^{-2}	24.5±0.2^e	5.8±0.1^{ab}	57.2±0.8^{abc}	17.2±0.6^a	3.5±0.3^{abc}	79.5±0.8^{ab}	58.5±2.2^{ab}
Day 14	Control	25.6±0.6^{bcde}	4.9±0.6^{bc}	50.8±1.9^e	13.4±1.9^c	2.6±0.3^d	75.0±4.4^{ab}	46.5±1.5^c
	1.7 kJ m^{-2}	27.8±1.3^{abc}	5.9±0.5^a	56.9±1.7^{abcd}	15.9±1.1^{abc}	3.1±0.2^{abcd}	85.1±1.9^a	55.1±1.2^{bc}
	3.4 kJ m^{-2}	28.0±0.3^{ab}	5.9±0.2^a	58.4±0.5^{ab}	15.7±0.9^{abc}	3.0±0.2^{bcd}	84.2±3.5^a	61.1±0.8^a

Means ± standard deviations followed by the same letter within a storage temperature regime are not significantly different according to Tukey's test ($p < 0.05$).

Table 6.2: Effect of postharvest UV-C treatments on macro- and micro nutrient contents of African nightshade leaves during storage at different temperature regime.

Storage days	UV-C dosage	Macro-nutrients (g kg^{-1})					Micro-nutrients (mg kg^{-1})	
		N	P	K	Ca	Mg	Fe	Zn
A. At 20 °C (retailer's simulation condition)								
Day 0	Control	46.8±2.8^a	6.8±0.2^a	47.6±1.2^a	32.0±1.4^a	3.4±0.2^a	121.6±3.4^a	50.0±0.8^a
Day 2	Control	37.7±3.9^{bc}	6.1±0.5^{ab}	43.6±2.6^{abc}	30.4±1.1^{ab}	3.1±0.3^{ab}	114.3±2.1^{bcd}	40.9±1.5^{bc}
	1.7 kJ m^{-2}	38.1±2.3^{bc}	5.8±0.0^c	42.2±1.2^{bc}	26.6±1.4^b	3.0±0.0^{ab}	110.5±2.3^d	37.3±0.6^c
	3.4 kJ m^{-2}	41.1±3.2^{abc}	6.0±0.1^{bc}	43.3±1.2^{abc}	31.0±0.7^{ab}	3.0±0.2^{ab}	113.0±4.0^{cd}	42.7±1.1^b
Day 4	Control	34.9±2.6^c	5.7±0.2^c	41.8±1.6^c	26.8±2.5^b	2.8±0.0^b	102.5±1.5^e	33.5±1.6^d
	1.7 kJ m^{-2}	43.3±1.7^{ab}	6.2±0.2^{abc}	47.3±2.8^{ab}	31.9±3.1^a	3.0±0.1^{ab}	119.4±1.4^{abc}	49.9±1.8^a
	3.4 kJ m^{-2}	43.0±3.5^{abc}	6.6±0.3^{ab}	46.9±2.1^{ab}	30.6±0.7^{ab}	3.3±0.1^a	120.8±1.7^{ab}	39.8±1.3^{bc}
B. At 5 °C (cold storage)								
Day 0	Control	46.8±2.8^a	6.8±0.2^a	47.6±1.2^a	32.0±1.4^a	3.4±0.2^a	121.6±3.4^a	50.0±0.8^a
Day 2	Control	37.3±2.9^{cde}	6.1±0.2^{ab}	43.5±1.9^{ab}	30.3±2.5^{ab}	3.1±0.1^a	114.4±2.9^{ab}	38.6±1.4^{bc}
	1.7 kJ m^{-2}	36.4±2.2^{cde}	5.9±0.4^b	41.5±3.6^{ab}	27.2±0.7^b	2.9±0.1^a	113.2±1.4^{abc}	33.3±2.7^c
	3.4 kJ m^{-2}	39.6±2.1^{abcde}	5.6±0.5^b	43.1±0.9^{ab}	25.5±1.8^b	2.9±0.1^a	114.2±4.5^{abc}	37.2±1.7^{bc}
Day 4	Control	35.9±3.1^{cde}	5.9±0.2^{ab}	43.1±2.8^{ab}	30.1±1.0^{ab}	3.0±0.1^a	104.7±3.4^{cd}	34.9±1.1^c
	1.7 kJ m^{-2}	38.0±2.4^{bcde}	6.0±0.2^{ab}	44.8±2.2^{ab}	30.0±0.6^a	3.0±0.2^a	110.6±4.2^{bcd}	38.9±4.3^{bc}
	3.4 kJ m^{-2}	41.9±3.3^{abcd}	5.8±0.4^{ab}	44.6±1.1^{ab}	29.5±1.7^{ab}	3.0±0.2^a	117.8±3.6^{abc}	37.7±1.6^{bc}
Day 10	Control	35.1±3.3^{de}	5.9±0.3^{ab}	41.4±0.6^{ab}	29.1±2.0^{ab}	3.0±0.1^a	103.3±2.4^d	32.9±1.3^c
	1.7 kJ m^{-2}	36.9±2.6^{cde}	6.2±0.9^{ab}	42.6±4.0^{ab}	31.4±1.7^a	3.2±0.2^a	116.1±6.0^{ab}	37.3±4.4^{bc}
	3.4 kJ m^{-2}	43.8±1.6^{abc}	6.5±0.2^{ab}	43.2±2.3^{ab}	31.8±0.7^a	3.4±0.2^a	118.4±4.1^{ab}	48.1±2.1^a
Day 14	Control	33.1±3.2^e	5.4±0.6^b	40.7±1.1^b	27.5±2.5^{ab}	3.0±0.2^a	101.3±1.9^d	33.3±3.1^c
	1.7 kJ m^{-2}	41.7±2.2^{abcd}	6.0±0.7^{ab}	44.2±3.4^{ab}	30.6±1.1^{ab}	2.8±0.3^a	119.1±1.8^{ab}	36.5±2.5^{bc}
	3.4 kJ m^{-2}	45.8±3.9^{ab}	6.5±0.1^{ab}	47.4±1.2^{ab}	31.7±2.9^a	3.2±0.4^a	118.7±2.2^{ab}	43.9±3.2^{ab}

Means ± standard deviations followed by the same letter within a storage temperature regime are not significantly different according to Tukey's test ($p < 0.05$).

Table 6.3: Effect of postharvest UV-C treatments on structural carbohydrate contents (g kg^{-1}) of vegetable amaranth and African nightshade leaves during storage at different temperature regime.

Storage days	UV-C dosage	Vegetable amaranth			African nightshade		
		Hemicellulose	Cellulose	Lignin	Hemicellulose	Cellulose	Lignin
A. At 20 °C (retailer's simulation condition)							
Day 0	Control	202.3±7.6^a	94.2±2.9^a	36.3±1.2^a	20.8±1.0^a	99.6±0.2^a	19.0±1.2^a
Day 2	Control	187.3±3.9^{ab}	80.6±2.9^b	35.7±2.5^a	19.3±0.6^{ab}	94.3±0.4^{abc}	15.3±0.3^{ab}
	1.7 kJ m^{-2}	193.1±1.0^{ab}	89.6±4.5^a	31.0±1.7^{bc}	18.6±1.6^{abc}	98.5±0.6^{ab}	16.9±1.4^{ab}
	3.4 kJ m^{-2}	189.3±9.5^{ab}	88.6±0.6^a	35.4±0.7^a	19.9±0.9^{ab}	94.2±2.9^{abc}	17.1±2.0^{ab}
Day 4	Control	185.5±5.2^b	80.5±1.4^b	34.7±0.8^{ab}	17.1±0.6^{bc}	89.9±0.2^c	15.1±1.5^b
	1.7 kJ m^{-2}	195.4±4.6^{ab}	93.3±1.1^a	28.7±1.2^c	16.2±1.7^c	93.3±3.9^{bc}	16.4±1.8^{ab}
	3.4 kJ m^{-2}	201.9±3.2^a	94.2±1.4^a	33.6±1.3^{ab}	19.4±0.8^{ab}	98.5±1.8^{ab}	15.4±1.0^{ab}
B. At 5 °C (cold storage)							
Day 0	Control	202.3±7.6^a	94.2±2.9^a	36.3±1.2^a	20.8±1.0^a	99.6±0.2^a	19.0±1.2^a
Day 2	Control	179.3±5.2^b	86.5±1.6^{abc}	35.0±1.1^{ab}	18.2±1.9^{abc}	96.8±0.6^{ab}	14.7±0.3^{cdef}
	1.7 kJ m^{-2}	198.6±2.8^a	89.9±2.9^{ab}	23.6±2.0^f	18.9±1.2^{ab}	98.3±1.5^{ab}	17.8±1.5^{ab}
	3.4 kJ m^{-2}	199.0±8.7^a	77.9±2.1^d	35.6±1.1^{ab}	17.3±0.6^{abc}	97.5±2.4^{ab}	18.5±0.8^a
Day 4	Control	166.4±7.6^{bcd}	86.1±2.8^{abcd}	34.3±3.0^{ab}	16.6±2.2^{bc}	95.5±0.7^{ab}	13.5±0.7^{efg}
	1.7 kJ m^{-2}	160.0±2.1^{cde}	92.7±0.8^a	25.5±2.3^{def}	15.7±0.7^{bc}	97.7±0.4^{ab}	14.5±1.2^{def}
	3.4 kJ m^{-2}	170.1±5.5^{bc}	88.0±6.2^{abc}	27.1±0.7^{def}	15.5±1.5^{bc}	98.3±2.0^{ab}	17.0±0.5^{abcd}
Day 10	Control	156.1±7.4^{cde}	82.1±1.2^{bcd}	30.7±0.6^{bc}	15.5±0.6^{bc}	94.1±1.3^b	12.4±1.1^{fg}
	1.7 kJ m^{-2}	159.2±3.8^{cde}	89.4±3.4^{ab}	27.2±1.1^{cdef}	14.2±1.2^c	97.8±1.0^{ab}	17.2±0.3^{abc}
	3.4 kJ m^{-2}	143.2±9.3^e	91.1±3.9^a	23.8±2.7^{ef}	16.2±0.9^{bc}	98.1±1.4^{ab}	17.6±0.3^{ab}
Day 14	Control	146.2±3.3^e	80.0±1.7^{cd}	29.1±0.7^{cd}	14.9±1.1^{bc}	94.1±0.3^b	11.3±0.9^g
	1.7 kJ m^{-2}	150.8±7.8^{de}	92.6±1.6^a	27.8±1.8^{cdef}	15.2±2.6^{bc}	96.9±2.4^{ab}	15.7±1.0^{bcde}
	3.4 kJ m^{-2}	142.8±5.8^e	92.1±1.1^a	28.6±1.1^{cde}	8.2±0.4^d	94.6±2.6^b	13.6±1.1^{efg}

Means ± standard deviations followed by the same letter within a storage temperature regime and a vegetable are not significantly different according to Tukey's test ($p < 0.05$).

the decline in chlorophylls was not inhibited by any of the UV-C treatments, whereas in contrast for carotenoids, the decline was retarded by higher UV-C dosages of 3.4 kJ m^{-2}. Carotenoid contents after 4 d of storage were even higher in comparison to the control (Table 6.4A). Total chlorophylls to total carotenoids ratio was significantly reduced with increase in UV-C dosage after 4 d compared to the control (Table 6.4A).

African nightshade leaves at 20 °C had significantly lower chlorophyll a contents for both UV-C treatments and lower chlorophyll b contents at 1.7 kJ m^{-2} after 2 d compared to the control while after 4 d, both UV-C had significantly higher chlorophyll (a and b) contents with significant increase with increase in UV-C dosage for chlorophyll a in comparison to the control. The ratio of chlorophyll a to b was significantly lower at 3.4 kJ m^{-2} after 2 d compared to the control while after 4 d, 3.4 kJ m^{-2} was significantly higher than 1.7 kJ m^{-2} although not different from the control. Total carotenoids were significantly higher with increasing UV-C dosages after 4 d compared to the control. The ratio of total chlorophylls to total carotenoids was only significantly lower at 3.4 kJ m^{-2} after 2 d, while the ratio of xanthophyll to carotene was significantly higher in both UV-C treatments after 4 d compared to the control (Table 6.5A).

At 5 °C, vegetable amaranth had significantly lower chlorophyll a and b contents in both UV-C treatments within 4 d compared to the control, while after 10 and 14 d, chlorophyll a was significantly higher with the increase in UV-C dosage and chlorophyll b was significantly higher at 1.7 kJ m^{-2} compared to the control. The ratio of chlorophyll a to b content was significantly lower at 1.7 kJ m^{-2} for 2 d but thereafter increased in both UV-C treatments. Similarly, total chlorophyll and total carotenoid contents were significantly lower in leaves of both UV-C treatments until 2 d. Thereafter (10 and 14 d), contents of both pigments were significantly higher with increasing UV-C dosages compared to the control. The ratio of total chlorophylls to total carotenoids was significantly higher at 1.7 kJ m^{-2} after 2 d, whereas after 14 d, both ratios, those of total chlorophylls to total carotenoids as well as of xanthophyll to carotene were significantly lower in both UV-C treatments compared to the control (Table 6.4B).

Similarly, in African nightshade plants, chlorophyll a content was significantly lower in both UV-C treatments after 2 d compared to the control with 3.4 kJ m^{-2} being significantly higher than 1.7 kJ m^{-2} after 4 d although not higher than the control. After 10 and 14 d, 3.4 kJ m^{-2} showed significantly higher chlorophyll a content compared to the control. Chlorophyll b content was significantly lower after 2 d in both UV-C treatments and after 4 d at 1.7 kJ m^{-2}, while after 4 d, 3.4 kJ m^{-2} had significantly higher chlorophyll b content compared to the control. No significant difference was observed for chlorophyll a to b ratio. Total chlorophyll was significantly lower after 2 d for both UV-C treatments with a significant increase with increase in UV-C dosage after 4 d. After 10 d, UV-C of 3.4 kJ m^{-2} resulted in a significantly higher total chlorophyll content compared to the control. Similarly, total carotenoids was significantly lower after 2 d for both UV-C treatments and after 4 d at 1.7 kJ m^{-2}, while after 10 and 14 d, 3.4 kJ m^{-2} had significantly

Table 6.4: Effect of postharvest UV-C treatments on chlorophyll and carotenoid contents (g kg^{-1}) of vegetable amaranth leaves during storage at different temperature regime.

Storage days	UV-C dosage	Total Chlorophylls	Chlorophyll a	Chlorophyll b	Chlorophyll a/ Chlorophyll b Ratio	Total Carotenoids	Total Chlorophylls/ Total Carotenoids Ratio	Xanthophyll/ Carotene Ratio
A. At 20 °C (retailer's simulation condition)								
Day 0	Control	17.6±1.7^a	12.9±1.2^a	4.7±0.5^a	2.83±0.05^a	5.7±0.4^a	3.10±0.13^a	1.05±0.00^c
Day 2	Control	7.5±0.9^b	5.4±0.6^{bc}	2.1±0.2^{bc}	2.63±0.12^{ab}	2.7±0.1^{cd}	2.72±0.26^{bc}	1.07±0.01^{ab}
	1.7 kJ m^{-2}	7.6±0.8^{bc}	5.5±0.6^{bc}	2.1±0.2^{bc}	2.55±0.07^{ab}	3.0±0.3^c	2.56±0.09^c	1.06±0.01^{bc}
	3.4 kJ m^{-2}	9.1±1.0^b	6.4±0.8^b	2.7±0.4^b	2.39±0.32^b	3.7±0.3^b	2.49±0.15^c	1.06±0.01^{bc}
Day 4	Control	6.7±0.7^c	4.9±0.5^c	1.7±0.2^c	2.83±0.10^{ab}	2.3±0.3^d	2.96±0.05^{ab}	1.07±0.01^{ab}
	1.7 kJ m^{-2}	7.1±1.4^c	5.0±0.8^c	2.1±0.6^{bc}	2.39±0.34^b	2.9±0.5^c	2.49±0.15^c	1.08±0.01^a
	3.4 kJ m^{-2}	8.5±0.8^{bc}	6.2±0.6^{bc}	2.3±0.2^{bc}	2.63±0.17^{ab}	3.8±0.4^b	2.23±0.03^d	1.08±0.01^a
B. At 5 °C (cold storage)								
Day 0	Control	17.6±1.7^a	12.9±1.2^a	4.7±0.5^a	2.83±0.05^{ab}	5.7±0.4^a	3.10±0.13^{bc}	1.05±0.00^b
Day 2	Control	14.9±1.2^{bc}	10.9±0.9^{bc}	4.0±0.3^{abc}	2.73±0.13^{ab}	4.9±0.4^{bc}	3.04±0.05^{bc}	1.05±0.00^b
	1.7 kJ m^{-2}	8.8±0.2^{fg}	5.9±0.3^{gh}	2.9±0.4^{cdf}	2.08±0.41^c	2.6±0.3^g	3.41±0.36^a	1.07±0.01^b
	3.4 kJ m^{-2}	7.9±0.8^g	5.9±0.6^{gh}	2.0±0.2^f	3.02±0.09^a	2.6±0.3^g	2.99±0.04^c	1.07±0.01^b
Day 4	Control	12.3±0.8^{de}	9.0±0.5^{de}	3.3±0.2^{de}	2.73±0.07^{ab}	4.0±0.2^{de}	3.10±0.05^{bc}	1.06±0.01^b
	1.7 kJ m^{-2}	8.8±0.5^{fg}	6.4±0.4^{fgh}	2.4±0.1^{cf}	2.74±0.22^{ab}	2.9±0.2^{fg}	3.01±0.05^c	1.06±0.00^b
	3.4 kJ m^{-2}	12.4±0.4^{de}	9.2±0.3^{de}	3.2±0.1^{cde}	2.84±0.06^a	4.2±0.2^{cd}	2.94±0.04^c	1.06±0.00^b
Day 10	Control	10.6±1.8^{ef}	7.2±0.9^{fg}	3.4±0.3^d	2.29±0.56^{bc}	3.5±0.4^{cf}	3.00±0.20^c	1.08±0.02^{ab}
	1.7 kJ m^{-2}	13.6±1.0^{cd}	10.0±0.7^{cd}	3.6±0.3^{bcd}	2.82±0.06^a	4.3±0.3^{cd}	3.12±0.06^{bc}	1.05±0.00^b
	3.4 kJ m^{-2}	16.6±1.5^{ab}	12.2±1.1^{ab}	4.4±0.4^{ab}	2.79±0.06^a	5.4±0.4^{ab}	3.08±0.12^{bc}	1.05±0.01^b
Day 14	Control	7.5±1.1^g	5.0±0.5^h	2.4±0.6^{cf}	2.15±0.39^c	2.3±0.3^g	3.27±0.09^{ab}	1.11±0.07^a
	1.7 kJ m^{-2}	11.0±0.8^{ef}	8.0±0.6^{cf}	3.0±0.2^{cd}	2.71±0.06^{ab}	3.7±0.3^{de}	2.97±0.05^c	1.05±0.01^b
	3.4 kJ m^{-2}	16.3±2.0^{ab}	11.9±1.4^{ab}	4.5±0.6^{ab}	2.67±0.11^{ab}	5.6±0.6^a	2.92±0.06^c	1.05±0.00^b

Means ± standard deviations followed by the same letter within a storage temperature regime and a vegetable are not significantly different according to Tukey's test ($p < 0.05$).

Table 6.5: Effect of postharvest UV-C treatments on chlorophyll and carotenoid contents (g kg^{-1}) of African nightshade leaves during storage at different temperature regime.

Storage days	UV-C dosage	Total Chlorophylls	Chlorophyll a	Chlorophyll b	Chlorophyll a/ Chlorophyll b Ratio	Total Carotenoids	Total Chlorophylls/ Total Carotenoids Ratio	Xanthophyll/ Carotene Ratio
A. At 20 °C (retailer's simulation condition)								
Day 0	Control	34.4±2.1^a	23.5±1.1^a	10.9±1.0^a	2.16±0.12^{ab}	11.2±1.0^a	3.09±0.11^a	0.99±0.01^{abc}
Day 2	Control	17.5±1.1^c	11.9±0.8^c	5.6±0.4^{cd}	2.13±0.02^{ab}	5.7±0.5^{cd}	3.09±0.07^a	0.98±0.01^{bc}
	1.7 kJ m^{-2}	12.6±0.9^d	8.4±0.5^d	4.1±0.4^e	2.05±0.14^{bc}	4.5±0.4^e	2.83±0.15^{ab}	0.98±0.01^{bc}
	3.4 kJ m^{-2}	13.4±0.5^d	8.7±0.5^d	4.7±0.1^{de}	1.86±0.12^c	4.9±0.2^{de}	2.76±0.10^b	0.99±0.01^{abc}
Day 4	Control	14.3±0.8^d	9.9±0.4^d	4.4±0.5^e	2.28±0.19^{ab}	4.6±0.4^{de}	3.08±0.11^a	0.97±0.02^c
	1.7 kJ m^{-2}	19.2±1.9^c	12.8±1.3^c	6.4±0.8^{bc}	2.03±0.19^{bc}	6.3±0.8^c	3.07±0.21^a	1.01±0.02^{ab}
	3.4 kJ m^{-2}	22.8±1.8^b	16.1±1.4^b	6.8±0.5^b	2.38±0.16^a	7.4±0.3^b	3.07±0.20^a	1.02±0.03^a
B. At 5 °C (cold storage)								
Day 0	Control	34.4±2.1^a	23.5±1.1^a	10.9±1.0^a	2.16±0.12^{abc}	11.2±1.0^a	3.09±0.11^{ab}	0.99±0.01^{bcd}
Day 2	Control	26.5±1.8^b	18.7±1.6^b	7.8±0.4^b	2.38±0.19^{ab}	8.5±0.5^b	3.13±0.07^a	1.00±0.00^{abc}
	1.7 kJ m^{-2}	15.5±0.5^{ef}	10.7±0.3^{def}	4.8±0.4^{fg}	2.24±0.17^{abc}	5.2±0.2^e	2.96±0.15^{abc}	0.99±0.00^{bcd}
	3.4 kJ m^{-2}	13.9±0.9^f	9.5±0.6^f	4.4±0.3^g	2.17±0.08^{abc}	4.6±0.3^e	3.00±0.04^{abc}	0.99±0.00^{bcd}
Day 4	Control	21.8±2.1^c	15.2±1.4^c	6.7±0.8^{cd}	2.29±0.20^{abc}	7.0±0.7^c	3.10±0.16^{ab}	0.98±0.01^d
	1.7 kJ m^{-2}	14.0±1.0^f	9.5±0.7^f	4.5±0.4^g	2.11±0.14^{bc}	4.9±0.3^e	2.87±0.03^{cd}	0.99±0.01^{bcd}
	3.4 kJ m^{-2}	18.6±0.6^d	12.4±0.6^{de}	6.3±0.4^{de}	1.99±0.16^c	6.5±0.1^{cd}	2.85±0.07^{cd}	0.99±0.02^{bcd}
Day 10	Control	17.1±0.8^{de}	11.8±0.5^{de}	5.2±0.5^{efg}	2.28±0.16^{abc}	5.7±0.2^{de}	3.00±0.05^{abc}	0.99±0.00^{bcd}
	1.7 kJ m^{-2}	18.7±1.6^d	12.8±1.2^d	5.8±0.5^{def}	2.21±0.19^{abc}	6.5±0.6^{cd}	2.89±0.07^{cd}	1.02±0.01^{ab}
	3.4 kJ m^{-2}	25.0±2.3^b	17.5±1.8^b	7.5±0.6^{bc}	2.34±0.13^{abc}	8.6±0.9^b	2.91±0.07^{bc}	1.01±0.01^{abc}
Day 14	Control	15.1±0.4^{ef}	10.5±0.3^{ef}	4.5±0.2^g	2.32±0.12^{abc}	4.8±0.2^e	3.15±0.10^a	1.00±0.00^{abc}
	1.7 kJ m^{-2}	16.3±1.9^{def}	11.6±1.4^{def}	4.7±0.5^g	2.46±0.09^{ab}	5.7±0.6^{de}	2.87±0.14^{cd}	1.03±0.01^a
	3.4 kJ m^{-2}	17.9±1.4^{de}	12.8±1.4^d	5.2±0.6^{efg}	2.50±0.44^a	6.6±0.7^{cd}	2.71±0.06^d	1.03±0.03^a

Means ± standard deviations followed by the same letter within a storage temperature regime and a vegetable are not significantly different according to Tukey's test ($p < 0.05$).

higher total carotenoids compared to the control. The ratio of total chlorophylls to total carotenoids was significantly lower after 4 and 14 d in both UV-C treatments compared to the control while the ratio of xanthophyll to carotene was not affected (Table 6.5B).

6.3.5. Effect of postharvest UV-C application on microbial counts

Postharvest UV-C application significantly influenced total bacterial (aerobic mesophilic microbes), yeast and mould counts of vegetable amaranth leaves at 20 °C. UV-C treated leaves (1.7 kJ m^{-2}) had significantly lower aerobic mesophilic and yeast counts only at day 0 (harvest day), while after 2 and 4 d, both microbial counts were not significantly different when compared to the control (Figure 6.4A and B). However, no significant difference was observed on moulds between the UV-C treatment and the control throughout the storage period (Figure 6.4C).

6.4. Discussion

In the present study, we investigated the effect of postharvest UV-C treatment on the nutritional quality, storability and shelf life of vegetable amaranth and African nightshade leaves during storage at different temperature regimes. The application of postharvest UV-C significantly contributed to reduced fresh weight loss of the studied AIVs. The studied AIVs exhibited a varied response to UV-C treatment on fresh weight loss basis with a more pronounced effect at cold temperature storage (5 °C) than at retailer's simulation storage conditions (20 °C); presumably due to reduced metabolic reaction rates. The reduction in fresh weight loss of the studied vegetables due to UV-C treatment could probably be due to reduced degradation of structural cell wall components (i.e. cellulose and lignin) as observed in the study due to stress mediated response (Huyskens-Keil et al., 2011). Such enhanced mechanical strength of the cell walls in UV-C treated AIVs may act as physical barriers to prevent excessive water loss (Stevens et al., 2004); hence reduction in weight loss leading to extended shelf life. However, differences in the studied AIVs in terms of fresh weight loss could be attributed to differences in UV-C sensitivity due to their variation in leaf structure and size. Vegetable amaranth leaves used in the study were light green, small and oval shaped, while African nightshade leaves were dark green, large and circular. Our results are corroborated by Karasahin et al. (2005) who observed a higher weight loss in eggplants (*Solanum melongena* L.) treated with UV-C at 3.6 kJ m^{-2}, following hot water treatment compared to the control. In another study, Lemoine et al. (2008) observed no effect on weight loss when broccoli was UV-C treated at 5, 8, and 10 kJ m^{-2} UV-C compared to the control.

In the present study, mineral elements and protein of vegetable amaranth and African nightshade were variedly affected by UV-C treatments. UV-C treatment resulted in higher N, P, K, Mg, Fe

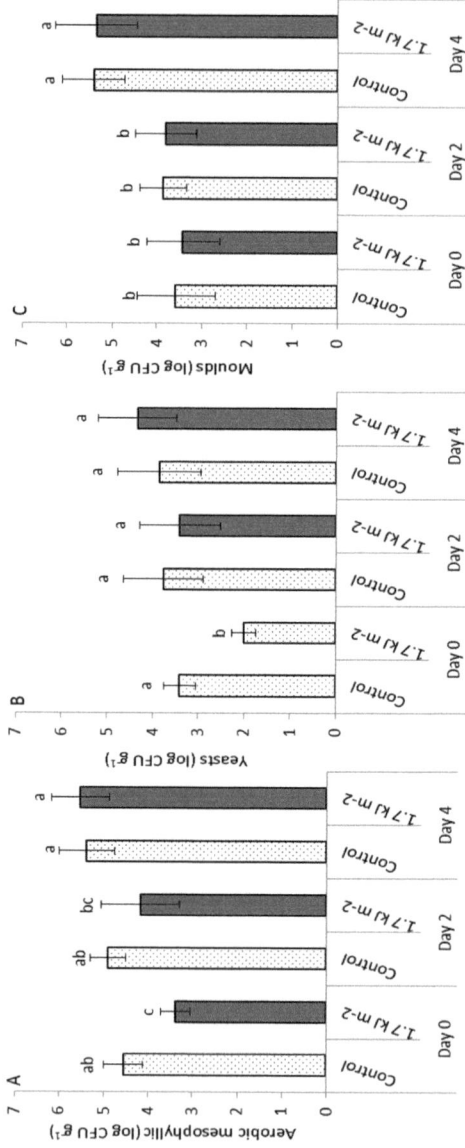

Figure 6.4: Effect of postharvest UV-C treatments on microbial counts on vegetable amaranth leaves at 20 °C storage temperature. Means ± standard deviations followed by the same letter within individual microbes are not significantly different according to Tukey's test ($p < 0.05$).

and protein contents for vegetable amaranth while for African nightshade additionally higher Zn contents were observed compared to the control treatments, depending on storage condition, especially during the advanced storage periods. This could be attributed to their involvement in plant stress defence mechanism as a result of UV-C treatment (Shabala and Munns, 2012). After UV-C application, it is assumed that the stress responsive mechanism is established by an initial stress signal being characterised by a decline in mineral elements content (e.g. P, K, and Mg in vegetable amaranth and Zn in African nightshade). Thereafter, the UV-C treated leaves try to re-establish homeostasis and to protect themselves against UV-C irradiation as indicated by an increase in specific mineral elements in the advanced storage durations. It is reported that N is involved as sink of reducing energy following metabolic disturbance (Shabala and Munns, 2012), P is involved in cytoplasmic homeostatic (Balemi and Negisho, 2012), K and proteins are important in plant stress resistance (Shabala and Munns, 2012; Wang et al., 2013), Mg is involved in various enzymatic activities and structural stabilization of tissues (Guo et al., 2016), while Fe and Zn are important for plant stress defence mechanisms especially in promoting high antioxidant enzyme activity such as Fe superoxide dismutase as well as Zn superoxide dismutase (Bowler et al., 1992). Vegetable amaranth displayed high contents of N, P, K, Mg and protein, while African nightshade showed high Ca, Fe and Zn contents which could be attributed to their physiological differences. UV-C treatment affected mineral elements and protein contents of African nightshade leaves more compared to vegetable amaranth leaves especially at 20 °C storage condition which could probably be due to their differences in leaf structural variation and sensitivity to UV-C treatment being demonstrated; e.g. higher hemicellulose content was observed in vegetable amaranth leaves compared to African nightshade. For instance, anthocyanin deficient maize (*Zea mays* L.) was observed to be more sensitive to UV-B than wild types (Stapleton and Walbot, 1994). Under various stress conditions including radiation, different plant species may induce specific changes in protein and mineral element synthesis that enable them to cope with such stress (Shabala and Munns, 2012). Barka et al. (2000) reported that after exposure of tomatoes to UV-C (3.7 kJ m^{-2}), the electrolyte leakage of K and Ca was in two phases. In the first phase (until 5 d of storage), radiation resulted in an immediate increase in tissue leakage. Thereafter, the pattern was reversed with higher leakage in control than in the UV-C treated fruits which persisted throughout the entire storage period. They attributed higher K and Ca leakage to perturbation of membrane transport after exposure to UV-C and the lower leakage rate in irradiated fruits after 5 d of storage to activation of a membrane repair mechanism including increased synthesis of membrane lipids. In addition, they reported higher protein content in UV-C treated tomato fruits which they attributed to increase in protease activity. In another study, Hemmaty et al. (2007) reported higher Ca content on apple fruits (*Malus domestica* Borkh.) treated with UV-C (1.435 × 10^{-4} W cm^{-2}) and hot water during storage compared to the control which they attributed to the increased electrolyte leakage after radiation.

UV-C irradiation treatment affected structural carbohydrates contents (hemicellulose, cellulose and lignin) in vegetable amaranth and African nightshade leaves variedly. Vegetable amaranth leaves had higher hemicellulose and lignin contents compared to African nightshade leaves which could be attributed to the different structural properties of the AIVs. Though not significantly different, until the later storage days, structural carbohydrates were higher in UV-C treated leaves compared to the control. This could be attributed to the changes in the textural cell wall properties of the AIVs as a result of UV-C treatment. This may contribute to a positive effect on dietary fibres. For instance, lignin is reported to play an important role in response of plants to environmental stress such as UV-C irradiation (Sharma et al., 2012). Denness et al. (2011) demonstrated a genetic network that enables plants to regulate lignin biosynthesis in response to cell wall damage using dynamic interactions between jasmonic acid and ROS as a plant defence response. Barka et al. (2000) reported a reduction in polygalacturonase, pectinmethylesterase, cellulase, xylanase, β-D-galactosidase, and protease activities in UV-C (3.7 kJ m^{-2}) treated tomato fruits compared to the untreated fruits. They suggested that such cell wall degrading enzyme could be one of the targets of UV-C irradiation contributing to a delay of the cell wall degradation. Similarly, Huyskens-Keil et al. (2011) reported a general increase in the cell wall components (cellulose, hemicellulose, pectic substances, and lignin) in UV-C treated white asparagus after 2 d of storage which they attributed to changes in the composition of the structural major cell wall components.

Changes in chlorophylls and carotenoids following UV-C application on vegetable amaranth and African nightshade leaves were observed during storage at different temperature conditions. Chlorophylls and carotenoids observed had a similar characteristic response in both vegetables. However, African nightshade leaves had a higher chlorophylls and carotenoids content compared to vegetable amaranth, probably attributed to their differences in leaf structural design. It has been reported that the physiological parameters such as species, variety, and cultivar may affect the response of plants to UV-C irradiation (Esnault et al., 2010). After UV-C application, there was a sharp decline in chlorophylls and carotenoids after 2 d of storage at 20 °C and until 4 d after storage at 5 °C which was subsequently followed by an increase in the later storage days, however, not higher than the leaves at harvest. Changes in chlorophylls a to b, xanthophyll to carotene and total chlorophylls to carotenoids ratios varied depending on AIV and storage conditions and were not significantly evident. The sudden decline in chlorophylls and carotenoids during the initial storage periods could be associated with the response to the induced stress brought about by the UV-C irradiation. Thereafter, the increase could be attributed to their role as a protective function against oxidative damage from ROS brought about by UV-C treatment. Similar results were reported by Liu et al. (2012), who observed a reduction in total phenolic content during the initial 7 d storage period, followed by an increase towards the end of the storage period (35 d) when tomato fruit were treated with UV-C (4 or 8 kJ m^{-2}) which they attributed to changes in antioxidant activity. Various studies suggest that chlorophylls and carotenoids are synthesized and degraded (photooxidation) under UV-C irradiation (Cazzaniga et al., 2016, 2012; Montané et al., 1998). In the initial stage of UV-C irradiation, the degradation rate overtakes the rate of synthesis resulting in lower chlorophyll and carotenoid concentration (Gonçalves et al., 2001). Thereafter, chlorophyll and/or carotenoid synthesis may increase to enhance photo-protection of plants to UV-C irradiation (Cazzaniga et al., 2012). Similarly, Chairat et al. (2013) reported higher chlorophyll contents as shown by a delay in leaf yellowing and lower activity of chlorophyllase, chlorophyll-degrading peroxidase and Mg-dechelatase in Chinese kale (*Brassica oleracea* L. var. alboglabra L.H. Bailey) treated with UV-C at 3.6 and 5.4 kJ m^{-2} as compared to the untreated leaves.

There is a continuously growing interest in alternative methods for postharvest decay management of horticultural crops in order to reduce the use of agrochemicals in reducing microbial contamination. In the present study, the postharvest application of UV-C to vegetable amaranth leaves at 1.7 kJ m^{-2} stored at 20 °C helped to reduce microbial population (aerobic mesophilic and yeast counts). Aerobic mesophilic and yeast counts were significantly reduced during the initial storage days (0 d) and mould counts were significantly different in the control and UV-C treatments throughout the storage period. Generally, microbial load increased with storage days, irrespective of the treatment applied. The use of postharvest UV-C application has been shown to alter the biotic relationship of plants by changes in plant disease susceptibility, and induction of plant tolerance mechanisms including the production of anti-microbial compounds (Ribeiro et al., 2012). The reduction in the studied microbial counts could be attributed to the germicidal effect of the UV-C irradiation and/or the plant defence response following UV-C treatment. Hassenberg et al. (2012) reported that the initial microbial load might be a potential influence to the responsiveness of plants treated with UV-C. The higher the initial load the more effective the spread of the pathogens and, consequently affecting the effectiveness of the treatment. In addition, water and sugar content of the produce might provide an optimal growing medium for microorganisms as well as pathogens. In another study, Stevens et al. (2004) demonstrated a 53% reduction in Rhizopus soft rot (*Rhizopons stolonifer*) infections after 72 h when tomatoes were treated with UV-C at 3.6 kJ m^{-2} compared to the untreated fruit which they attributed to induced tomato resistance following UV-C treatment due to polygalacturonase activity suppression. In another study, Escalona et al. (2010) demonstrated delayed growth of *Listeria monocytogenes* and *Salmonella enterica* at 5 °C for 14 and 4 d, respectively; when UV-C was applied to baby spinach leaves at 2.4 kJ m^{-2}. Thereafter, a significant increase in microbial growth was observed on radiated leaves compared to the control. They attributed the reduction in microbial load to the physical protection barrier due to the presence of an amorphous epicuticular wax, and prism-shaped crystals following UV-C application.

6.5. Conclusion and recommendation

The study demonstrates the possibility of efficient use of hormic UV-C dosages in improving nutritional qualities, storability and shelf life of vegetable amaranth and African nightshade leaves. However, the studied AIVs responded variedly to UV-C treatment. Fresh weight loss was significantly reduced by postharvest UV-C application with the effect being more pronounced in cold temperature storage especially between 4 and 10 d of storage which is an indication of a prolonged shelf life using a combined treatment of UV-C at low temperature storage. Postharvest UV-C application was found to maintain or improve nutrient content of vegetable amaranth (N, P, K, Ca, Mg, Fe and protein) and African nightshade (N, P, K, Ca, Mg, Fe, Zn and protein), especially on the advanced storage duration. Postharvest application of UV-C to the studied AIVs helped to maintain or even increase hemicellulose and cellulose content in vegetable amaranth and lignin content in African nightshade leaves with the effect being more dominant under cold temperature storage conditions (5 °C), except in African nightshade leaves, where hemicellulose content was significantly reduced after 14 d of storage at higher UV-C dosage (3.4 kJ m^{-2}). Increase in hemicellulose and cellulose contents is an indication of increase in dietary fibre content, beneficial for nutritional value. On the other hand, increase in lignin (lignification process) might have a negative impact on sensory textural properties. Postharvest application of UV-C to both AIVs resulted in a general decline in antioxidative compounds such as chlorophylls a and b and total carotenoids during the early storage periods after which there was a sharp increase compared to the untreated leaves. Postharvest UV-C application to vegetable amaranth leaves at 1.7 kJ m^{-2} and stored at 20 °C helped to reduce microbial contamination by reducing aerobic mesophilic and yeast counts during the initial storage days (at harvest). It is hypothesized that the UV-C mediated increase of the nutritional components of the studied AIVs could be a result of the plant physiological stress response induced by hormic UV-C application. Improving mineral elements (e.g. Ca, Fe and Zn) and structural carbohydrate contents following UV-C treatment could help in enhancing their nutritional quality, and hence beneficial to consumers of the studied AIVs. Deficiencies of such mineral elements have been the main cause of 'hidden hunger'. Thus, using postharvest UV-C application in maintaining and/or improving nutritional quality and shelf life in AIVs may serve as a vital step in improving food security, health, and nutrition and contributing in reducing food losses in developing countries like Kenya. However, there is need for the study on the ecophysiological impacts and its effect on postharvest UV-C application, especially on open field cultivated AIVs.

Acknowledgment

The study is part of the project Horticultural Innovations and Learning for Improved Nutrition and Livelihood in East Africa (HORTINLEA) which is being funded by the German Federal Ministry of Education and Research (BMBF) and the German Federal Ministry of Economic Cooperation and Development (BMZ) in the framework of the GlobE – Global Food Security program. We gratefully acknowledge the financial support of BMBF and BMZ.

7. Hormic postharvest UV-C application to improve health promoting secondary plant compound pattern in vegetable amaranth

Gogo, E.O., Förster, N., Dannehl, D., Frommherz, L., Trierweiler, B., Opiyo, A.M., Ulrichs, Ch., Huyskens-Keil, S., Postharvest Biology and Technology - submitted (Ref: POSTEC_2017_437).

Abstract

Vegetable amaranth (*Amaranthus cruentus* L.) is among the African indigenous leafy vegetables (AIVs) important in the diets of many households in Africa. It is known for supplying adequate amounts of nutrients, including health promoting plant secondary compounds as well as creating job opportunities, particularly for the youth and women. However, improper processing, handling, and storage of AIVs might result in quality deterioration and high quality losses including reduced availability of these health promoting plant compounds. Low dosages of UV-C have been shown to induce beneficial biological responses. The present study was conducted to evaluate the effects of hormic postharvest UV-C application on health promoting secondary plant compounds of vegetable amaranth cv. Madiira. Eight weeks after planting, leaves were harvested and treated with UV-C (254 nm) at either 1.7 kJ m^{-2} or 3.4 kJ m^{-2} while untreated leaves served as control. The leaves were kept for 2-4 d at 20 °C (65% RH) and for 2-14 d at 5 °C (85% RH). Characteristic health promoting plant compounds, such as vitamin E, carotenoids, flavonoids, phenolic acids, total phenolics as well as glutathione peroxidase (GPOX) activity and antioxidant capacity (TEAC) and their correlations were analyzed. Results showed that the accumulation of secondary metabolites was dependent on UV-C dosage, storage temperature and duration. Vitamin E, carotenoids (e.g. lycopene, β-carotene and lutein), flavonoids (e.g. quercetin and kaempferol derivatives), phenolic acids (e.g. ferulic, coumaric and caffeic acid derivatives) as well as GPOX activity and TEAC increased in UV-C treated vegetable amaranth leaves compared with the untreated samples. Furthermore, there was a significant relationship in most studied secondary compounds and TEAC. The UV-C effects at both storage conditions were comparable in most studied compounds while storage duration variedly affected the accumulation of the compounds studied. The increase in the studied secondary plant compounds is attributed to their plant defence mechanism against oxidative damage of plant tissues by UV-C irradiation. This could be an important strategy in reducing the loss of secondary plant compounds, hence health promotion during AIVs postharvest supply chain.

7.1. Introduction

Vegetable amaranth (*Amaranthus cruentus* L.) is one of the African indigenous leafy vegetables (AIVs) characterized by fast growing and a high tolerance towards arid conditions and poor soils in comparison to other exotic (introduced) crops cultivated under unfavourable conditions in

Kenya (Abukutsa-Onyango, 2003). Therefore, it is part of the diets supplying adequate amounts of protein, vitamins, dietary fibre, and other important nutrients, and furthermore contributing to the incomes of rural and urban households in Africa (Chelang'a et al., 2013; Muhanji et al., 2011). Moreover, AIVs are known for their health promoting properties, such as anticarcinogenic, antiinflammatoric, antihistaminic, and antitumor activities (Nana et al., 2012). In fact, especially vegetable amaranth has been used curatively for diarrhoea, dysentery, ulcers, and intestinal haemorrhaging (Nana et al., 2012). The curative effects are attributed to secondary plant metabolites, such as vitamins, carotenoids, flavonoids, and phenolic acids (Nana et al., 2012; Noori et al., 2015; Suffo et al., 2016). As such, it can play an important role in improving food health, nutrition, and security, especially in Sub-Saharan Africa. Secondary plant metabolites are also of interest because of their use as dyes, fibres, glues, oils, waxes, flavouring agents, and drugs, and they are viewed as potential sources of new natural drugs, antibiotics, replacement of synthetic food additives, insecticides, and herbicides (Kasote et al., 2015). Recently, there has been an upsurge of interest focussing on secondary metabolites in fruits and vegetables and their human health related impacts. This is mainly based on global health awareness campaigns, whereby consumers have become more interested in foods that support and promote health rather than focussing on superior external quality attributes, as some years ago (Kasote et al., 2015). However, improper processing, handling, and storage of AIVs might result in quality deterioration and losses including reduced availability of these health promoting plant compounds (Gogo et al., 2016). This has promoted research in the field of postharvest technology to determine how the content of secondary plant metabolites can be maintained or even improved during the postharvest supply chain (Schreiner and Huyskens-Keil, 2006). The concentration of various secondary plant compounds is controlled by genetic processes, in addition to being influenced by environmental factors, e.g. UV irradiation, temperature, irrigation, and soil and nutrients amendment (Castrillón-Arbeláez and Délano-Frier, 2016). Among various environmental factors, UV-C (200-280 nm) irradiation is reported to be one of the most important variables affecting secondary metabolite contents in plants (Ribeiro et al., 2012).

Treatments based on UV-C have been widely used with sterilization purposes in the fields of health, microbiology, and food processing due to its germicidal properties (Ribeiro et al., 2012). However, it is possible to apply an appropriate low dose of UV-C to induce beneficial responses in biological systems and particularly in plant tissues, where the concept underlying the strategy is known as hormesis (Shama, 2007). Postharvest treatment of fruits and vegetables with relatively low doses of UV-C have proven to be effective in delaying ripening and senescence, diminishing decay, and even in increasing the content of health promoting plant compounds in fruit and vegetables, both in whole and fresh-cut products (Pataro et al., 2015; Ribeiro et al., 2012; Schreiner and Huyskens-Keil, 2006; Turtoi, 2013). The latter plant responses are caused due to the fact that UV-C acts as an abiotic physical elicitor of stress resistance mechanisms leading to a rapid stimulation of the synthesis of secondary plant compounds, such as vitamins, carotenoids, flavonoids, and phenolic acids (Ribeiro et al., 2012). Studies on UV-C mediated increase in secondary metabolites (e.g. vitamins, carotenoids, flavonoids, and phenolic acids) and antioxidative potential (e.g. glutathione peroxidase activity) have been reported (Pataro et al., 2015; Ribeiro et al., 2012). These studies have been demonstrated on various vegetables such as red cabbage (*Brassica oleracea* var. capitata f. *rubra*) (Zhang et al., 2016), broccoli (*Brassica oleracea* L. var. italica) (Costa et al., 2006; Khalili et al., 2017; Lemoine et al., 2008, 2007), Chinese kale (*Brassica oleracea* var. alboglabra) (Chairat et al., 2013), tatsoi (*Brassica rapa* L. var. rosularis) (Tomás-Callejas et al., 2012), and spinach (*Spinacia oleracea* L.) (Artés-Hernández et al., 2009; Higashio et al., 2001). In addition, treatments with UV-C potentially present several advantages for the food producing industry as it does not leave residues on the products, have no legal restrictions, and does not require complex equipment (Ribeiro et al., 2012; Shama, 2007).

Based on the advantages of postharvest UV-C application on fruits and vegetables and the lack of knowledge on its effects on AIVs, the present study focussed on the impact of hormic postharvest UV-C treatments on the secondary metabolites of vegetable amaranth. The study focussed on compounds such as vitamin E, carotenoids, flavonoids, and phenolic acids, as well as glutathione peroxidase activity (GPOX), and trolox equivalent antioxidant capacity (TEAC). In order to determine and evaluate the dynamics of these compounds, various storage conditions and UV-C treatments were applied. Furthermore, the contents of secondary metabolites in vegetable amaranth leaves were compared to those contained in other leafy vegetables to evaluate their health potential of a diet rich in UV-C treated vegetable amaranth plants.

7.2. Material and methods

7.2.1. Plant material

Vegetable amaranth cv. Madiira seeds were sourced from world vegetable centre (Arusha, Tanzania). The plants were grown under greenhouse conditions in 2015 and 2016, both during May to June in the experimental greenhouse at Humboldt-Universität zu Berlin, Germany. Sowing was done in small tray cells and after 14 d; the seedlings were transplanted in to 6-L pots. Growing medium (Profi-Substrate + Ton + Fe, Gramoflor GmbH and Co., Vechta, Germany) was used for planting. Watering was done daily using an automatic drip irrigation system. All other good agricultural practices were conducted uniformly when deemed necessary. In 2015, the weekly mean temperatures, relative humidity and PAR were between 16.9-26.7 °C, 66.8-83.2%, 400.5-627.6 $\mu mol\ m^{-2}\ s^{-1}$, respectively (Figure 7.1A), while in 2016, the

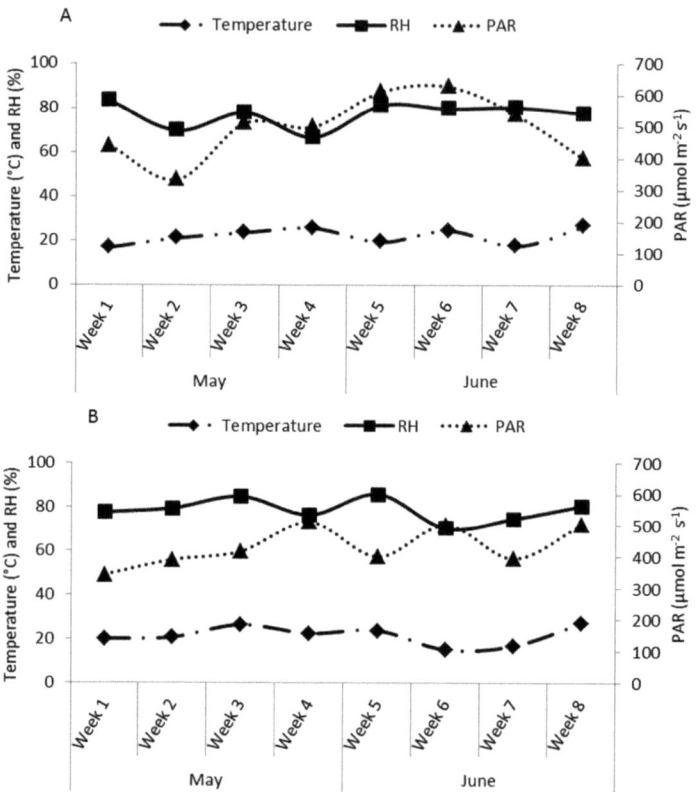

Figure 7.1: Greenhouse microclimate conditions (A-2015 and B-2016) during the production of vegetable amaranth at Humboldt-Universität zu Berlin, Germany.

microclimate conditions were 15.1-27.1 °C, 70.2-85.7%, 389.6-510.7 µmol m^{-2} s^{-1} for temperature, relative humidity, and PAR, respectively (Figure 7.1B).

7.2.2. Experimental set-up and treatment application

Eight weeks after sowing, the vegetable leaves were harvested and immediately treated with UV-C in an UV-C chamber (ABOX® UV Technology, UMEX GmbH, Germany), where temperature and relative air humidity were kept constant at 5 °C and 85%, respectively. UV-C dosage was achieved with medium pressure mercury vapour discharge lamps with a peak emission at 254 nm

(VL-6C, 6 W-254 nm Tube, Power: 11 W, Vilber Lourmat GmbH, Germany). The lamps were placed at a distance of 0.4 m to leaves. The dosage was calculated from the product of exposure time and irradiance, as measured by a portable handheld digital radiometer (UVPAD-E, Opsytec Dr. Gröbel GmbH, Germany). Based on this, two different dosages were applied, i.e. 1.7 kJ m^{-2} and 3.4 kJ m^{-2}. The dosages were chosen based on preliminary experiments and the commonly applied UV-C dosages on leafy vegetables and were found not to negatively affect their visual quality (Chairat et al., 2013). Untreated leaves served as control. Each treatment was applied in three replications with each containing 30 leaves arranged in a completely randomized design. During UV-C treatment, the leaves were carefully arranged one after the other and facing upwards to eliminate possible shadow effects and ensure each leaf received equal dosage. The leaves were stored at 20 °C and 5 °C for a possible maximum shelf life of 4 and 14 d, respectively. After UV-C treatment application, the leaves were stored on trays under controlled temperature in a retailing simulated water vapour saturated atmosphere condition. Samples were evaluated at harvest, 2 and 4 d after storage at 20 °C, while those stored at 5 °C, samples were evaluated at harvest 2, 4 and 14 d after storage.

7.2.3. Sample preparation and analysis

At each data collection period, samples were immediately shock frozen in liquid nitrogen and kept at -80 °C. Carotenoids content was determined using fresh frozen material. The remaining samples were freeze-dried for 72 h at 0.003 mbar (Alpha 1-4, Martin Christ Gefriertrocknungsanlagen GmbH, Germany), ground, mixed to a fine homogenized powder, and stored in a desiccator for further analyses of vitamin E, flavonoids, phenolic acids, total phenolic compounds, GPOX, and TEAC. Preliminary analysis on total phenolic compounds, GPOX and TEAC did not show appreciable difference due to the treatments during storage especially at 5 °C. Therefore, the analysis was done at 0-4 d of storage at 20 °C in order to detect the difference of the extreme variants. All the results are presented on dry matter basis.

7.2.3.1. Determination of vitamin E content

Vitamin E content was determined using the analytical set-up and HPLC-FLD method as described in Knecht et al. (2015) for the C30-phase column (Develosil RP Aqueous C30, 150 x 3 mm, 3 μm, Phenomenex, Aschaffenburg, Germany). Vitamin E was directly extracted out of 100 mg freeze-dried plant powder with 100% acetone containing 0.0025 butylhydroxytoluene (BHT). An aliquot of the extract was dried under a stream of nitrogen, reconstituted in a mixture of methanol/acetone/water (54/40/6, v/v/v) and filtered (PTFE, 0.2 μm, Phenomenex, Aschaffenburg, Germany) prior to HPLC-FLD analysis. The C30-HPLC parameters were as follows: column temperature 18 °C; flow rate 0.5 mL min^{-1}; gradient elution with methanol/water (91:9, v/v; eluent A) and tert-methyl- butylether/methanol/water (80:18:2; v/v/v; eluent B): 0–20.5 min 0% B, 20.5–25 min 0–10% B, 25–36 min 10% B, 36–46 min 10–55% B, 46–48 min 55–

80% B, 48–51 min 80% B, 51–53 min 80–0% B, 53–63 min 0% B. Vitamin E were expressed as α-Tocopherol equivalents (α-TE) and calculated as mg α-TE kg^{-1} on dry matter basis.

7.2.3.2. Determination of carotenoids content

Extraction and determination of lycopene, β-carotene, and lutein was conducted according to the method of Goodwin and Britton (1988), with slight modification. An aliquot of 0.5 g fresh samples was homogenized using a digital homogenizer (Ultra-Turrax® T 25, IKA®-Werke GmbH and Co. KG, Germany) in acetone/hexane (4:5, v:v) for 1 min at 18,000 rpm, and centrifuged (Multifuge X1R, Thermo Fisher Scientific, Heraeus Holding GmbH, Germany) for 10 min (4,000 rpm) in duplicate. The supernatants were collected in a 25 mL volumetric flask and brought to volume using the acetone/hexane mixture. Three replications of all samples per treatment were measured spectrophotometrically (UV-Mini-1240, Shimadzu, Japan) in duplicate at wavelengths of 505 nm (lycopene), 453 nm (β-carotene), and 445 nm (lutein). The results were expressed in g kg^{-1} on dry matter basis.

7.2.3.3. Determination of flavonoids and phenolic acids

Three replications of each UV-C treated samples as well as of control samples were used to determine the content of flavonoids and phenolic acids using the modified HPLC method described by Förster et al. (2015). An aliquot of 20 mg lyophilized, grinded leaf samples was extracted in 300 μL of 70% methanol (pH 4.0, acetic acid) for 15 min in an ice water ultrasonic bath (Sonorex Super AG 102H; Bandelin electronic GmbH & Co. KG, Germany). The sample was re-extracted twice using 300 μL of the extraction solvent for 10 min. After each extraction, the samples were centrifuged for 5 min at 10,000 rpm at 4 °C (Multifuge X1R, Thermo Fisher Scientific, Heraeus Holding GmbH, Germany). Supernatants were combined and further concentrated in a vacuum concentrator (Thermo Scientific Savent SVC3000; Vacuubrand GmbH & Co. KG, Germany) and thereafter dissolved in 50% methanol. The samples were filtered through SpinX tubes using centrifugation (10 min at 3,000 rpm at 20 °C; Costar SpinX tubes), and transferred to HPLC vials. As internal standards for phenolic acids and flavonoids, 4-methoxy cinnamic acid (1 mM) and apigenin-7-glucoside (1 mM) were used, respectively. HPLC-system (Ultimate 3000) was used for the qualitative and quantitative analysis of extracts. The extract was separated using a 150 × 2.1 mm, 3 μm, C16 column (AcclaimPA, Thermo Fisher Scientific, Idstein, Germany). The eluent gradient used was as follows: 0−1 min, 0.5% B; 1−10 min, 0.5−40% B; 10−12 min, 40% B; 12−18 min, 40−80% B; 18−20 min, 80% B; 20−24 min, 80−99% B; 24−30 min, 99-100% B; 30−34 min, 100−0.5% B; and 34−39 min, 0.5% B at a flow rate of 0.4 mL min^{-1}. Two solvents (solvent A, H$_2$O (0.5% formic acid) and solvent B, 40% acetonitrile) were used for analysis. The oven temperature was 35 °C. Detection was carried out at 290 nm for phenolic acids and 370 nm for flavonoids on a photodiode array detector. The compounds were quantified against internal standards. Identification of flavonoids and phenolic acids compounds was done according to molecular mass (MS measurement performed on selected samples), UV-spectrum, retention time and available standards. Flavonoids identified were quercetin 3-glucoside, quercetin 3-rutinoside, and kaempferol 3-rutinoside, whereas phenolic acids were feruloyl derivates, coumaroyl derivates, and caffeoyl derivatives. Results were expressed as mmol kg^{-1} on dry matter basis.

7.2.3.4. Determination of total phenolic compounds

The total phenolic compounds were determined in control and UV-C treated vegetable amaranth leaves during storage for 4 d. Hereby, the main focus was placed on the higher temperature effect (20 °C) due to previous experiments, where a typical temperature regulated pattern of the total phenolic compounds occurred. The total phenolic compounds in the vegetable amaranth leaves were determined using the modified method of Slinkard and Singleton (1997). At first, the same number of leaf samples as described above was extracted using acidified methanol (0.1% (v/v) hydrochloric acid). An aliquot of 0.5 g of finely grinded lyophilized sample was extracted with 10 mL of 80% acidified methanol, and centrifuged for 15 min at 4,000 rpm. The supernatant was collected in a 25 mL volumetric flask and the plant residue was extracted again with 10 mL 80% acidified methanol and centrifuged for 15 min. The supernatants were collected in the same volumetric flask and filled up to a final volume of 25 mL. The extracted samples were diluted with distilled water at 1:9. The same extracts were also used for the determination of TEAC. After the extraction procedure, 1 mL of the diluted extracts was filled in a 10 mL tube and was supplemented with 5 mL of working solution (i e. solution A (100 mL of 2 g sodium carbonate and 80 mg potassium sodium tartrate) and solution B (2 mL of 0.5% (w/v) copper sulphate) at a ratio of 5:1), followed by the addition of 0.5 mL of Folin-Ciocalteu's phenol reagent (Merck, Germany). Subsequently, the sample solutions were mixed with a vortex mixture developing a dark blue colour during the reaction time. After 1 h of reaction, the samples were measured spectrophotometrically at 765 nm (Spectrophotometer, Model 690, Gamma Analysen Technik GmbH; Bremerhaven-Lehe, Germany). Gallic acid was used as standard (Riedel-de Häen) and the total phenolic content was expressed as g equivalents gallic acid per kg on dry matter basis (GAE g kg^{-1}).

7.2.3.5. Determination of Trolox equivalent antioxidant capacity (TEAC)

The same extraction samples used for the total phenolics analysis were taken in order to determine the antioxidant capacity in vegetable amaranth leaves using the TEAC assay according to the modified method of Rohn et al. (2004). An aliquot of 500 µL working solution of 0.5 mmol L^{-1} 2,2'-azino-bis (3-ethylbenzothiazoline- 6-sulphonic acid) diammonium salt (ABTS), prepared in phosphate buffer, pH 7.2 (Sigma–Aldrich–Taufkirchen, Germany) was added into glass cuvettes containing 100 µL diluted sample extracts (1:9). To generate the ABTS radical cation, 200 µL potassium persulfate (10 mmol L^{-1} in phosphate buffer, pH 7.2) was pipetted to the sample mixtures to start the reaction. The absorbance of the sample mixtures was measured spectrophotometrically (Spectrophotometer, Model 690, Gamma Analysen Technik GmbH; Bremerhaven-Lehe, Garmany) in duplicate at 734 nm, exactly 6 min after start of the reaction. The reaction of the vegetable amaranth leaf extracts was compared to that of Trolox (6-hydroxy-2,5,7,8-tetramethylchroman-2-carboxilic acid) as the set standard. The results were expressed as mmol Trolox kg^{-1} on dry matter basis.

7.2.3.6. Glutathione peroxidase activity assay (GPOX)

The activity of glutathione peroxidase (GPOX, EC 1.11.1.9) was determined in control and UV-C treated vegetable amaranth leaves during storage for 4 d. However the present study focused on the higher temperature effect (20 °C) on GPOX based on previous experiments, where we experienced a typical temperature regulated pattern of GPOX activity. The activity of GPOX was determined according to the modified procedure of Schopfer (1989). A sample of 2.5 g was homogenized (Ultra-Turrax® T 25, IKA®-Werke GmbH and Co. KG, Germany) in 20 mL of 0.05 M cold sodium phosphate buffer (pH 6.0). The homogenate was stirred for 10 min in an ice-bath and thereafter centrifuged at 11,000 rpm for 15 min at 4 °C. The supernatant was filtered through miracloth (calbiochem), filled to a volume of 50 mL with 0.05 M cold sodium phosphate buffer (pH 6.0), filtered again, and finally served as enzyme source. The extractions were done in replicates. The reaction mixture consisted of 3.0 mL of a mixture containing 2 mL of 20 mmol guaiacol, 800 µL of 0.05 M sodium phosphate buffer (pH 6.0), 100 µL of 1 mmol H_2O_2, and 100 µL of sample. For the initiation of the reaction, 100 µL of 1 mmol H_2O_2 was added to the samples and immediately (60 s) measured spectrophotometrically (Spectrophotometer, Model 690, Gamma Analysen Technik GmbH; Bremerhaven-Lehe, Garmany) in triplicates at 436 nm. The enzyme activity was calculated in terms of the protein content of the sample, and is reported in nano katals per mg of protein on dry matter basis (nkat mg^{-1} protein), where 1 kat is the conversion of 1 mol of substrate per s.

7.2.4 Data analysis

The univariate procedure of SAS (version 9.4; SAS Institute, USA) was used to check for normality of the data before analysis. Since there were non-significant differences between the seasons, data for 2015 and 2016 were pooled and subjected to analysis of variance (ANOVA) using the procedure for general linear model (proc GLM). Significant differences were calculated using Tukey's test. Multiple correlation analysis was done on secondary plant compounds vis a vis their antioxidant capacity using restricted maximum likelihood (REML) estimator. All statistical analysis was performed at $p < 0.05$. Data are presented as mean values ± standard deviations.

7.3. Results

7.3.1. Vitamin E content

Postharvest UV-C application significantly influenced vitamin E content of vegetable amaranth leaves during storage, however only to a certain extent (Figure 7.2). At 20 °C (retailer's simulated condition), vitamin E content did not change significantly compared with the control at harvest (day 0). During storage, vitamin E content remained significantly unaffected irrespective of the treatments applied, except after 4 d where the control leaves had significantly higher vitamin E content (24.5%) compared with the UV-C treated leaves at 1.7 kJ m^{-2}. At 5 °C (cold storage), vitamin E content varied significantly compared with the control (day 0). An increase of vitamin E was observed after 2 and 4 d of storage for 1.7 kJ m^{-2} UV-C treated leaves, both at 16.2%, while a reduction was observed in all treatments after 14 d at 46.0, 40.6, and 39.2% in the control, 1.7 kJ m^{-2} and 3.4 kJ m^{-2} UV-C treated leaves, respectively, compared with the control at day 0. Treating vegetable amaranth leaves with UV-C did not significantly affect vitamin E content during storage, except after 14 d where leaves treated with 3.4 kJ m^{-2} UV-C had significantly higher vitamin E content (30.8%) compared with the control. However, both UV-C treatments did not significantly differ with each other (Figure 7.2). Generally, cold storage (at 5 °C) of vegetable amaranth leaves helped to retain vitamin E content longer and revealed a higher content by 1.9-9.7% compared with the simulated retailer's storage condition (at 20 °C), however depending on the storage days and UV-C treatments.

7.3.2. Carotenoids content

Carotenoid contents (lycopene, β-carotene, and lutein) of vegetable amaranth leaves were significantly influenced by storage duration and postharvest UV-C treatments (Figure 7.3). During the storage at 20 °C, all the carotenoid compounds significantly decreased by 43.6-61.8%, 33.7-60.5%, and 31.7-59.6% for lycopene, β-carotene, and lutein contents, respectively, compared with the control on day 0. There was no significant difference in all the studied carotenoids between 2 and 4 d of storage except for the lycopene content of the control treatment that was significantly reduced by 25.2% after 4 d of storage. UV-C treatment at 3.4 kJ m^{-2} resulted in significantly higher β-carotene (33.6%) and lutein (31.8%) contents compared with the control after 2 d of storage while there was no significant difference between the control and 1.7 kJ m^{-2} UV-C treatments in all the studied carotenoids. Similarly, after 4 d of storage, lutein content was significantly increased by 26.5-68.8% with increasing UV-C dosage while lycopene (47.6%) and β-carotene (67.6%) contents were significantly higher in 3.4 kJ m^{-2} UV-C treatments compared with the control. At 5 °C all the carotenoid compounds significantly decreased by 11.2-65.7%, 13.4-61.1%, and 13.2-58.7% for lycopene, β-carotene, and lutein contents, respectively during storage, compared with the control on day 0. UV-C treatments resulted in a significant reduction in lutein (45.6-46.8%), β-carotene (46.6-47.6%) and lycopene (53.5-59.5%) contents compared with the control after 2 d of storage. After 4 d of storage, the

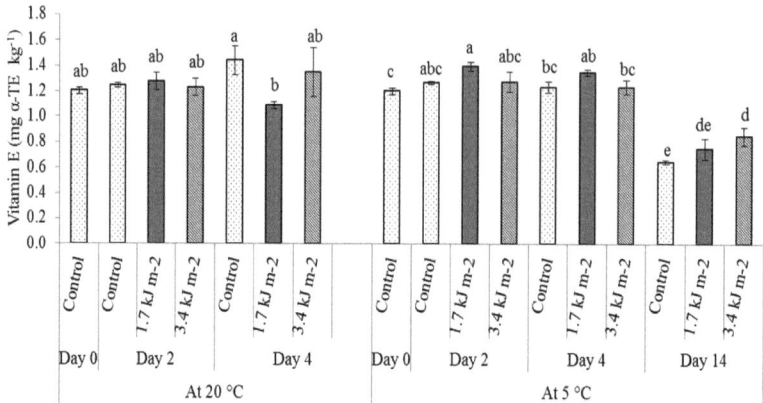

Figure 7.2: Effect of postharvest UV-C application dosage on vitamin E content on dry matter basis of vegetable amaranth leaves during storage. Means ± standard deviations followed by the same letter within storage temperature regime are not significantly different according to Tukey's test ($p < 0.05$).

significant reduction was still observed for 1.7 kJ m^{-2} UV-C treated leaves in terms of lutein (26.0%), β-carotene (26.0%), and lycopene (18.2%) contents compared with the control treatments, whereas no significant difference was observed between control and 3.4 kJ m^{-2} UV-C treatments for all the studied carotenoids. On the contrary, after 14 d of storage, both UV-C treatments resulted in significantly higher lutein (58.3-139.8%), β-carotene (67.3-153.6%) and lycopene (79.2-203.2%) contents in leaves, with increasing dosage compared with the control (Figure 7.3). In general, 5 °C storage revealed a negative influence on carotenoid contents especially on UV-C treated leaves during the initial storage days compared with 20 °C temperature storage.

7.3.3. Flavonoids content

With some exceptions, the contents of all analyzed flavonoids in control leaves were relatively constant during the entire storage period at both storage temperatures. However, flavonoid contents (quercetin and kaempferol derivatives, as well as total flavonoids) increased within the storage period and depending on the UV-C irradiation dosage and storage temperature (Figure 7.4). At 20 °C, contents of quercetin derivatives and total flavonoids content were significantly increased in the control and UV-C treatments at 3.4 kJ m^{-2}, only after 2 d (27.7-28.1%) and 4 d (69.8-72.5%) of storage, respectively as well as for the UV-C treatment at 1.7 kJ m^{-2} both after 2 d (29.5%) and 4 d (30.8-34.0%) of storage, compared to the control at day 0. Kaempferol derivatives were not significantly affected by the treatments applied after 2 d of storage.

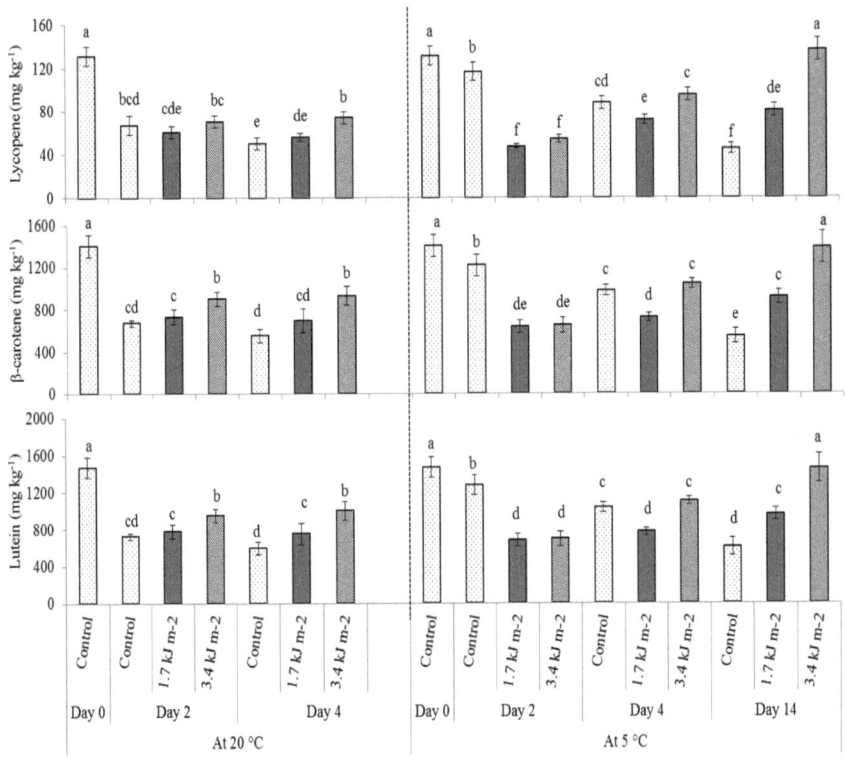

Figure 7.3: Effect of postharvest UV-C application dosage on carotenoid content on dry matter basis of vegetable amaranth leaves during storage. Means ± standard deviations followed by the same letter within a carotenoid type and storage temperature regime are not significantly different according to Tukey's test ($p < 0.05$).

However after 4 d of storage, kaempferol derivatives were significantly increased by 142.5% and 165.0% for 1.7 kJ m^{-2} and 3.4 kJ m^{-2} UV-C treated leaves, respectively when compared with the control on day 0. At 5 °C, there was a significant increase in quercetin derivatives and flavonoid contents on the UV-C treated leaves at 1.7 kJ m^{-2} (16.7-44.2%) and 3.4 kJ m^{-2} (19.1-412.2%) throughout the storage when compared with the control at day 0. However, there was a significant decline on the quercetin derivatives and total flavonoids contents on the control treatment after 2 d (17.1-17.4%) of storage, in comparison to control at day 0. For the kaempferol derivatives, the control treatments only tendentiously remained affected throughout

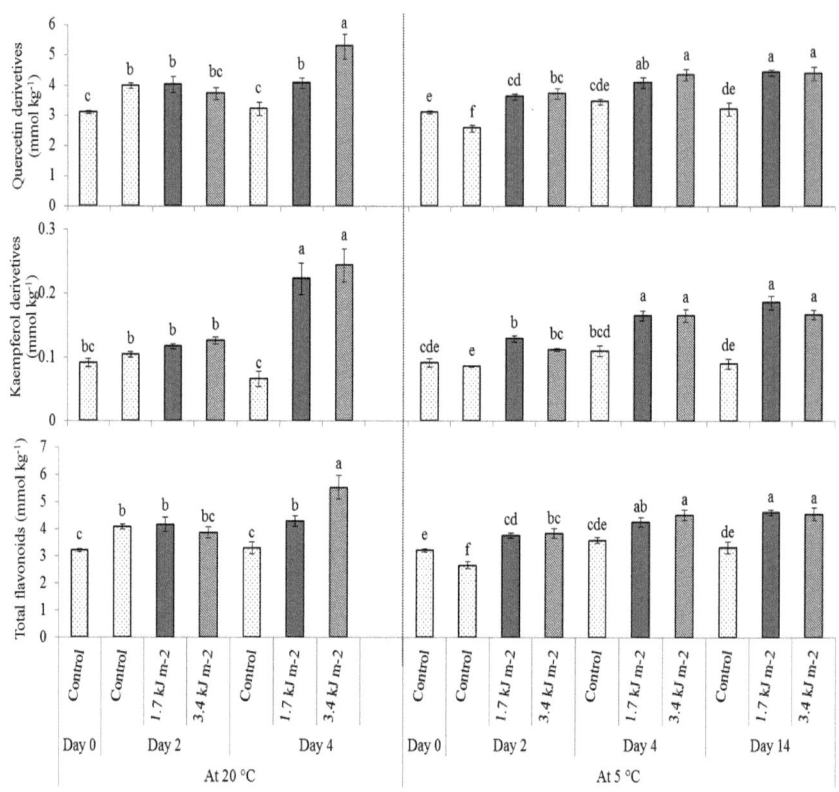

Figure 7.4: Effect of postharvest UV-C application dosage on flavonoids content on dry matter basis of vegetable amaranth leaves during storage. Means ± standard deviations followed by the same letter within a flavonoid type and storage temperature regime are not significantly different according to Tukey's test ($p < 0.05$).

the storage period, while all the UV-C treatments were significantly higher throughout the storage compared with the control. The higher UV-C dosage (3.4 kJ m^{-2}) influenced the flavonoids to a larger extent, i e. the increase of quercetin derivatives and total flavonoids were twice as high as found for the flavonoid ratio between the lower UV-C dosage and control. Quercetin and kaempferol derivatives as well as total flavonoids content effects were comparable at both storage conditions as they had almost a similar behavioural pattern.

7.3.4. Quercetin to kaempferol ratio

At 20 °C, quercetin to kaempferol ratio was only significantly increased for the control treatment (44.3%) and significantly reduced for the UV-C treatments (36.2-46.0%) after 4 d of storage when compared with the control on day 0 (Figure 7.5). During storage, no significant difference was observed among the treatments after 2 d of storage while after 4 d of storage, the control treatments had a significantly higher quercetin to kaempferol ratio (55.8-62.6%) compared with the UV-C treatments. At 5 °C, no significant difference was observed in all the treatments after 2 d as well as for the control after 4 d and 14 d of storage; however, there was significant reduction in the quercetin to kaempferol ratio for the UV-C treatments after 4 d (22.4-27.3%) and 14 d (22.6-30.0%) of storage compared with the control on day 0. During storage, the control treatment had a significantly higher quercetin to kaempferol ratio (21.6%) compared with the UV-C treatments at 1.7 kJ m^{-2} after 4 d of storage while after 14 d of storage, the content was significantly higher in the control treatment (26.9-36.5%) compared with the UV-C treatments. Regardless of the storage temperature and days, increasing UV-C dosage did not significantly improve the quercetin to kaempferol ratio. No marked difference of the quercetin to kaempferol ratio was observed at both storage temperature conditions.

7.3.5. Phenolic acid content

Postharvest UV-C application significantly influenced phenolic acids (ferulic, coumaric, and caffeic acid derivatives and as well as total phenolic acids) content of vegetable amaranth leaves during storage (Table 7.1A-B). At 20 °C, ferulic and coumaric acid derivatives as well as total phenolic acid content remained unaffected in the control treatments throughout the storage when compared with the control on day 0 (Table 7.1A). Generally, both UV-C treatments had significantly higher (16.2-37.0%) contents of these phenolic acids when compared with the contents on day 0. During storage, both UV-C treatments (19.4-32.6%) increased phenolic acid compounds compared with the control at the corresponding storage period. Similarly, at 5 °C, all the phenolic acid compounds were significantly increased (22.8-51.9%) depending on storage duration and treatments, with highest increase observed in UV-C treated leaves compared with the control on day 0 (Table 7.1B). During storage, all the studied phenolic acid compounds were significantly higher in the UV-C treated leaves (18.0-53.5%) compared with the control on the corresponding storage days. Cold temperature storage (at 5 °C) helped to maintain the phenolic acid contents longer; however, it did not have appreciable advantage with respect to the treatments when compared with the simulated retailer's storage condition (at 20 °C).

7.3.6. Total phenolic compounds

Postharvest UV-C application significantly influenced total phenolic compounds on vegetable amaranth leaves during storage at 20 °C. Total phenolic compounds significantly increased (27.0-38.3%) throughout the storage, especially for UV-C treated leaves compared with the

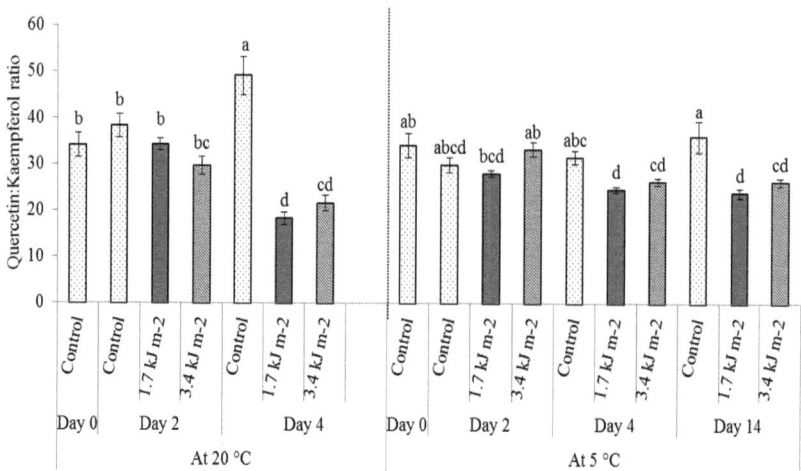

Figure 7.5: Effect of postharvest UV-C application dosage on quercetin to kaempferol ratio of vegetable amaranth leaves during storage. Means ± standard deviations followed by the same letter within a storage temperature regime are not significantly different according to Tukey's test ($p < 0.05$).

control on day 0. During storage, both UV-C treatments had significantly higher total phenolic content (30-41.6%) after 2 d of storage, with a significant increase of 30.8-50.6% 4 d of storage, with increasing UV-C dosage, compared with the control at the corresponding storage days (Figure 7.6).

7.3.7. Trolox equivalent antioxidant capacity (TEAC)

Postharvest UV-C application significantly influenced TEAC of vegetable amaranth leaves during storage at 20 °C. The TEAC activity of the control treatments was unaffected during storage, whereas for UV-C treated leaves, it significantly increased (14.1-42.3%) with the highest content observed after 2 d of storage at 3.4 kJ m^{-2} when compared with the control at harvest. During storage, TEAC significantly increased (11.2-38.7%) with increasing UV-C dosage compared with the control after 2 d of storage. After 4 d of storage, the trend was the same with both UV-C treated vegetable amaranth leaves revealing significantly higher TEAC (13.8-16.5%) compared with the control; however, both UV-C treatments were not significantly different (Figure 7.7).

Table 7.1: Effect of postharvest UV-C application dosage on phenolic acids content, on dry matter basis (mmol kg^{-1}) of vegetable amaranth leaves during storage.

Storage days	UV-C dosage	Ferulic acid derivatives	Coumaric acid derivatives	Caffeic acid derivatives	Total phenolic acid
		A. At 20 °C			
Day 0	Control	10.57±0.44^b	0.46±0.03^c	1.64±0.16^d	12.67±0.28^c
Day 2	Control	10.59±0.36^b	0.52±0.02^{bc}	2.15±0.09^c	13.26±0.40^{bc}
	1.7 kJm^{-2}	12.78±0.62^a	0.58±0.02^{ab}	2.70±0.12^{ab}	16.06±0.57^a
	3.4 kJm^{-2}	12.64±0.66^a	0.63±0.04^a	2.67±0.22^{ab}	15.94±0.57^a
Day 4	Control	10.48±0.14^b	0.46±0.04^c	2.30±0.19^{bc}	13.25±0.21^{bc}
	1.7 kJm^{-2}	12.53±0.83^a	0.63±0.02^a	2.85±0.10^a	16.01±0.98^a
	3.4 kJm^{-2}	11.65±0.39^{ab}	0.57±0.02^{ab}	2.50±0.09^{abc}	14.72±0.48^{ab}
		B. At 5 °C			
Day 0	Control	10.57±0.44^{bcd}	0.46±0.03^{bcd}	1.64±0.16^{cd}	12.67±0.28^{cd}
Day 2	Control	11.00±0.58^{bc}	0.43±0.01^{cd}	1.99±0.18^{bc}	13.41±0.43^{bc}
	1.7 kJm^{-2}	11.36±0.31^b	0.50±0.04^{bc}	2.50±0.16^a	14.36±0.41^b
	3.4 kJm^{-2}	12.98±0.97^a	0.66±0.02^a	2.61±0.05^a	16.25±1.03^a
Day 4	Control	9.27±0.56^{de}	0.44±0.01^{cd}	2.28±0.10^{ab}	11.99±0.46^{cde}
	1.7 kJm^{-2}	10.25±0.15^{bcde}	0.53±0.02^b	2.45±0.09^a	13.23±0.13^{bc}
	3.4 kJm^{-2}	10.36±0.24^{bcde}	0.50±0.02^{bc}	2.45±0.18^a	13.31±0.43^{bc}
Day 14	Control	9.00±0.36^e	0.40±0.03^d	1.40±0.06^d	10.79±0.39^e
	1.7 kJm^{-2}	9.86±0.34^{bcde}	0.45±0.04^{bcd}	1.67±0.15^{cd}	11.98±0.34^{cde}
	3.4 kJm^{-2}	9.51±0.86^{cde}	0.41±0.03^d	1.73±0.15^{cd}	11.65±0.74^{de}

Means ± standard deviations followed by the same letter within a phenolic acid type and storage temperature regime are not significantly different according to Tukey's test ($p < 0.05$).

7.3.8. Glutathione peroxidase (GPOX) activity

The activity of GPOX was significantly influenced by postharvest UV-C application on vegetable amaranth leaves during storage at 20 °C for 4 d. When compared with the control at harvest, all the treatments resulted in the significant increase in GPOX activity (23.2-43.6%). During storage, vegetable amaranth leaves treated with 3.4 kJ m^{-2} UV-C dosage had significantly higher GPOX activity (16.5%) compared with the control treatment (Figure 7.8). However, there was no significant difference of the GPOX activity in vegetable amaranth leaves between the control and 1.7 kJ m^{-2} UV-C dosage treatments and between the two UV-C treatments.

7.3.9. Relationships between Trolox equivalent antioxidant capacity (TEAC) and plant secondary compounds

Postharvest UV-C application variably influenced relationships between TEAC and secondary compounds of vegetable amaranth leaves during storage at 20 °C (Table 7.2). Postharvest UV-C treatment resulted in a significant relationship between TEAC and total phenolic compounds

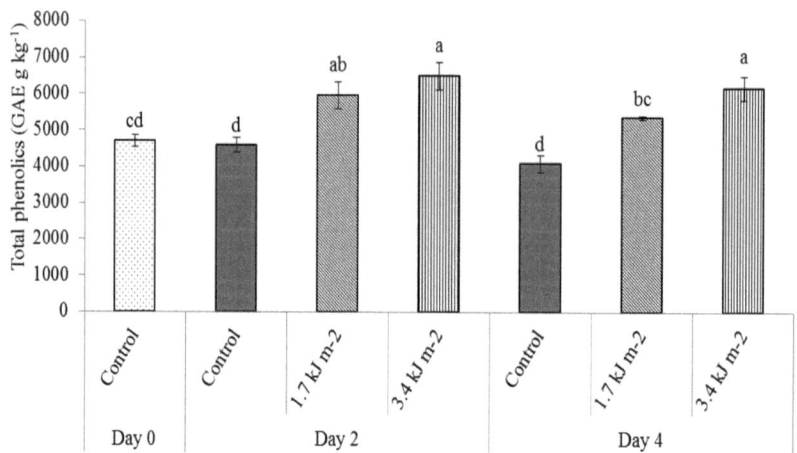

Figure 7.6: Effect of postharvest UV-C application dosage on total phenolic content on dry matter basis of vegetable amaranth leaves during storage at 20 °C. Means ± standard deviations followed by the same letter are not significantly different according to Tukey's test ($p < 0.05$).

($r = 0.82, p < 0.0001$), total phenolic acid ($r = 0.75, p < 0.0001$), and GPOX ($r = 0.81, p < 0.0027$). Total phenolic compound exhibited a significant relationship between TEAC ($r = 0.82$, $p < 0.0001$), total phenolic acid ($r = 0.75, p < 0.0001$), total flavonoids ($r = 0.56, p = 0.0080$) and GPOX ($r = 0.70$, $p = 0.0387$) as a result of the UV-C treatment. Postharvest UV-C treatments resulted in a significant relationship between TEAC ($r = 0.75, p < 0.0001$) and total phenolic compounds ($r = 0.73, p = 0.0001$). UV-C treatment resulted in a significant relationship between total flavonoids and total phenolic compounds ($r = 0.56$, $p = 0.0080$) and GPOX ($r = 0.75$, $p = 0.0051$). Similarly, postharvest UV-C treatment resulted in a significant relationship between GPOX and TEAC ($r = 0.81, p < 0.0027$), total phenolic compound ($r = 0.70, p = 0.0387$), and total flavonoids ($r = 0.75, p = 0.0051$).

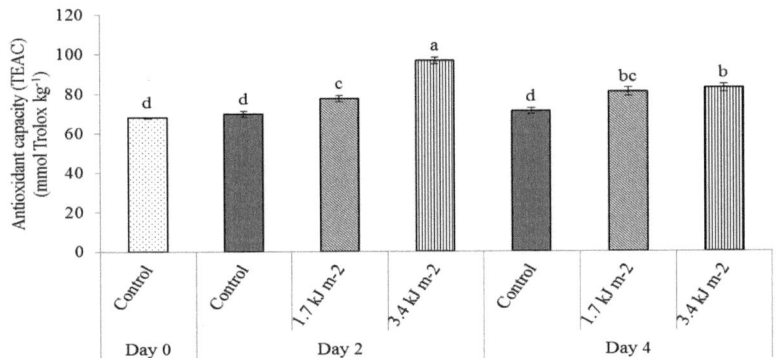

Figure 7.7: Effect of postharvest UV-C application dosage on Trolox equivalent antioxidant capacity (TEAC) on dry matter basis of vegetable amaranth leaves during storage at 20 °C. Means ± standard deviations followed by the same letter are not significantly different according to Tukey's test ($p < 0.05$).

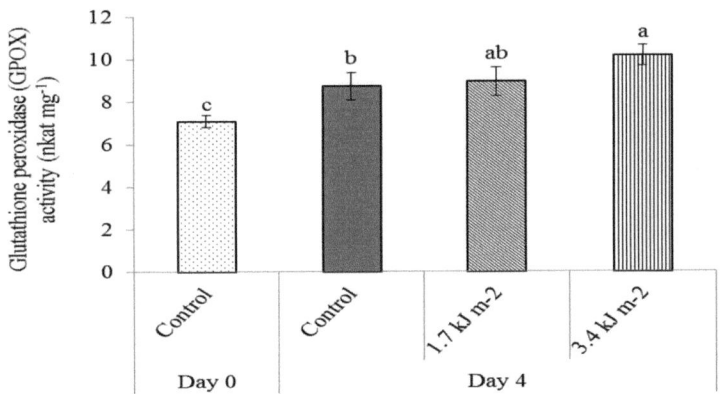

Figure 7.8: Effect of postharvest UV-C application dosage on glutathione peroxidase (GPOX) activity on dry matter basis of vegetable amaranth leaves during storage at 20 °C. Means ± standard deviations followed by the same letter are not significantly different according to Tukey's test ($p < 0.05$).

Table 7.2: Multiple correlations of secondary plant compounds and antioxidant capacity of postharvest UV-C treated vegetable amaranth leaves during storage at 20 °C.

Variables	Antioxidant capacity (TEAC) (mmol Trolox kg^{-1})	Total phenolic (g kg^{-1})	Total phenolic acid (mmol kg^{-1})	Total flavonoids (mmol kg^{-1})	Total carotenoids (mg kg^{-1})	Vitamin E (mg α-TE kg^{-1})	Glutathione peroxidase activity (GPOX) (nkat mg^{-1})
Antioxidant capacity (TEAC) (mmol Trolox kg^{-1})	1.0000	0.8184 $p < 0.0001^*$	0.7489 $p < 0.0001^*$	0.3880 $p = 0.0822$	-0.0739 $p = 0.7502$	-0.1105 $p = 0.6334$	0.8110 $p < 0.0027^*$
Total phenolic (g kg^{-1})	0.8184 $p < 0.0001^*$	1.0000	0.7323 $p = 0.0001^*$	0.5622 $p = 0.0080^*$	0.0805 $p = 0.7288$	-0.2083 $p = 0.3650$	0.6986 $p = 0.0387^*$
Total phenolic acid (mmol kg^{-1})	0.7489 $p < 0.0001^*$	0.7323	1.0000	0.4124	-0.2732	-0.3338	0.5645 $p = 0.0753$
Total flavonoids (mmol kg^{-1})	0.3880 $p = 0.0822$	0.5622 $p = 0.0080^*$	0.4124 $p = 0.0632$	1.0000	-0.1304 $p = 0.5733$	0.0899 $p = 0.6984$	0.7490 $p = 0.0051^*$
Total carotenoids (mg kg^{-1})	-0.0739 $p = 0.7502$	0.0805 $p = 0.7288$	-0.2732 $p = 0.2308$	-0.1304 $p = 0.5733$	1.0000	-0.1849 $p = 0.4223$	-0.5496 $p = 0.0641$
Vitamin E (mg α-TE kg^{-1})	-0.1105 $p = 0.6334$	-0.2083 $p = 0.3650$	-0.3338 $p = 0.1392$	0.0899 $p = 0.6984$	-0.1849 $p = 0.4223$	1.0000	0.1895 $p = 0.5553$
Glutathione peroxidase activity (GPOX) (nkat mg^{-1})	0.8110 $p < 0.0027^*$	0.6986 $p = 0.0387^*$	0.5645 $p = 0.0753$	0.7490 $p = 0.0051^*$	-0.5496 $p = 0.0641$	0.1895 $p = 0.5553$	1.0000

*Significant at $p < 0.05$.

7.4. Discussion

UV-C irradiation has an important role in various physiological processes, especially in the secondary metabolism, as plant defence mechanisms against oxidative damage (Xi et al., 2014). Evidences suggest that plant secondary metabolites increase during stress conditions, acting as antioxidants in plant defence system (Caverzan et al., 2016; Rohanie and Ayoub, 2012). These compounds are also important in human health promotion (Kasote et al., 2015). In this study, the effect of targeted postharvest UV-C application on secondary metabolites of vegetable amaranth leaves during storage at different temperature regimes was evaluated. Postharvest UV-C application effects on the studied secondary metabolites changed depending on dosage, storage duration, and temperature.

Vitamin E (α-tocopherol) was significantly reduced by applying UV-C at 1.7 kJ m^{-2} when the leaves were stored at 20 °C, compared with the control, after 4 d of storage. At 5 °C, UV-C at 3.4 kJ m^{-2} had significantly higher vitamin E content compared with the control after 14 d of storage. Soriano-Melgar et al. (2014) found an increase in vitamin E in damiana (*Turnera diffusa* Willd) leaves treated with UV-C at 0.38 mW cm^{-2} (253.7 nm, 4.56 kJ m^{-2}) for 20 min day^{-1}, which was attributed to its protection against oxidative damage. Das and Roychoudhury (2014) found changes in α-tocopherol levels during plant responses to environmental stress, such as UV-C irradiation, which is characterized by two phases. In the first phase there is an increase in α-tocopherol synthesis, followed by a second phase of net α-tocopherol loss. This observation was confirmed with the changes in vitamin E content during storage in the present study. This could probably be attributed to the adaptation mechanisms of vegetable amaranth to UV-C stress. Furthermore, reports indicate that temperature and UV-C dosage affects vitamin E synthesis, hence its UV-C scavenging and absorbing properties (Kasote et al., 2005; Rivera-Pastrana et al., 2014). This could be associated with the effects of temperature on the plant physiological activities, explaining the differences in results at both storage temperature regimes as found in the present study. Moreover, vitamin E has the ability to protect plants against photoinhibition and photooxidation by quenching for reactive oxygen species (ROS) (Havaux et al., 2005); which increases during UV-C irradiation (Zhang et al., 2016). This could possibly explain its increase on 3.4 kJ m^{-2} UV-C treated vegetable amaranth leaves during storage at 5 °C, as observed in the present study.

Carotenoids (e.g. lycopene, β-carotene and lutein) content initially declined followed by a gradual increase during storage with the effect being more pronounced in the UV-C treatments with increasing dosage. Our findings are contrary to Zhang et al. (2016) who reported lower total carotenoids content of UV-C treated (1-5 kJ m^{-2}) fresh-cut red cabbage compared with the control, where contents decreased with increasing UV-C dosage. These responses were attributed to UV-C photobleaching and carotenoid photoinhibition effects, respectively. However, Gogo et al. (2017) demonstrated that UV-C treatment affects changes in carotenoids content depending on plant species and varieties being attributed to their differences in physiological stress adaptation mechanisms. In the present study, the increase in the carotenoids content in the UV-C treated samples may be part of the antioxidant system, where carotenoids are involved in the protection of chloroplast against photooxidation. However, the initial decline could be associated with storage temperature and photobleaching effects. Carotenoids can be degraded (photobleaching) or synthesized (photoinhibition) under UV-C irradiation (Gogo et al., 2017; Zhang et al., 2016). In the initial stages the degradation may probably overtake synthesis, presumably due to UV-C biological system disturbance, resulting in lower carotenoid concentration. Thereafter, carotenoid synthesis may occur to enhance photoprotection of plants against UV-C irradiation. Both explanations are very likely, since UV-C irradiation affects the content of carotenoids, with the effect being highly dependent on the species, dosage, storage temperature and duration (Cvetkovic and Markovic, 2008; Gogo et al., 2017; Havaux et al., 2005; Kacharava et al., 2009).

Flavonoids (e.g. quercetin, kaempferol derivatives) were significantly improved with postharvest UV-C treatments while the ratio of quercetin to kaempferol was reduced in vegetable amaranth leaves during storage compared with the control. Costa et al. (2006) reported higher flavonoid content after 0-2 d of storage and lower content after 4-6 d on UV-C treated (10 kJ m^{-2}) broccoli florets compared with the untreated samples at 20 °C. In another study, UV-C (3 kJ m^{-2}) stimulated accumulation of total flavonoids on red cabbage after 8 d of storage and thereafter decreased during 4 d compared with the untreated samples (Zhang et al., 2016). Both studies are contrary to the present study because it was found that flavonoids increased with increasing UV-C dosage and storage duration at both storage temperatures. The former and latter scientists used the exact storage temperature (20 °C) and almost the same UV-C dosage (3 kJ m^{-2}) respectively, as in our study. However, it is important to note that plant responses to UV-C, especially on the accumulation of flavonoids depend on physiological stage of development as well as species and variety specific (Kacharava et al., 2009). The UV-C mediated accumulation of flavonoids in amaranth leaves could be attributed to the activation of flavonoid biosynthesis as defence mechanisms in scavenging for free radicals due to the reactivity of the hydroxyl groups induced by the UV-C treatment. In this context, genes coding for key regulatory steps of the phenylpropanoid pathway, such as phenylalanine ammonia-lyase, have been shown to be upregulated in response to UV-C irradiation (Pongprasert et al., 2011; Tomás-Barberán and Espín, 2001). It has been found that there is considerable increase in flavonoid synthesis following abiotic stresses, such as UV irradiation which might be attributed to their radical scavenging and UV absorbing ability (Kasote et al., 2015). In addition, UV-C irradiation may enhance the accumulation of quercetin more than that of kaempferol as observed in the study. This is because; quercetin is a better reactive oxygen species scavenger than kaempferol (Husain et al., 1987). This would explain the lower quercetin to kaempferol ratio of UV-C treated leaves as observed in the present study.

Postharvest UV-C treatment of vegetable amaranth leaves helped to improve phenolic acids content (e.g. ferulic, coumaric, caffeic acids derivatives) throughout the storage with the effect being more pronounced at 20 °C temperature storage. This could be attributed to the changes in plant physiological responses which are temperature dependent. Studies suggest that the biological actions of phenolic acids against environmental stresses (e.g. UV-C irradiation) involve scavenging or quenching for free radicals and acting as UV-C filters (Saxena et al., 2012). This helps in reducing the penetration and protection potential towards UV-C damaging effects (Saxena et al., 2012; Younis et al., 2010). Therefore, the increased accumulation of phenolic acids of UV-C treated vegetable amaranth leaves might be drawn from this explanation.

Similar to the pattern of flavonoids and phenolic acids, total phenolic compounds significantly increased with increasing dosages of UV-C after 4 d of storage at a storage temperature of 20 °C, whereas as expected no major difference was found in terms of the low storage temperature of 5 °C (data not shown). Artés-Hernández et al. (2009) observed that UV-C effects on plant physiological responses, particularly on phenolic compound accumulation, depend on storage temperature and duration. The changes during storage duration and temperature could be attributed to plant stress adaptation and physiological mechanisms, respectively. In agreement with the present results, UV-C (4-14 kJ m^{-2}) treatments resulted in a significant increase in total phenolic compounds in broccoli florets during storage at 20 °C (Costa et al., 2006; Lemoine et al., 2008, 2007). These plant responses are assumingly based on the activation of the key enzyme phenylalanine ammonia lyase, which is temperature dependent (Engelsma, 1970) and associated synthesis of phenolic compounds caused by UV-C irradiation as also reported earlier (Artés-Hernández et al., 2009; Pluskota et al., 2005). The accumulation of plant phenolic compounds indicates a defence response, acting as singlet oxygen quenchers and therefore serving as UV-C protective filters on plants (Caverzan et al., 2016).

The antioxidant capacity (TEAC) of UV-C treated vegetable amaranth leaves was significantly increased compared with the untreated leaves stored at 20 °C during the entire storage period. The effect of a higher UV-C irradiation was more pronounced after 2 d of storage compared to 4 d of storage. This could be associated with the increase in plant secondary compounds and therefore, their antioxidative activities during storage as observed in the study. Similarly, UV-C irradiation (1.0-14 kJ m^{-2}) resulted in significant increase in antioxidant capacity on broccoli florets (Costa et al., 2006; Khalili et al., 2017; Lemoine et al., 2008, 2007), Chinese kale leaves (Chairat et al., 2013) and red cabbage (Zhang et al., 2016). However, UV-C (4.54 kJ m^{-2}) did not significantly affect antioxidant activity of tatsoi leaves stored at 5 °C (Tomás-Callejas et al., 2012), which was confirmed by in the present study when no significant antioxidant activity was observed in UV-C treated vegetable amaranth leaves at low temperatures of 5 °C (data not shown) . These results might be due to the fact that plants have efficient complex secondary metabolites as enzymatic (e.g. GPOX) and non-enzymatic (e.g. vitamin E, carotenoids, flavonoids, phenolic acids) antioxidant defence systems to avoid toxic effects of free radicals (Kasote et al., 2015). The activities of these plant secondary compounds are temperature and storage duration dependent (Artés-Hernández et al., 2009). The presence of these compounds makes plants efficient against uncontrolled oxidation of essential biomolecules, especially under environmental stress conditions, such as UV-C irradiation (Kasote et al., 2015). The increase in antioxidant capacity in the present study might be therefore attributed to be a defence response against free radicles caused by UV-C. Therefore, by a moderate targeted UV-C stress application, the increase in secondary plant compounds also implies an increase in health promoting compounds as a contribution to improved, food nutrition and health in the food supply chain.

Glutathione peroxidase activity (GPOX) was significantly enhanced in UV-C treated vegetable amaranth leaves after 4 d of storage at 20 °C, but only at higher dosage of 3.4 kJ m^{-2}. Plants exposed to other treatments, especially at a storage temperature of 5 °C, remained unaffected (data not shown). In support of the present results, peroxidase activity increased on UV-C treated Chinese kale leaves (1.8-7.2 kJ m^{-2}) (Chairat et al., 2013) and red cabbage (1-5 kJ m^{-2}) (Zhang et al., 2016) during storage for 8 d at 5 °C and for 12 d at 4 °C, respectively. These studies further confirm that plant response to UV-C treatment especially on GPOX activity is species, dose, storage duration and temperature specific; attributed to differences in their physiological characteristics. Antioxidant enzymes with peroxidase activity, such as GPOX, are mainly involved in the protection of plant cells from oxidative stress against lipid peroxidation by reducing lipid hydroperoxides to their corresponding alcohols as well as free hydrogen peroxide to water (Navrot et al., 2006; Passaia and Margis-Pinheiro, 2015). Therefore, the increase in GPOX activity as observed in UV-C treated vegetable amaranth leaves could be attributed to their role in the enzymatic catabolism against lipid peroxidation as a result of UV-C induced stress (Passaia and Margis-Pinheiro, 2015).

Significant positive correlations were observed between most of the studied plant secondary compounds and antioxidant capacity (e g. TEAC, total phenolic acids, total phenolic compounds, total flavonoids, and GPOX), except for total carotenoids and vitamin E. Khalili et al. (2017) similarly observed positive correlations between the antioxidant capacity and total phenolic compounds of UV-C treated (1.5-10 kJ m^{-2}) broccoli florets. Furthermore, some researchers also reported that total antioxidant activity cannot be significantly related to all antioxidative compounds, because of existing differences in their synergistic actions (Pataro et al., 2015). This would explain the higher and lower correlations between the antioxidant capacity and the respective secondary plant compound obtained in the present study.

7.5. Conclusion and recommendation

Hormic postharvest UV-C application significantly affected secondary metabolites content in vegetable amaranth leaves depending on dosage, storage duration and temperature. Contents of vitamin E, carotenoids (e.g. lycopene, β-carotene and lutein), flavonoids (e.g. quercetin and kaempfero derivatives), phenolic acids (e.g. ferulic, coumaric and caffeic acids derivatives), as well as GPOX activity and antioxidant capacity (TEAC) were increased in UV-C treated vegetable amaranth leaves compared with the untreated samples. However, the quercetin to kaempferol ratio was significantly reduced in UV-C treated vegetable amaranth leaves, confirming there involvement in antioxidative activities. Furthermore, there were significant correlations between plant secondary compounds and antioxidant capacity (e.g. TEAC, total phenolic acids, total phenolic compounds, flavonoids and GPOX), while no significant correlations were observed in terms of vitamin E and total carotenoids. The relationships among the plant secondary compounds indicate their synergistic effects in antioxidative activities in quenching for free radicles. The UV-C effects at both storage conditions were comparable, while storage duration variedly affected the accumulation of the studied compounds. The increase in the studied secondary compounds is attributed to their plant defence mechanism against oxidative damage of plant tissues caused by UV-C irradiation. Based on the fact that plant secondary metabolites have been shown to possess an antioxidant effect on human and associated chronic diseases and cancer prevention, targeted UV-C treatments of vegetable amaranth leaves may contribute not only to an increase in secondary metabolites but also to an associated health promotion. The latter assumption has to be investigated in more detail.

Acknowledgment

The study is part of the project Horticultural Innovations and Learning for Improved Nutrition and Livelihood in East Africa (HORTINLEA) which is being funded by the German Federal Ministry of Education and Research (BMBF) and the German Federal Ministry of Economic Cooperation and Development (BMZ) in the framework of the GlobE – Global Food Security program. We gratefully acknowledge the financial support of BMBF and BMZ. The authors appreciate the support of Susanne Meier in conducting an excellent job in the laboratories.

8. Discussion

The present study evaluated the emerging pre- and postharvest treatment technologies for the quality assurance of AIVs with the special emphasis on Vegetable amaranth and African nightshade. AIVs have a great potential in alleviating food insecurity, nutrition and health problems as well as creating job opportunities for women and youth in the developing countries such as Kenya. However, they are highly perishable resulting in significant loss of nutrients and income, during production and postharvest. By 2050, 33% more human mouths are expected to be fed, implying that food supplies would need to increase by 60% (McGuire, 2015). Food availability and accessibility can be increased by increasing production, improving distribution, and reducing the losses. Thus, reduction of postharvest food losses is a critical component of ensuring present and future global food security. Over the past decades, significant focus and resources have been allocated to increase food production. Increasing agricultural productivity is critical for ensuring global food security, but this may not be sufficient. Food production is currently being challenged by limited land, water and increased weather variability due to climate change. To sustainably achieve the goals of food security, food availability needs to be also increased through reductions in the postharvest losses at farm, retail and consumer levels. Food losses do not merely reduce food available for human consumption but also cause negative externalities to society through costs of waste management, greenhouse gas production, and loss of scarce resources used in their production. Food loss is estimated to be equivalent to 6-10% of human-generated greenhouse gas emissions (Gustavasson et al., 2011). A significant contributor of this problem is through methane gas generation in landfills where food waste decomposes anaerobically (Buzby and Hyman, 2012). Given the significant role food loss reductions could have toward sustainably contributing to global food security, it is important to have reliable measures of these losses. Unfortunately, most of the available postharvest loss and food waste estimates are based on the anecdotal stories with few actual measured or estimated numbers (Affognon et al., 2015). Moreover, these numbers in turn, feed into estimates of food availability which are widely used in food security assessments and policy analyses. In Kenya, about 25% of the country's population suffers chronic food insecurity and poor nutrition, and over $ 1.3 billion (€ 1.2 billion) is used to import food annually, in an attempt to satisfy the demand (Ndaka et al., 2012). Furthermore, about 5% of the country's population is constantly sustained on food aid. Huge losses in the overall quantity harvested create seasonal and geographical shortages, as well as fluctuations in price commodities (Affognon et al., 2015). Quality losses, often associated with deterioration, result in loss of market opportunity, nutritional value, and safety. On several occasions, losses in quality have resulted in serious health hazards such as consumption of aflatoxin contaminated food and large quantities of contaminated produce have had to be discarded. Traditional methods such as blanching (Habwe et al., 2008), fermentation, solar drying, and sun drying (Muchoki et al., 2007) are available, but there are challenges associated with these technologies, especially loss of nutritional quality and organoleptic properties (Chelang'a et al., 2013). Packaging is also an area where efforts have been made by researchers especially on modified atmosphere packaging; however, this has been a problem to farmers because of cost implications. Packaging bags are mostly made from plastic materials which are non-biodegradable, becoming a challenge to environmental pollution (Mampholo et al., 2015). Based on this, Kenya has proposed to ban the use of plastic bags by September, 2017 (The Economist, 2017). This calls for urgent interventions, especially on the alternative postharvest loss management technologies which are affordable, safe and sustainable.

Therefore, it was necessary to conduct a survey to assess the problems of AIV farmers and how they would wish the problems to be addressed. This is important for the technology adoption and sustainability purposes. In the first study, we assessed the situation of postharvest losses along the entire AIV supply chain in Kenya (from farmers in peri-urban and urban areas, transportation to marketing) to develop and initiate new strategies for reducing such postharvest losses. The study was done in the three main AIV producing counties in Kenya i.e. Nakuru, Kisii and Kakamega. These counties were chosen based on their diversity in AIV distribution and marketing in the peri-urban and urban centres. AIVs from Nakuru were sold at supermarket in cold storage conditions and the distance to the market was approximately 10 km; AIVs from Kisii were sold in the Nakuru county closed market under ambient conditions and the distance to the market was approximately 210 km and AIVs from Kakamega were sold at Kakamega county open market under ambient conditions and the market distance was approximately 5 km. From this study, it became obvious that quantitative as well as qualitative postharvest losses occurred throughout the postharvest supply chain. These losses were attributed to pre-harvest factors (e.g. poor quality seeds, unfavourable weather conditions, inadequate plant nutrition, irrigation and crop protection) which affect yield, harvest and postharvest quality (e.g. rapid physiological deterioration and microbiological decay of products) during transport, storage and marketing. Inadequate harvest techniques and facilities for storage and transport, insufficient application of processing or treatment methods where AIVs supply chain actors were still relying on traditional methods (e.g. poor packaging, fermentation, solar drying or blanching), insufficient hygiene conditions, poor infrastructure as well as lack of knowledge on postharvest handling practices among the AIVs supply chain actors aggravate these problems. The commonly used traditional preservation methods such as blanching, air-drying, solar-drying and fermentation are reported to result in significant loss of nutritional product quality (Muchoki et al., 2007). Moreover, there is also lack of quality control and food safety regulations, calling for regulatory policies and mechanisms. In many developing countries, non-existent or unreliable grid connected electricity hinder a power supply for cold storage facilities. Furthermore, smallholder farmers who are the main actors cannot afford such expensive cold storage facilities and/or the use of refrigerated trucks. Therefore, affordable and sustainable alternative technologies could be explored for adoption (Gogo et al., 2016). Thus, there is need to optimise, adopt and implement emerging affordable postharvest handling technologies in order to manage AIV losses along the supply chain. Furthermore, development of standard guidelines for optimised and simple adapted postharvest handling procedures considering quality and safety guidelines of AIVs along the supply chain by policy makers in cooperation with researchers; with dissemination and continuous knowledge transfer to smallholder farmers and stakeholders along the supply chain strongly need consideration.

While the direct measurement of loss by tracking approach may focus only on discarded quantitative losses, the estimate by survey approach may not give true representative values because of the possibility of either underestimating or overestimating actual losses (Hodges et al., 2011). Currently, an up to date database on postharvest losses especially on AIVs are non-existent, making the intervention process difficult (Gogo et al., 2016). Therefore, there was need to evaluate the actual quantitative, nutritional and economic losses of AIVs along the supply chain. Significant quantitative (chlorophylls), nutritional (e.g. carotenoids and mineral elements) and economic losses of AIVs along the supply chain were observed. The losses could be attributed to a combination of many factors with some unique to specific supply chain stage and county. At harvest, losses were due to lack of certified seeds, weather conditions, insect pest and diseases as well as inappropriate harvesting method or time. Farmers are still relying on traditional seed production methods which affect yield and quality of AIVs. Climate change has also affected rainfall patterns becoming unpredictable with increasing drought problems. This has become a serious problem to AIV farmers who rely on rainfall for production. Water stress has an influence on yield and quality of AIVs. Liu and Stützel (2004) observed a significant reduction in dry mass, and leaf area on drought stressed vegetable amaranth genotypes. They demonstrated that drought affects sink-source relationship; hence biomass partitioning which eventually impacts on AIV yield and quality. AIV producers are mainly smallholder farmers hence resource limited. Therefore, they cannot afford irrigation facilities, conventional fertilizers and other chemicals for insect pest and disease management. For instance, it was observed that diseases such as bacterial soft rot (*Erwinia* spp.) and grey mould (*Botrytis cinerea*) and insect pests such as aphids (*Aphis* spp.), white flies (*Trialeurodes vaporariorum*), flea beetles (*Phyllotreta* spp.), and red spider mites (*Tetranychus urticae*) caused serious problems to AIVs. These diseases and insect pests resulted in lower yield at harvest as well as postharvest losses during AIV distribution. These disease problems may be present at harvest but not visible until later stages of the supply chain based on the prevailing conditions i.e. high temperature and relative humidity (Bhat et al., 2010). The management of this problem is even much challenging at postharvest level because of health related issues (chemical residues). This therefore requires interventions that are environmentally sound, especially to consumers. There is still no clear guideline on the optimal harvesting stage of AIVs as well as harvesting time and method. It was observed that AIVs are harvested 4-8 weeks after planting. This mainly depends on consumer requirement and harvesting method. For example, some consumers prefer tender AIVs (less bitter) while others prefer much mature stage (more bitter) AIVs. Studies have demonstrated varying nutritional and phytochemicals (responsible for bitterness) contents with maturity stage of AIVs (Abugre et al., 2011; Flyman and Afolayan, 2008). The main harvesting method was uprooting (one time) or by sequential or pinching (multiple). Harvesting method physiologically affects yield and quality of AIVs (Wangolo et al., 2015). It was also observed that AIVs were harvested at any time of the day.

However, this has an influence on disease development as well as heat build-up that eventually affect quality of AIVs. For instance, harvesting early in the morning may result to disease build-up during AIV distribution, as a result of accumulated dew on leaf surface, while harvesting late in the afternoon may result in field heat accumulation affecting metabolic activities hence quality of AIVs. During transportation losses were due to poor road conditions, poor handling as well as disease contamination. Roads in most of the developing countries are still in poor condition resulting in constant vehicle breakdown, impact damage due to pot holes while AIVs were taking longer time than expected to reach intended destination. During transportation, AIVs suffer from mechanical injuries such as bruising, surface abrasions, and cuts resulting in significant postharvest losses especially vitamin C (Mampholo et al., 2016; Lee and Kader, 2000). Farmers do not have a clue on how to handle AIVs as sprinkling of cold water in order to maintain freshness during distribution was a common activity, not considering the quality of water used and the disease related problems. This could be one of the entry points for AIV contamination resulting in postharvest losses (Banach et al., 2015). At the market, the losses were attributed to poor handling (handling non-packaged AIVs with bare hands, rough handling), unhygienic market conditions, inappropriate packaging (non-perforated polythene bags), lack of cold storage facilities, and seasonal gluts. There are no recommended storage, transportation facilities and packaging materials for AIVs. For instance, AIVs were transported using varying transportation modes such as pedestrian, bicycles, motorbikes, vehicles (e.g. lorries, pick-ups) and packaging materials such as gunny bags and non-perforated polythene bags (ordinary polythene bags). AIVs were kept in varying storage conditions in supply chain. Storage conditions such as temperature and relative humidity management are the most important factors to maintain quality of AIVs. In other situations, the AIVs especially in the open markets were traded in ambient conditions hence exposed to dust and smoke. It was observed that buyers and sellers were frequently handling the AIVs with their bare hands which could cause serious contamination problems. AIVs are packed in non-perforated polythene bags that enhance heat and water accumulation as a result of respiration. This situation provides favourable conditions for pathogen development hence loss of AIV quality. However, studies have demonstrated that nutritional quality of AIVs are better maintained using modified atmosphere packaging materials compared with non-perforated packaging and non-packaged AIVs (Mampholo et al., 2015). Furthermore, since most of the AIV farmers rely on rain during production, all the AIVs are harvested and available at the market about the same time leading to great loss and wastage. All these problems translate to quantitative, nutritional and economic losses along the AIV supply chain. This study provides highly valuable information on postharvest losses to farmers, researchers, policy makers, and all the actors in the AIV supply chain for the intervention purposes. In order to encourage and sustain AIV commercial farming, there is need for more studies on affordable, safe and easy to apply postharvest treatments combined with training of farmers on appropriate postharvest handling practices, i.e. appropriate harvest technologies, issues of optimised transportation and postharvest preservation and postharvest treatments ensuring the maintenance of high quality AIVs during distribution and marketing.

Based on the above studies and the need for intervention, it was necessary to evaluate the effects of emerging pre- and postharvest technologies (e.g. electric current, UV-C irradiation) for reducing postharvest losses and maintaining or improving the quality of AIVs during distribution, which is being addressed in the subsequent studies. The electric field has long been used to manage insect pests, weed, disease and frost as well as improving growth and development, yield and quality of crops (Diprose et al., 1984; Scott, 1967). In fact, the technology can also reduce the requirements for fertilizer or pesticides (Diprose et al., 1984). Currently, the practise has emerged as a pre- and postharvest treatment technology especially in enhancing bioactive compounds in vegetable crops (Dannehl et al., 2012). In this regard, we focused on investigating effects of direct-electric-current (DC) on growth parameters and bioactive compounds in different morphological sections, i.e. leaves and stems of African nightshade plants during growth. It was important to study the different morphological sections in order to understand their different physiological behaviour to DC which may have an influence on the targeted bioactive compounds. Generally, the findings of this study demonstrated that the application of weak dosages of DC (8 and 16 V) can improve growth, and quality in terms of health protecting plant compounds (e.g. chlorophylls, carotenoids, hemicellulose, and selected mineral elements). The composition of bioactive compounds varied in the studied morphological sections. A higher content of N, C, Ca, Mg, Fe, and Zn was observed in leaves while stems had higher K contents. The changes in nutrient composition in the different morphological sections could be attributed to their physiological role during plant stress. For instance, the higher content of K in the stems is important for its biochemical and physiological role in plant stress defence (Shabala and Munns, 2012; Wang et al., 2013). This is specifically true because the DC was directly applied to the stem, which needed more protection. Although DC was directly applied on the stem, the greatest increase of the bioactive compounds was observed on leaves. This is important because leaf is the most economical part in AIVs, although tender stems are occasionally consumed. The difference in bioactive compounds in the morphological sections could be attributed to differential in tissue electrolyte leakage. The results showed that DC induced plant defence response which may have altered the cell membrane properties and hence physiological processes resulting in better yield and quality. The AIVs produced using this technology are also considered safe since the accumulation of heavy metals were within acceptable limits for human consumption. This study provides timely information with the recent change in consumer eating habits, with attention being directed to vegetables rich in bioactive compounds. AIV farmers in Kenya commonly practice small-scale farming or kitchen gardening, where they cultivate vegetables in small plots or in pots, especially for home consumption. Therefore, the findings of the study may be beneficial to such farmers because they can use alternative sources of power. On the other hand, large scale farmers may also benefit from the technology because they can afford electricity. Furthermore, this technology is also applicable in areas where electricity is absent or unstable which is the situation in most cases in developing countries as farmers can use alternative power sources, e.g. batteries, solar cells, or dynamos.

As a result of global health awareness campaigns, consumers have become more interested in foods that support and promote health rather than focussing on superior external quality attributes, as was the case some years ago (Kasote et al., 2015). Therefore, there has been an upsurge of interest focussing on improving secondary metabolites in fruits and vegetables and their human health related impacts. Although the use of UV-C is well established for water treatment, air disinfection, and surface decontamination (Fonseca and Rushing, 2008), its use is still limited in postharvest technology particularly in fresh leafy vegetables. UV-C treatment has a potential for commercial use as a surface treatment on fresh products. Recent studies have demonstrated that UV-C treatment may be an effective tool to extend shelf life and maintain or even improve nutritional value of fresh produce (Huyskens-Keil et al., 2011; Kang et al., 2013; Katerova et al., 2012; Lu et al., 2016; Stevens et al., 2004). However, this application has only been done on fruit, stem and root vegetables with limited studies on leafy vegetables especially AIVs. Therefore, we evaluated the effect of postharvest UV-C (1.7 and 3.4 kJ m^{-2}) postharvest application dosage on primary compounds and microbial safety of two AIVs (i.e. vegetable amaranth and African nightshade) and secondary compounds of vegetable amaranth. The AIVs were stored at 5 °C and 20 °C for their maximum possible storage life of 14 and 6 days, respectively. The storage temperatures i.e. 5 °C and 20 °C were selected to simulate cold storage and retailer's conditions, respectively. From the study, we observed that the UV-C dosages applied affected nutrient patterns (i.e. N, P, K, Ca, Mg, Fe, Zn, and proteins) in the AIVs differently with the contents being maintained or even improved during storage at 5 °C and 20 °C. The nutritional contents were comparable in both storage conditions. This is advantageous to AIV smallholder farmers who are mainly resource limited and cannot afford cold storage facilities. Shelf life was improved exhibited by reduced weight loss and microbiological status, especially in the initial stages. Furthermore, it was observed that a targeted postharvest UV-C application of the AIV resulted in accumulation of carotenoids, flavonoids, phenolic acids, total phenolic compounds, antioxidant capacity, and glutathione peroxidase activities with the effect varying with storage temperature and duration. Studies have suggested that, UV-C plant responses are caused by an abiotic physical elicitor of stress resistance mechanisms leading to a rapid stimulation of the synthesis of secondary plant compounds, such as vitamins, carotenoids, flavonoids, and phenolic acids (Ribeiro et al., 2012). The increase in the studied secondary plant compounds is attributed to their plant defence mechanism against oxidative damage of plant tissues by UV-C irradiation. Although UV-C application is targeted to influence the synthesis of bioactive compounds, it could have negative impacts to the plants. However, this is plant and dosage specific. Low dosages of UV-C (1.7-3.4 kJ m^{-2}) stimulate the ability of the plant to scavenge and/or control the level of cellular ROS that consequently activate primary and secondary compounds (Cetin, 2014; Salama et al., 2011) which may contribute to extended shelf life, enhanced nutritional quality and reduced microbiological population in the studied AIVs (Huyskens-Keil et al., 2011; Ramakrishna and Ravishankar, 2011; Tarek et al., 2016).

The UV-C treatment is generally recognized as safe (GRAS status), hence without legal restrictions and it does not require complex equipment, hence easy to use with no chemical residue on the treated produce (Hassenberg et al., 2012). In fact, there are already recommendations for its application for commercialization (Ribeiro et al., 2012; Shama, 2007). However, for the purposes of scale-up or commercialization of UV-C treatments, suitable measures would have to be put into place to protect any personnel working in the vicinity of UV sources. These issues have already been addressed with reference to UV transilluminators which are commonly used in molecular biology laboratories (Klein, 2000). Instructing personnel in the hazards associated with UV-C would be an important first step. It is also important to create awareness of the hazards associated with UV-C which is as important as the implementation of adequate protective measures and the technology itself. UV-C is already being applied in gastronomy or on big cruising ships, in addition to laboratory use thus easy and safe equipment already exist.

UV-C source manufacturers always quote intensities at a fixed distance from the source. This enables the intensity at any other point in the UV-C field to be derived theoretically, as intensity varies as the reciprocal of the square of the distance from the source. This information together with the length of time the product remains within the UV-C field will enable the theoretical dose to be obtained. In practice, the true emission from the source will depend on numerous factors such as the transmittance of the quartz glass envelope and the actual voltage at the electrodes. UV-C emission will also depend on the age of the source, i.e. how many hours the discharge has been struck, and will decline according to some exponential. The cumulative effect of all possible variations may well result in appreciable differences in emission between apparently identical sources from the same manufacturer, and therefore the theoretical emissivity should only be used as a rough guide at the design stage rather than as a scale-up parameter. In addition, it should be pointed out that such methods can only give estimates of the dosage delivered as opposed to the dose absorbed. It is therefore essential to be able to measure the dosage.

9. Conclusion and recommendation

The greatest challenge globally especially in developing countries is how to feed the ever increasing population with adequate and quality food (Parfitt et al., 2010). Attention has been mostly geared towards increasing food production. However, one important and complementary factor that is often forgotten is reducing food loss and waste (Hodges et al., 2011). More alarmingly, evidence suggests that postharvest losses tend to be highest in developing countries like Kenya (McGuire, 2015). Under these circumstances, in a malnutrition and increasingly competitive world, reducing postharvest food losses and waste is a major developmental goal (McGuire, 2015). As observed in the study, farmers still rely on traditional methods in AIV production and postharvest handling, resulting in massive postharvest quantitative, nutritional, and economic losses. These losses are aggravated by inadequate harvest techniques and facilities for storage and transport, insufficient application of postharvest treatment methods for AIV preservation, insufficient hygiene conditions in the markets as well as poor infrastructure along the supply chain. Moreover, there is also a lack of quality control and food safety regulations, calling for urgent interventions. Consequently, the study provides timely information for researchers and policy makers for intervention. From the study, emerging pre-harvest treatment technologies (e.g. direct-electric-current) and targeted postharvest treatment technologies (e.g. UV-C) helped in improving nutritional, health promoting compounds as well as reducing quantitative and economic losses during AIV distribution. This could help in improving food security, health and nutrition especially in the current situation where consumer eating habits have shifted resulting in a high demand of quality, safe and healthy food products. The study provides affordable postharvest treatments technologies for implementation and adoption in assuring quality of AIVs in rural, peri-urban and urban areas that will help to strengthen a quality product oriented food supply chain. Thus, the pre- and postharvest treatment technologies will help in assuring quality food availability and accessibility along the entire AIV supply chain. This will ultimately improve the food nutrition and health situation of the people, resulting in better living standards hence, a healthy working nation. It will be important to conduct consumer acceptability surveys in order to win over the minds of the consumer; this is ultimately as important as being assured of the science underlying the treatment. For instance, the term 'irradiate' means to treat with any type of electromagnetic radiation. In the popular mind it has become synonymous with ionizing radiation, which is generally held to be 'a bad thing'. The use of electric current in crop production may not sound well with consumers. Therefore, if these pre- and postharvest treatment technologies are to be applied on a commercial basis, ways must be found of promoting its benefits without arousing negative reactions by the consumers. However, the application of these technologies brings in additional cost to farmers and other AIV value chain actors, especially in terms of maintenance and expertise. It is important to note that in context of developing countries, most of the farmers are resource limited and may not have sufficient financial power. In this case, they may form cooperatives where they can take advantage of economies of scale and have a central treatment unit in the main AIVs producing areas. This could help in pulling resources hence cutting on costs. Furthermore, in the assessment of cost benefit analysis, which we highly recommend, allowance would need to be made for the additional nutritional (improved minerals, proteins, dietary fibre and secondary compounds) and economic benefits (reduction in postharvest losses) as well as reductions in the use of chemical fungicide applications as a result of the control of microorganisms, brought about by these technologies.

10. Summary

Postharvest loss has been a huge problem to food nutrition, health and security, especially in developing countries. We have explored the situation of postharvest losses with more emphasis on causes and types along the AIV supply chain. Major problems identified were inappropriate harvesting and handling techniques, inadequate postharvest treatment and preservation methods, poor roads, lack of cold storage facilities, unhygienic market conditions, and lack of implementation by regulatory bodies on AIV handling, quality and safety standards, and was affected by county (location) and supply chain stage. Yellowing, wilting, presence of foreign bodies, mechanical damage and insect pest and disease damage were major postharvest problems along the supply chain. On average, farmers experienced loss between 10-50% with some experiencing >50%, and this varied with county and supply stage. Shorter AIV shelf life (1-2 d) is a major concern. Postharvest loss is unique for specific counties and supply chain stage, and attributed to AIV production, harvesting, handling, distribution and marketing dynamics. In addition, we studied the actual losses both quantitative (physical loss) and qualitative (nutritional loss). The losses varied depending on counties and supply chain stage. The mineral elements and protein were reduced by between 3.2-29.4%, while chlorophylls and carotenoids were reduced by between 70.9-90.9% and 70.4-91.9%, respectively. Cumulative weight loss was between 71.8-292.4% while the economic loss was between 12.6-34.4%.

Based on the above results, a series of studies were conducted on pre-harvest treatments (DC) and postharvest treatments (UV-C) on the quality assurance of AIVs. On the DC experiment, different morphological sections, i.e., leaves and stems of African nightshade. Applying DC (8 and 16 V) increased leaf fresh (11.5-14.4%) and dry (12.1-24.2%) weight as well as marketable leaves (29.1-55.3%). Biosynthesis of chlorophylls and carotenoids was enhanced by increased DC. Furthermore, dietary fibre fractions such as hemicellulose was promoted (23.3-45.3%) by DC applications, while cellulose and lignin remained unaffected. Minerals accumulated with increasing DC. On the UV-C experiment, the accumulation of primary compounds (chlorophylls, mineral elements, proteins and dietary fibre) and secondary metabolites (carotenoids, flavonoids, phenolic acids, phenolic compounds, and glutathione peroxidase (GPOX), and vitamin E), microbial status and antioxidant capacity (TEAC) was dependent on UV-C dosage (1.7 kJ m^{-2} or 3.4 kJ m^{-2}), storage temperature (5 °C or 20 °C) and duration (0-14 d) as well as the studied AIVs. Mineral elements and proteins were variedly affected with a general decline in the initial stages followed by an increase compared to the untreated leaves. Hemicellulose and cellulose was significantly increased in vegetable amaranth and lignin content was significantly increased in African nightshade following UV-C treatment. Chlorophyll and carotenoid contents declined within 2-4 d during storage, depending on storage conditions; but thereafter increased again significantly compared to the control. Aerobic mesophylic and yeast counts were significantly reduced by UV-C treatment, while mould counts were not affected. Vitamin E, carotenoids (e.g. lycopene, β-carotene and lutein), flavonoids (e.g. quercetin and kaempferol derivatives), phenolic acids (e.g. ferulic, coumaric and caffeic acid derivatives) as well as GPOX activity and TEAC increased with increasing UV-C dosage compared with the untreated samples. Furthermore, there was a significant relationship in most studied secondary compounds and TEAC. The applied pre-harvest (DC) or postharvest (UV-C) treatments induces plant stress biosynthesis pathway, resulting in the accumulation of plant primary and secondary compounds. These technologies could play a vital role in reducing postharvest losses, assurance AIV quality thereby improving food security, health and nutrition, especially in the developing countries such as Kenya, where the vegetables are mostly consumed.

Zusammenfassung

Nach der ernte Verlust war ein großes Problem für Lebensmittel Ernährung, Gesundheit und Sicherheit, vor allem in den Entwicklungsländern. Wir haben die Lage der Nachverlustverluste mit mehr Betonung auf Ursachen und Typen entlang der Afrikanisches indigenes Blattgemüse Lieferkette erforscht. Wesentliche Probleme waren unangemessene Ernte- und Handhabungstechniken, unzureichende Nachbehandlungs- und Konservierungsmethoden, schlechte Straßen, fehlende Kühllager, unhygienische Marktbedingungen und mangelnde Umsetzung durch die Regulierungsstellen auf Afrikanisches indigenes Blattgemüse Handhabung, Qualitäts- und Sicherheitsstandards Grafschaft (Standort) und Lieferkette Stufe. Gelbfärbung, Verwelken, Vorhandensein von Fremdkörpern, mechanischer Beschädigung und Insektenschädlings- und Krankheitsschäden waren wichtige Nachernteprobleme entlang der Lieferkette. Im Durchschnitt erlebten die Landwirte einen Verlust zwischen 10-50% und einige erlebten >50%, und dies variierte mit der Grafschaft und der Versorgungsbühne. Kürzere Afrikanisches indigenes Blattgemüse Haltbarkeit (1-2 Tage) ist ein wichtiges Anliegen. Nach der ernte Verlust ist einzigartig für bestimmte Grafschaften und Versorgung Kette Bühne, und zugeschrieben Afrikanisches indigenes Blattgemüse Produktion, Ernte, Handhabung, Vertrieb und Marketing-Dynamik. Darüber hinaus untersuchten wir die tatsächlichen Verluste sowohl quantitativen (physischen Verlust) und qualitativen (Ernährungsverlust). Die Verluste variierten je nach Landkreise und Lieferkettenstadium. Die Mineralstoffe und das Eiweiß wurden um 3,2-29,4% reduziert, während Chlorophylle und Carotinoide um 70,9-90,9% bzw. 70,4-91,9% reduziert wurden. Der kumulative Gewichtsverlust lag zwischen 71,8-292,4%, während der wirtschaftliche Verlust zwischen 12,6-34,4% lag.

Basierend auf den obigen Ergebnissen wurde eine Reihe von Studien über Vorernte Behandlungen (DC) und Nach der ernte Behandlungen (UV-C) über die Qualitätssicherung von Afrikanisches indigenes Blattgemüse durchgeführt. Auf dem DC-Experiment, verschiedene morphologische Abschnitte, d.h. Blätter und Stämme der afrikanischen Nachtschatten. Die Anwendung von DC (8 oder 16 V) erhöhte Blatt frisch (11,5-14,4%) und trocken (12,1-24,2%) Gewicht sowie marktfähige Blätter (29,1-55,3%). Die Biosynthese von Chlorophyllen und Carotinoiden wurde durch erhöhte DC erhöht. Darüber hinaus wurden diätetische Faserfraktionen wie Hemicellulose durch DC-Anwendungen gefördert (23,3-45,3%), während Cellulose und Lignin unberührt blieben. Minerale mit zunehmendem DC angesammelt. Bei dem UV-C-Experiment wird die Akkumulation von Primärverbindungen (Chlorophylle, Mineralstoffe, Eiweiß und Ballaststoffe) und Sekundärmetaboliten (Carotinoide, Flavonoide, Phenolsäuren, Phenolverbindungen und Glutathionperoxidase (GPOX) und Vitamin E) mikrobiell Status und Antioxidationsmittel (TEAC) war abhängig von UV-C-Dosierung (1,7 kJ m^{-2} oder 3,4 kJ m^{-2}), Lagertemperatur (5 °C oder 20 °C) und Dauer (0-14 Tage) sowie Die studierten Afrikanisches indigenes Blattgemüse. Mineralische Elemente und Eiweiß wurden mit einem allgemeinen Rückgang der Anfangsphasen, gefolgt von einer Zunahme im Vergleich zu den unbehandelten Blättern, stark beeinflusst. Hemicellulose und Cellulose wurden im pflanzlichen Amaranth signifikant erhöht und der Lignigehalt wurde in der afrikanischen Nachtschatten nach UV-C-Behandlung signifikant erhöht. Chlorophyll- und Carotinoidinhalte sanken innerhalb von 2-4 Tage während der Lagerung je nach Lagerungsbedingungen; Aber danach wieder deutlich gegenüber der Kontrolle erhöht. Aerobe Mesophyl- und Hefezählungen wurden durch UV-C-Behandlung signifikant reduziert, während die Formzahlen nicht beeinträchtigt wurden. Vitamin E, Carotinoide (z. B. Lycopin, β-Carotin und Lutein), Flavonoide (z. B. Quercetin und Kaempferolderivate), Phenolsäuren (z. B. ferulische, Cumar- und Caffeinsäurederivate) sowie die GPOX-Aktivität und TEAC erhöhten sich mit zunehmender UV-C-Dosis im Vergleich zu den unbehandelten Proben. Darüber hinaus gab es eine signifikante Beziehung in den meisten untersuchten Sekundärverbindungen und TEAC. Die angewandten Vorernte (DC) oder Nach der ernte (UV-C) Behandlungen induzieren den Pflanzenspannungs-Biosyntheseweg, was zur Akkumulation von pflanzlichen Primär- und Sekundärverbindungen führt. Diese Technologien könnten eine entscheidende Rolle bei der Verringerung der Nachverlustverluste spielen, die Sicherheit der Afrikanisches indigenes Blattgemüse Qualität, wodurch die Ernährungssicherheit, die Gesundheit und die Ernährung verbessert werden, vor allem in den Entwicklungsländern wie Kenia, wo das Gemüse meist verbraucht wird.

11. Publications

Gogo E.O., Opiyo, A., Ulrichs, C., Huyskens-Keil, S., 2017. Analysis on postharvest losses along the supply chain of African indigenous leafy vegetables in Kenya. International Journal of Vegetable Science (submitted).

Gogo, E.O., Förster, N., Dannehl, D., Frommherz, L., Trierweiler, B., Opiyo, A.M., Ulrichs, Ch., Huyskens-Keil, S., 2017. Hormic postharvest UV-C application to improve health promoting secondary plant compound pattern in vegetable amaranth. Postharvest Biology and Technology (submitted).

Gogo E.O., Opiyo, A., Ulrichs, C., Huyskens-Keil, S., 2017. Improving shelf life and carotenoid content of vegetable amaranth (*Amaranthus cruentus* L.) cv. Madiira 1 using short-term pre-harvest UV-B application. Egerton Journal of Science and Technology (in press).

Gogo, E.O., Trierweiler, B., Opiyo, A.M., Frommherz, L., Frechen, M., Ulrichs, C., Huyskens-Keil., S., 2017. Reducing Postharvest Losses using Modified Atmosphere Packaging Bags on African Nightshade (*Solanum scabrum* Mill.) Leaves. Acta Horticulturae (in press).

Gogo E.O., Opiyo, A.M., Ulrichs, Ch., Huyskens-Keil, S., 2017. Nutritional and economic postharvest loss analysis of African indigenous leafy vegetables along the supply chain in Kenya. Postharvest Biology and Technology 130, 39–47.

Gogo E.O., Opiyo, A.M., Hassenberg, K., Ulrichs, Ch., Huyskens-Keil, S., 2017. Postharvest UV-C treatment for extending shelf life and improving nutritional quality of African indigenous leafy vegetables. Postharvest Biology and Technology 129, 107–117.

Gogo E.O., Opiyo, A., Ulrichs, Ch., Huyskens-Keil, S., 2016. Postharvest treatments of African leafy vegetables for food security in Kenya: A review. African Journal of Horticultural Sciences 9, 32–39.

Gogo, E.O., Huyskens-Keil, S., Krimlowski, A., Ulrichs, C., Schmidt, U., Opiyo, A., Dannehl, D., 2016. Impact of direct-electric-current on growth and bioactive compounds of African nightshade (*Solanum scabrum* Mill.) plants. Journal of Applied Botany and Food Quality 89, 60–67.

12. References

Abugre, C., Appiah, F., Kumah, P., 2011. The effect of time of harvest and drying method on the nutritional composition of spider flower (*Cleome gynandra* L.). Int. J. Postharvest Technol. Innov. 2, 221–232.

Abukutsa-Onyango, M.O., 2003. Unexploited potential of indigenous African vegetables in Western Kenya. Maseno J. Educ. Arts Sci. 4, 103–122.

Adebooye, O.C., Ajayi, S.A., Baidu-Forson, J.J., Opabode, J.T., 2005. Seed constraint to cultivation and productivity of African indigenous leaf vegetables. Afr. J. Biotechnol. 4, 1480–1484.

Ade-Omowaye, B.I.O., Rastogi, N.K., Angersbach, A., Knorr, D., 2002. Osmotic dehydration of bell peppers: influence of high intensity electric field pulses and elevated temperature treatment. J. Food Eng. 54, 35–43.

Affognon, H., Mutungi, C., Sanginga, P., Borgemeister, C., 2015. Unpacking postharvest losses in Sub-Saharan Africa: A meta-analysis. World Dev. 66, 49–68.

Allende, A., Artés, F., 2003. UV-C radiation as a novel technique for keeping quality of fresh processed 'Lollo Rosso' lettuce. Food Res. Int. 36, 739–746.

Allende, A., McEvoy, J.L., Luo, Y., Artes, F., Wang, C.Y., 2006. Effectiveness of two-sided UV-C treatments in inhibiting natural microflora and extending the shelf life of minimally processed 'Red Oak Leaf' lettuce. Food Microbiol. 23, 241–249.

Angesbach, A., Heinz, V., Knorr, D., 2000. Effects of pulsed electric fields on cell membranes in real food systems. Innov. Food Sci. Emerg. Technol. 1, 135–149.

AOAC., 1999. Official methods of analysis. 14th ed. Washington: Association of Official Analytical Chemists.

Artés-Hernández, F., Escalona, V.H., P.A. Robles, Martínez-Hernández, G.B., Artés, F., 2009. Effect of UV-C radiation on quality of minimally processed spinach leaves. J. Sci. Food Agric. 89, 414–421.

Atungulu, G., Nishiyama, Y., Koide, S., 2004. Electrode configuration and polarity effects on physicochemical properties of electric field treated apples postharvest. Biosyst. Eng. 87, 313–323.

Ayanwale, A.B., Amusan, C.A., 2014. Livelihood strategies of female indigenous vegetable farmers' in Osun State, Nigeria. J. Agr. Sci. 6, 96–107.

Ayua, A., Omware, J., 2013. Assessment of processing methods and preservation of African leafy vegetables in Siaya County, Kenya. Global J. Biol. Health Sci. 2, 46–48.

Babalola, S.O., Akinwande, B.A., 2014. Determination of minerals by ICP-AES in indigenous vegetables from Southwest Nigeria. Nutr. Food Sci. 44, 249–257.

Bailey, V.A., Townsend, J.S., 1921. The motion of electrons in gases. Phil. Mag. 42, 873–891.

Baldermann, S., Blagojevic, L., Frede, K., Klopsch, R., Neugart, S., Neumann, A., Ngwene, B., Norkeweit, J., Schröter, D., Schröter, A., Schweigert, F.J., Wiesner, M., Schreiner, M., 2016. Are neglected plants the food for the future? CRC Crit. Rev. Plant Sci. 35, 106–119.

Balemi, T., Negisho, K., 2012. Management of soil phosphorus and plant adaptation mechanisms to phosphorus stress for sustainable crop production: a review. J. Soil Sci. Plant Nutr. 12, 547–561.

Banach, J.L., Sampers, I., Haute, S.V., van der Fels-Klerx, H.J., 2015. Effect of disinfectants on preventing the cross-contamination of pathogens in fresh produce washing water. Int. J. Environ. Res. Public Health. 12, 8658–8677.

Barka, E.A., Kalantari, S., Makhlouf, J., Arul, J., 2000. Impact of UV-C illumination on the cell wall-degrading enzymes during ripening of tomato (*Lycopersicon esculentum* L.) fruit. J. Agric. Food Chem. 48, 667–671.

Ben-Ammar, J., Lanoisellé, J.L., Lebovka, N., Van Hecke, E., Vorobiev, E., 2011. Impact of a pulsed electric field on damage of plant tissues: effects of cell size and tissue electrical conductivity. J. Food Sci. 76, 90–97.

Bhat, K.A., Masood, S.D., Bhat, N.A., Bhat, M.A., Razvi, S.M., Mir, M.R., Akhtar, S., Wani, N., Habib, M., 2010. Currrent status of postharvest soft rot in vegetables: A review. Asian J. Plant Sci. 9, 200–208.

Biesalski, H.K., 2013. Hunger: A baseline study of the current situation: Hidden hunger. Springer-Verlag Berlin Heidelberg, pp. 25–50.

Black, J.D., Forsyth, F.R., Fensom, D.S., Ross, R.B., 1971. Electrical stimulation and its effects on growth and ion accumulation in tomato plants. Canad. J. Bot. 49, 1809–1815.

Bowler, C., Van Montagu, M., Inzé, D., 1992. Superoxide dismutase and stress tolerance. Annu. Rev. Plant Physiol. Plant Mol. Biol. 43, 83–116.

Bratton, B.O., Henry, E.W., 1977. Electrical stimulation and its effects on indoleacetic acid and peroxidase levels in tomato plants (*Lycopersicon esculentum*). J. Exp. Bot. 28, 338–344.

Brückner, M., Caglar, G., 2016. Understanding meal cultures – Improving the consumption of African indigenous vegetables: Insights from sociology and anthropology of food. Afr. J. Hortic. Sci. 9, 53–61.

Burana, C., Srilaong, V., 2010. Effect of UV-C irradiation on chlorophyll degradation and quality changes in Chinese kale (*Brassica oleracea* var. alboglabra). Acta Hortic. 875, 119–126.

Buzby, J.C., Hyman, J., 2012. Total and per capita value of food loss in the United States. Food Policy 37, 561–570.

Castrillón-Arbeláez, P.A., Délano-Frier, J.P., 2016. Secondary metabolism in *Amaranthus* spp. A Genomic approach to understand its diversity and responsiveness to stress in marginally studied crops with high agronomic potential, in: Shanker, A.K. Shanker, C. (Eds.). Abiotic and Biotic Stress in Plants - Recent Advances and Future Perspectives. InTech, pp. 187–227. ISBN 978-953-51-2250-0.

Caverzan, A., Casassola, A., Brammer, S.P., 2016. Reactive oxygen species and antioxidant enzymes involved in plant tolerance to stress, in: Shanker, A.K., Shanker, C. (Eds.). Abiotic and Biotic Stress in Plants - Recent Advances and Future Perspectives. InTech, pp. 463–480. ISBN 978-953-51-2250-0.

Cazzaniga, S., Bressan, M., Carbonera, D., Agostini, A., Dall'Osto, L., 2016. Differential roles of carotenes and xanthophylls in photosystem I photoprotection. Biochem. 55, 3636–3649.

Cazzaniga, S., Li, Z., Niyogi, K.K., Bassi, R., Dall'Osto, L., 2012. The Arabidopsis szl1 mutant reveals a critical role of β-carotene in photosystem I photoprotection. Plant Physiol. 159, 1745–1758.

Cetin, E.S., 2014. Induction of secondary metabolite production by UV-C radiation in *Vitis vinifera* L. Öküzgözü callus cultures. Biol. Res. 47, 1–7.

Chairat, B., Nutthachai, P., Varit, S., 2013. Effect of UV-C treatment on chlorophyll degradation, antioxidant enzyme activities and senescence in Chinese kale (*Brassica oleracea* var. alboglabra). Int. Food Res. J. 20, 623–628.

Chege, P., Kuria, E., Kimiywe, J., Nyambaka, H., 2014. Changes in nutrient content for β-carotene, iron and zinc in solar dried and stored *Amaranthus cruentus* vegetables. Int. J. Agric. Innov. Res. 3, 880–882.

Chelang'a, P.K., Obare, G.A., Kimenju, S.C., 2013. Analysis of urban consumers' willingness to pay a premium for African leafy vegetables (ALVs) in Kenya: A case of Eldoret town. Food Sec. 5, 591–595.

Costa, L., Vicente, A.R., Civello, P.M., Chaves, A.R., Martínez, G.A., 2006. UV-C treatment delays postharvest senescence in broccoli florets. Postharvest Biol. Technol. 39, 204–210.

Costanzo, E., 2008. The influence of an electric field on the growth of soy seedlings. J. Electrostat. 66, 417–420.

Cvetkovic, D., Markovic, D., 2008. UV-effects on antioxidant activity of selected carotenoids in the presence of lecithin estimated by DPPH test. J. Serb. Chem. Soc. 73, 1051–1061.

Dannehl, D., Huyskens-Keil, S., Eichholz, I., Ulrichs, C., Schmidt, U., 2009. Effects of intermittent-direct-electric-current (IDC) on polyphenols and antioxidant activity in radish (*Raphanus sativus* L.) during growth. J. Appl. Bot. Food Qual. 83, 54–59.

Dannehl, D., Huyskens-Keil, S., Eichholz, I., Ulrichs, C., Schmidt, U., 2011. Effects of direct-electric-current on secondary plant compounds and antioxidant activity in harvested tomato fruits (*Solanum lycopersicon* L.). Food Chem. 126, 157–165.

Dannehl, D., Huyskens-Keil, S., Wendorf, D., Ulrichs, C., Schmidt, U., 2012. Influence of intermittent-direct-electric-current (IDC) on phytochemical compounds in garden cress during growth. Food Chem. 131, 239–246.

Das, K., Roychoudhury, A., 2014. Reactive oxygen species (ROS) and response of antioxidants as ROS- scavengers during environmental stress in plants. Front. Environ. Sci. 2, 1–13.

Denness, L., McKenna, J.F., Segonzac, C., Wormit, A., Madhou, P., Bennett, M., Mansfield, J., Zipfel, C., Hamann, T., 2011. Cell wall damage-induced lignin biosynthesis is regulated by a reactive oxygen species- and jasmonic acid-dependent process in arabidopsis. Plant Physiol. 156, 1364–1374.

DIN-ISO-10694, 1995. Soil quality –Determination of organic and total carbon after dry combustion (elementary analysis). ISO 10694:1995.

DIN-ISO-13878, 1998. Soil quality –Determination of total nitrogen content by dry combustion (elemental analysis). ISO 13878:1998.

Diprose, M.F., Benson, F.A., Willis, A.J., 1984. The effect of externally applied electrostatic fields, microwave radiation and electric currents on plants and other organisms, with special reference to weed control. Bot. Rev. 50, 171–223.

Dörnenburg, H., Knorr, D., 1993. Cellular permeabilisation of cultured plant tissues by high electric field pulses or ultra high pressure for the recovery of secondary metabolites. Food Biotechnol. 7, 35–48.

Duarte-Sierra, A., Corcuff, R., Angers, P., Arul, J., Forney, C., 2012. Influence of UV-C on colour development and free amino acid profile in broccoli florets during postharvest storage. Acta Hortic. 945, 97–104.

Dymek, K., Dejmek, P., Galindo, F.G., 2014. Influence of pulsed electric field protocols on the reversible permeabilization of rucola leaves. Food Bioproc. Technol. 7, 761–773.

EFSA., 2008. Safety of aluminium from dietary intake. Eur. J. Food Safety Author 754, 1–34.

Engelsma, G., 1970. Low-temperature effects on phenylalanine ammonia-lyase activity in gherkin seedlings. Planta 91, 246–254.

Escalona, V.H., Aguayo, E., Martínez-Hernández, G.B., Artés, F., 2010. UV-C doses to reduce pathogen and spoilage bacterial growth in vitro and in baby spinach. Postharvest Biol. Technol. 56, 223–231.

Eshtiaghi, M.N., Knorr, D., 2002. High electric field pulse pretreatment: potential for sugar beet processing. J. Food Eng. 52, 265–272.

Esnault, M.A., Legue, F., Chenal, C., 2010. Ionizing radiation: Advances in plant response. Environ Exper. Bot. 68, 231–237.

FAO., 2011. Global Food Losses and Food Waste – Extent, Causes and Prevention. Rome. ISBN 978-92-5-107205-9.

Ferruzzi, M.G., Failla, M.L., Schwartz, S.J., 2001. Assessment of degradation and intestinal cell uptake of carotenoids and chlorophyll derivatives from spinach puree using an in vitro digestion and Caco-2 human cell model. J. Agric. Food Chem. 49, 2082–2089.

Fiedor, J., Fiedor, L., Haeßner, R., Scheer, H., 2005. Cyclic ednoperoxides of β-carotene, potential pro-oxidants, as products of chemical quenching of singlet oxygen. Biochim. Biophys. Acta. 1709, 1–4.

Fincan, M., DeVito, F., Dejmek, P., 2004. Pulsed electric field treatment for solid-liquid extraction of red beetroot pigment. J. Food Eng. 64, 381–388.

Finger, F.L., Endres, L., Mosquim, P.R., Puiatti, M., 1999. Physiological changes during postharvest senescence of broccoli. Pesq. Agropec. Bras. 34, 1565–1569.

Flyman, M.V., Afolayan, A.J., 2008. Effect of plant maturity on the mineral content of the leaves of *Momordica balsamina* L. and *Vigna unguiculata* subsp. *sesquipedalis* (L.) Verdc. J. Food Qual. 31, 661–671.

Fonseca, J.M., Rushing, J.W., 2008. Application of ultraviolet light during postharvest handling of produce: Limitations and possibilities. Fresh Produce 2, 41–46.

Forney, C.F., Fan, L., Hildebrand, P.D., Song, J., 2001. Do negative air ions reduce decay of fresh fruits and vegetables? Acta Hortic. 553, 421–424.

Förster, N., Ulrichs, C., Schreiner, M., Arndt, N., Schmidt, R., Mewis, I., 2015. Ecotype variability in growth and secondary metabolite profile in *Moringa oleifera*: Impact of sulfur and water availability. J. Agric. Food Chem. 63, 2852−2861.

Friis, H., Gomo, E., Michaelsen, K.F., 2002: 'Micronutrient interventions and the HIV pandemic, in: Friis H (Ed.) Micronutrients and HIV infection, CRC, Florida, pp. 220−245.

Gall, H.L., Philippe, F., Domon, J.M., Gillet, F., Pelloux, J., Rayon, C., 2015. Cell wall metabolism in response to abiotic stress. Plants 4, 112–166.

Gaspar, T., Franck, T., Bisbis, B., Kevers, C., Jouve, L., Hausman, J.F., 2002. Concepts in plant stress physiology. Application to plant tissue cultures. Plant Growth Reg. 37, 263–285.

Goering, H.K., Van Soest, P. J., 1972. Forage fibre analyses. Agriculture handbook 379 (20 pp.). Washington: USDA.

Gogo E.O., Opiyo, A.M., Hassenberg, K., Ulrichs, Ch., Huyskens-Keil, S., 2017. Postharvest UV-C treatment for extending shelf life and improving nutritional quality of African indigenous leafy vegetables. Postharvest Biol. Technol. 129, 107–117.

Gogo, E.O., Opiyo, A., Ulrichs, C., Huyskens-Keil, S., 2016. Postharvest treatments of African leafy vegetables for food security in Kenya: A review. Afr. J. Hortic. Sci. 9, 32–40.

Gonçalves, J.F.D.C., Marenco, R.A., Vieira, G., 2001. Concentration of photosynthetic pigments and chlorophyll fluorescence of mahogany and Tonka bean under two light environments. Rev. Bras. Fisiol. Veg. 13, 149–157.

Gonzalez, M.E., Barrett, D.M., 2010. Thermal, high pressure and electric field processing effects on plant cell membrane integrity and relevance to fruit and vegetable quality. J. Food Sci. 75, 121–130.

Gonzalez, M.E., Barrett, D.M., 2010. Thermal, high pressure and electric field processing effects on plant cell membrane integrity and relevance to fruit and vegetable quality. J. Food Sci. 7, 121–130.

Goodwin, T.W., Britton, G., 1988. Distribution and analysis of carotenoids, in: Goodwin, T.W. (Ed.), Plant Pigments. Academic Press, London, pp. 61–132. ISBN 0-12-289847-8.

Guo, W., Nazimc, H., Lianga, Z., Yanga, D., 2016. Magnesium deficiency in plants: An urgent problem. Crop J. 4, 83–91.

Gürsul, I., Gueven, A., Grohmann, A., Knorr, D., 2016. Pulsed electric fields on phenylalanine ammonia lyase activity of tomato cell culture. J. Food Eng. 188, 66–76.

Gustavsson, J., Cederberg, C., Sonesson, U., van Otterdijk, R., Meybeck, A., 2011. Global Food Losses and Food Waste: Extent Causes and Prevention. Rome, Food and Agriculture Organization (FAO) of the United Nations.

Habwe, F.O., Walingo, K.M., Onyango, M.O.A., 2008. Food processing and preparation technologies for sustainable utilization of African indigenous vegetables for nutrition security and wealth creation in Kenya. Int. Union Food Sci. Technol. 3, 1–9.

Hailu, G., Derbew, B., 2015. Extent, causes and reduction strategies of postharvest losses of fresh fruits and vegetables – A review. J. Biol. Agric. Healthc. 5, 49–64.

Hassenberg, K., Huyskens-Keil, S., Herppich, W.B., 2012. Impact of postharvest UV-C and ozone treatments on microbiological properties of white asparagus (*Asparagus officinalis* L.). J. Appl. Bot. Food Qual. 85, 174–181.

Havaux, M., Eymery, F., Porfirova, S., Rey, P., Dömann, P., 2005. Vitamin E protects against photoinhibition and photooxidative stress in *Arabidopsis thaliana*. Plant Cell. 17, 3451–3469.

Heinz, V., Alvarez, I., Angersbach, A., Knorr, D., 2002. Preservation of liquid foods by high intensity pulsed electric fields-basic concepts for process design. Trends Food Sci. Technol. 12, 103–111.

Hemmaty, S., Moallemi, N., Naseri, L., 2007. Effect of UV-C radiation and hot water on the calcium content and postharvest quality of apples. Span. J. Agric. Res. 5, 559–568.

Higashio, H., Ippoushi, K., Ito, H., Azuma, K., 2001. Effect of UV Irradiation on content of flavonoids in spinach leaves. Acta Hortic. 553, 567–568.

Hinojosa, A., Gatica, I., Bustamante, A., Cárdenas, D., Escalona, V., 2015. Effect of the combined treatment of UV-C light and modified atmosphere packaging on the inactivation of *Escherichia coli* inoculated watercress. J. Food Process Preserv. 39, 1525–1533.

Hodges, R.J., Buzby, J.C., Bennett, B., 2011. Postharvest losses and waste in developed and less developed countries: Opportunities to improve resource use. J. Agric. Sci. 149, 37–45.

Hox, J.J. Boeije, H.R., 2015. Data collection - Primary vs secondary. Encyclopaedia for Social Measurement 1, 593–599.

Hu, H., Sparks, D., 1991. Zinc deficiency inhibits chlorophyll synthesis and gas exchange in 'stuart' pecan. HortSci. 26, 267–268.

Husain, R.S., Cillard, J., Cillard, P., 1987. Hydroxyl radical scavenging activity of flavonoids. Phytochem. 26, 2489–2491.

Huyskens-Keil, S., Hassenberg, K., Herppich, W.B., 2011. Impact of postharvest UV-C and ozone treatment on textural properties of white asparagus (*Asparagus officinalis* L.). J. Appl. Bot. Food Qual. 84, 229–234.

Inaba, A., Gao, J.P., Nakamura, R., 1991. Induction by electric currents of ethylene biosynthesis in cucumber (*Cucumis sativus* L.) fruit. Plant Physiol. 97, 1161–1165.

Irungu, C., Mburu, J., Maundu, P., Grum, M., Hoeschle-Zeledon, I., 2007. Marketing of African leafy vegetables in Nairobi and its implications for on-farm conservation of biodiversity. Acta Hortic. 752, 197–202.

Jones, T.B., 1978. Electrohydrodynamically enhanced heat transfer in liquids (review). Adv. Heat Transf. 14, 107–148.

Kacharava, N., Chanishvili, Sh., Badridze, G., Chkhubianishvili, E., Janukashvili, N., 2009. Effect of seed irradiation on the content of antioxidants in leaves of kidney bean, cabbage and beet cultivars. Aust. J. Crop Sci. 3, 137–145.

Kader, A.A., 2005. Increasing food availability by reducing postharvest losses of fresh produce. Acta Hortic. 682, 2169–2176.

Kaguongo, W., Maingi, G., Giencke, S., 2014. Post-harvest losses in potato value chains in Kenya. Analysis and recommendations for reduction strategies, in: Lohr, K., Pickardt, T., Ostermann, H. (Eds.). Top Kopie GmbH, Frankfurt, GIZ, Germany.
https://www.giz.de/fachexpertise/.../PHL_in_potato_value_chains_in_Kenya_web.pdf

Kamga, R.T., Kouamé, C., Atangana, A.R., Chagomoka, T., Ndango, R., 2013. Nutritional evaluation of five African indigenous vegetables. J. Hort. Res. 21, 99–106.

Kang, J.H., Chun, H., Song, N.B., Kim, M.S., Park, J., Oh, D.H., Song, K.B., 2013. Effects of electron beam and ultraviolet-C radiation on quality and microbial populations of leafy vegetables during storage. J. Korean Soc. Appl. Bi. 56, 301–307.

Karasahin, I., Pekmezci, M., Erkan, M., 2005. Combined hot water and UV-C treatments reduces postharvest decay and maintains quality of eggplants. In: Post-Harvest Technol. 12–16 September, Montpellier France.

Kareem, S.A., 1999. Stimulation of plant growth by means of electric shock application. Nigerian J. Pure Appl. Sci., 4, 855–860.

Karki, S.K., Fasse, A, Grote, U., 2016. The role of standards in domestic food value chains in Sub-Saharan Africa: A review article. Afr. J. Hortic. Sci. 9, 41–53.

Kasangi, D.M., Shitandi A.A., Shalo P.L., Mbugua S.K., 2010. Effect of spontaneous fermentation of cowpea leaves (*Vigna unguiculata*) on proximate composition, mineral content, chlorophyll content and beta-carotene content. Int. Food Res. J. 17, 721–732.

Kasote, D.M., Katyare, S.S., Hegde, M.V., Bae, H., 2015. Significance of antioxidant potential of plants and its relevance to therapeutic applications. Int. J. Biol. Sci. 11, 982–991.

Katerova, Z., Todorova, D., Tasheva, K., Sergiev, I., 2012. Influence of ultraviolet radiation on plant secondary metabolite production. Genet. Plant Physiol. 2, 113–144.

Khalili, F., Shekarchi, M., Razavi, K., Rastegar, H., 2017. Postharvest UV-C irradiation delays senescence and maintains nutritional properties of broccoli florets. Int. J. Veg. Sci. 23, 158–170.

Kharel, G.P., Hashinaga, F., Shitani, R., 1996. Effect of high electric field on some fruits and vegetables. J. Jpn. Soc. Cold Food Preserv. 22, 17–22.

Kimiywe, J., Waudo, J., Mbithe, D., Maundu, P., 2007. Utilization of medicinal value of indigenous leafy vegetables consumed in urban and peri-urban Nairobi. Afr. J. Food Agric. Nutr. Dev. 7, 15–19.

Kinyuru, J.N., Konyole, S.O., Kenji, G.M., Onyango, C.A., Owino, V.O., Owuor, B.O., Estambale, B.B., Friis, H., Roos, N., 2012. Identification of traditional foods with public health potential for complementary feeding in Western Kenya. J. Food Res. 1, 148–158.

Kitinoja, L., AlHassan, H.Y., 2012. Identification of appropriate postharvest technologies for small-scale horticultural farmers and marketers in Sub-Saharan Africa and South Asia - Part 1. postharvest losses and quality assessments. Acta Hortic. 934, 31–40.

Kitinoja, L., Saran, S., Roy, S.K., Kader, A.A., 2011. Postharvest technology for developing countries: Challenges and opportunities in research, outreach and advocacy. J. Sci. Food Agric. 91, 597–603.

Klein, R.C., 2000. Ultraviolet light hazards from transilluminators. Health Phys. 78, S48–S50.

Knecht, K., Sandfuchs, K., Kulling, S. E., Bunzel, D., 2015. Tocopherol and tocotrienol analysis in raw and cooked vegetables: A validated method with emphasis on sample preparation. Food Chem. 169, 20–27.

Koraddi, V.V., Devendrappa, S., 2011. Analysis of physiological loss of weight of vegetables under refrigerated conditions. J. Farm Sci. 1, 61–68.

Kotaka, S., Krueger, A.P., 1968. Studies on the air-ion-induced growth increase in higher plants. Adv. Front. Plant Sci., 20, 115–208.

Koukouli, S., Vlachonikolis, I.G., Philalithis, A., 2002. Socio-demographic factors and self-reported functional status: the significance of social support. BMC Health Serv. Res. 2, 1–13.

Kurkdjian, A., Guern, J., 1989. Intracellular pH: measurement and importance in cell activity. Annu. Rev. Plant Physiol. Mol. Biol. 40, 271–303.

Kusnadi, C., Sastry, S.K., 2012. Effect of moderate electric fields on salt diffusion into vegetable tissue. J. Food Eng. 110, 329–336.

Lado, B.H., Yousef, A.E., 2002. Alternative food preservation technologies: Efficacy and mechanisms. Microb. Infect. 4, 433–440.

Lee, J.H., Chun, H.H., Oh, D.H., Park, J., Won, M., Song, K.B., 2012. Sensory and microbiological qualities of romaine lettuce and kale affected by a combined treatment of aqueous chlorine dioxide and ultraviolet-C. Hort. Environ. Biotechnol. 53, 387–396.

Lee, K.S, Kader, A., 2000. Pre-harvest and postharvest factors influencing vitamin C content of horticultural crops. Postharvest Biol. Technol. 20, 207–220.

Lemoine, M.L., Civello, P.M., Chaves, A.R., Martínez, G.A., 2008. Effect of combined treatment with hot air and UV-C on senescence and quality parameters of minimally processed broccoli (*Brassica oleracea* L. var. italica). Postharves Biol. Technol. 48, 15–21.

Lemoine, M.L., Civello, P.M., Martínez, G.A., Chaves, A.R., 2007. Influence of a postharvest UV-C treatment on refrigerated storage of minimally processed broccoli (*Brassica oleracea* var italica). J. Sci. Food Agric. 87, 1132–1139.

Liu, C., Cai, L., Han, X., Ying, T., 2011. Temporary effect of postharvest UV-C irradiation on gene expression profile in tomato fruit. Gene, 486, 56–64.

Liu, C., Cai, L., Lu, X., Han, X., Ying, T., 2012. Effect of postharvest UV-C irradiation on phenolic compound content and antioxidant activity of tomato fruit during storage. J. Integr. Agric. 11, 159–165.

Liu, F., Stützel, H., 2004. Biomass partitioning, specific leaf area, and water use efficiency of vegetable amaranth (*Amaranthus* spp.) in response to drought stress. Sci. Hortic. 102, 15–27.

Lu, Y., Zhang, J., Wang, X., Lin, Q., Liu, W., Xie, X., Wang, Z., Guan, W., 2016. Effects of UV-C irradiation on the physiological and antioxidant responses of button mushrooms (*Agaricus bisporus*) during storage. Int. J. Food Sci. Technol. 51, 1502–1508.

Mampholo, B.M., Sivakumar, D., Thompson, A.K., 2016. Maintaining overall quality of fresh traditional leafy vegetables of Southern Africa during the postharvest chain. Food Rev. Int. 32, 400–416.

Mampholo, M.B., Sivakumar, D., Rensburg, J.V., 2015. Variation in bioactive compounds and quality parameters in different modified atmosphere packaging during postharvest storage of traditional leafy vegetables (*Amaranthus cruentus* L. and *Solanum retroflexum* Dunal.). J. Food Qual. 38, 1–12.

Masinde, P.W., Ojiewo, C.O., Murakami, K., Agong, S.G., 2007. Scaling up production of traditional green leafy vegetables in Kenya: Perspectives on water and nitrogen management. Dyn. Soil. Dyn. Plant 1, 105–111.

Maundu, P.M., Njiro, E.I., Chweya, J.A., Imungi, J.K., Seme, E.N., 1999. The Kenyan case study, in: Chweya, J.A., Eyzaguirre, P.B., (Eds.). The biodiversity of traditional leafy vegetables. International Plant Genetic Resources Institute, Rome. pp. 51-84.

McGuire, S., 2015. FAO, IFAD, and WFP. The state of food insecurity in the world 2015, In: Meeting the 2015 International Hunger Targets: Taking Stock of Uneven Progress, Rome: FAO, 2015. Adv. Nutr. 6, 623–624.

Mibei, E. K., Ojijo, N.K.O., Karanja, S.M., Kinyua, J.K., 2012. Phytochemical and antioxidant analysis of methanolic extracts of four African indigenous leafy vegetables. Ann. Food Sci. Technol. 13, 37–42.

Montané, M.H., Tardy, F., Kloppstech, K., Havaux, M.l., 1998. Differential control of xanthophylls and light-induced stress proteins, as opposed to light-harvesting chlorophyll a/b proteins, during photosynthetic acclimation of barley leaves to light irradiance. Plant Physiol. 118, 227–235.

Montavon, M., El Toukhi, M., Auderset, G., Greppine, H., 1987. Effect of photoperiod and electrical potentials applied to petioles on the glucose-6-phosphate dehydrogenase activity used as marker of floral induction in shoot apices of spinach. Ann. Bot. 60, 225–230.

Montavon, M., Penel, C., Greppin, H., 1988. Peroxidase activity in relation to photoperiodic induction and electric potentials applied to petioles of spinach. Plant Sci. 56, 93–97.

Morris, D.A., 1980. The influence of small direct electric currents on the transport of auxin in intact plants. Planta 150, 431–434.

Motsa, N.M., Modi, A.T., Mabhaudhi, T., 2015. Influence of agro-ecological production areas on antioxidant activity, reducing sugar content, and selected phytonutrients of orange-fleshed sweet potato cultivars. Food Sci. Technol. 35, 32–37.

Muchoki, C.N., Imungi, J.K., Lamuka, P.O., 2007. Changes in beta-carotene, ascorbic acid and sensory properties in fermented, solar-dried and stored cowpea leaf vegetables. Afr. J. Food Agric. Nutr. Dev. 7, 1–20.

Muhanji, G., Roothaert, R.L., Webo, C., Stanley, M., 2011. African indigenous vegetable enterprises and market access for small-scale farmers in East Africa. Int. J. Agr. Sustain. 9, 194–202.

Murr, L.E., 1963. Plant growth response in a simulated electric field environment. Nature 200, 490–491.

Murr, L.E., 1964. Mechanism of plant-cell damage in an electrostatic field. Nature 201, 1305–1306.

Murr, L.E., 1965. Plant growth response in an electrokinetic field. Nature 207, 1177–1178.

Nagata, M., Yamashita, I., 1992. Simple method for simultaneous determination of chlorophyll and carotenoids in tomato fruit. J. Japan Soc. Food Sci. Technol. 39, 925–928.

Nana, F.W., Hilou, A., Millogo, J.F., Nacoulma, O.G., 2012. Phytochemical composition, antioxidant and xanthine oxidase inhibitory activities of *Amaranthus cruentus* L. and *Amaranthus hybridus* L. Extracts. Pharm. 5, 613–628.

Navrot, N., Collin, V., Gualberto, J., Gelhaye, E., Hirasawa, M., Rey, P., Knaff, D.B., Issakidis, E., Jacquot, J.-P., Rouhier, N., 2006. Plant glutathione peroxidases are functional peroxiredoxins distributed in several subcellular compartments and regulated during biotic and abiotic stresses. Plant Physiol. 142, 1364–1379.

Ndaka, D., Macharia, I., Mutungi, C., Affognon, H., 2012. Postharvest losses in Africa – Analytical review and synthesis: the case of Kenya. International Centre for Insect Physiology and Ecology, Nairobi, Kenya.

Noori, M., Talebi, M., Nasiri, Z., 2015. Seven Amaranthus L. (Amaranthaceae) taxa flavonoid compounds from Tehran Province, Iran. Int. J. Mod. Bot. 5, 1–7.

Nyaura, J.A, Sila, D.N, Owino, W.O., 2014. Post-harvest stability of vegetable amaranthus (*Amaranthus dubius*) combined low temperature and modified atmospheric packaging. Food Sci. Qual. Manage. 30, 66–72.

Odongo, G.A., Schlotz, N., Herz, C., Hanschen, F.S., Baldermann, S., Neugart, S., Trierweiler, B., Frommherz, L., Franz, C.M.A.P., Ngwene, B., Luvonga, A.W., Schreiner, M., Rohn, S., Lamy, E., 2017. The role of plant processing for the cancer preventive potential of Ethiopian kale (*Brassica carinata*), Food Nutr. Res. 61, 1–11,

Ojiewo, C.O., Mbwambo, O., Swai, I., Samali, S., Tilya, M.S., Mnzava, R.N., Mrosso, L., Minja, R., Oluoch, M., 2013. Selection, evaluation and release of varieties from genetically diverse African nightshade germplasm. Int. J. Plant Breed. 7, 76–89.

Okpalamma, F., Ojimelukwe, P.C., Mazi, E.A., 2013. Post-harvest storage and processing changes in carotenoids and micronutrients in fluted pumpkin (*Telferia occidentalis* Hook F.). IOSR J. Agric. Vet. Sci. 6, 34–39.

Oniang'o, R., Grum, M., Obel-Lawson, E., 2008. Developing African leafy vegetables for improved nutrition. Regional workshop, 6–9 December 2005. Rural Outreach Program, Nairobi, Kenya.

Onyango, C.M., Imungi J.K., 2007. Postharvest handling and characteristics of fresh-cut traditional vegetables sold in Nairobi-Kenya. Afr. Crop Sci. J. 8, 1791–1794.

Onyango, C.M., Imungi, J.K., Mose, L.E., Harbinson, J., Van Kooten, O., 2009. Feasibility of commercial production of amaranth leaf vegetable by small-scale farmers in Kenya. Afr. Crop Sci. J. 9, 767–772.

Opiyo, A.M., Mungai, N.W., Nakhone, L.W., Lagat, J.K., 2015. Production, status and impact of traditional leafy vegetables in household food security: A case study of Bondo district-Siaya county-Kenya. ARPN J. Agric. Biol. Sci. 10, 330–338.

Page, T., Griffiths, G., Buchanan-Wollaston, V., 2001. Molecular and biochemical characterization of postharvest senescence in broccoli. Plant Physiol. 125, 718–727.

Parfitt, J., Barthel, M., Macnaughton, S., 2010. Food waste within food supply chains: quantification and potential for change to 2050. Philos. Trans. R. Soc. Lond. B Biol. Sci. 365, 3065–3081.

Passaia, G., Margis-Pinheiro, M., 2015. Glutathione peroxidases as redox sensor proteins in plant cells. Plant Sci. 234, 22–26.

Pataro, G., Donsi, G., Ferrari, G., 2015. Post-harvest UV-C and PL irradiation of fruits and vegetables. Chem. Eng. Trans., 44, 31–36.

Phoon, P.Y., Galindo, F.G., Vicente, A., Dejmek, P., 2008. Pulsed electric field in combination with vacuum impregnation with trehalose improves the freezing tolerance of spinach leaves. J. Food Eng. 88, 144–148.

Picchioni, G.A., Valenzuela-Vazquez, M., Armenta-Sanchez, S., 2001. Calcium-activated root growth and mineral nutrient accumulation of *Lupinus havardii*: Ecophysiological and horticultural significance. J. Amer. Soc. Hort. Sci. 126, 631–637.

Pluskota, W. E., Michalczyk, D. J., Gorecki, J., 2005. Control of phenylalanine ammonia-lyase gene promoters from pea by UV radiation. Acta Physiol. Plant 27, 229–236.

Pohl, H.A., 1978. Electroculture. J. Biol. Physics 5, 3–23.

Pongprasert, N., Sekozawa, Y., Sugaya, S., Gemma, H., 2011. The role and mode of action of UV-C hormesis in reducing cellular oxidative stress and the consequential chilling injury of banana fruit peel. Int. Food Res. J. 18, 741–749.

Ramakrishna, A., Ravishankar, G.A., 2011. Influence of abiotic stress signals on secondary metabolites in plants. Plant Signal. Behav. 6, 1720–1731.

Rastogi, N.K., Eshtiagi, M.N., Knorr, D., 1999. Accelerated mass transfer during osmotic dehydration of high intensity electrical field pulse pretreated carrots. J. Food Sci. 64, 1020–1023.

Ribeiro, C., Canada, J., Alvarenga, B., 2012. Prospects of UV radiation for application in postharvest technology. Emir. J. Food Agric. 24, 586–597.

Rivera-Pastrana, D.M., Gardea, A.A., Yahia, E.M., Martínez-Téllez, M.A., González-Aguilar, G.A., 2014. Effect of UV-C irradiation and low temperature storage on bioactive compounds, antioxidant enzymes and radical scavenging activity of papaya fruit. J. Food Sci. Technol. 51, 3821–3829.

Rohanie, M., Ayoub, M., 2012. Significance of UV-C hormesis and its relation to some phytochemicals in ripening and senescence process, in: Montanaro, G., Dichio, B. (Eds.). Advances in Selected Plant Physiology Aspects. InTech, pp. 251–268. ISBN 978-953-51-0557-2.

Rohn, S., Rawel, H. M., Kroll, J., 2004. Antioxidant activity of protein-bound quercetin. J. Agric. Food Chem. 52, 4725–4729.

Rosegrant, M.W., Sarah, A.C., Weibo, L., Timothy, B.S., Rowena, A.V., 2005. Looking ahead: Long-term prospects for Africa's agricultural development and food security. 2020, Washington, D.C., IFPRI, Discussion Paper No. 41.

Salama, H.M.H., Al-Watban, A.A., Al-Fughom, A.T., 2011. Effect of ultraviolet radiation on chlorophyll, carotenoid, protein and proline contents of some annual desert plants. Saudi J. Biol. Sci. 18, 79–86.

Saxena, M., Saxena, J., Pradhan, A., 2012. Flavonoids and phenolic acids as antioxidants in plants and human health. Int. J. Pharm. Sci. Rev. Res., 16, 130–134.

Schopfer, P., 1989. Experimentelle Pflanzenphysiologie, Band 2. Springer-Verlag, Berlin.

Schreiner, M., Huyskens-Keil, S., 2006. Phytochemicals in fruit and vegetables: health promotion and postharvest elicitors. Crit. Rev. Plant Sci. 25, 267–278.

Scott, B.I.H., 1967. Electric fields in plants. Ann. Rev. Plant Physiol. 18, 409–418.

Shabala, S., Munns, R., 2012. Salinity stress: Physiological constraints and adaptive mechanisms, in: Shabala, S. (Eds.). Plant stress physiology. CAB International, London, UK, pp. 59–94. ISBN 978-1-84593-995-3.

Shama, G., 2007. Process challenges in applying low doses of ultraviolet light to fresh produce for eliciting beneficial hormetic responses. Postharvest Biol. Technol. 44, 1–8.

Sharma, P., Jha, A.B., Dubey, R.S., Pessarakli, M., 2012. Reactive oxygen species, oxidative damage, and antioxidative defence mechanism in plants under stressful conditions. J. Bot. 1, 1–26.

Shayanfar, S., Chauhan, O.P., Toepfl, S., Heinz, V., 2014. Pulsed electric field treatment prior to freezing carrot discs significantly maintains their initial quality parameters after thawing. Int. J. Food Sci. Technol. 49, 1224–1230.

Shiundu, K.M., Oniang'o, R., 2007. Marketing African leafy vegetables, challenges and opportunities in the Kenyan context. Afr. J. Food Agric. Nutr. Dev. 17, 4–12.

Sidaway, G.H., 1966. Influence of electrostatic fields on seed germination. Nature 203, 303.

Slinkard, K., Singleton, V.L., 1997. Total phenol analysis: Automation and comparison with manual methods. Am. J. Enol. Vitic. 28, 49–55.

Smith, I.F., Eyzaguirre, P., 2007. African leafy vegetables: Their role in the world health organization's global fruit and vegetable initiative. Afr. J. Food Agric. Nutr. Dev. 7, 1684–5374.

Soliva-Fortuny, R., Balasa, A., Knorr, D., Martín-Belloso, O., 2009. Effects of pulsed electric fields on bioactive compounds in foods: a review. Trends Food Sci. Technol. 20, 544–556.

Soriano-Melgar, L.A.A., Alcaraz-Meléndez, L., Méndez-Rodríguez, L.C., Puente, M.E., Rivera-Cabrera, F., Zenteno-Savín, T., 2014. Antioxidant responses of damiana (*Turnera diffusa* Willd) to exposure to artificial ultraviolet (UV) radiation in an in vitro model; part I; UV-C radiation. Nutr. Hosp. 29, 1109–1115.

Sosulski, F.W., Imafidon, G.I., 1990. Amino acid composition and nitrogen-to-protein conversion factors for animal and plant foods. J. Agr. Food Chem. 38, 1351–1356.

Spanswick, R.M., 1981. Electrogenic ion pumps. Ann. Rev. Plant Physiol. 32, 267–289.

Stapleton, A.E., Walbot, V., 1994. Flavonoids can protect maize DNA from the induction of ultraviolet radiation damage. Plant Physiol. 105, 881–889.

Stevens, C., Liua, J., Khana, V.A., Lua, J.Y., Kabwea, M.K., Wilsonb, C.L., Igwegbea, E.C.K., Chalutzc, E., Drobyc, S., 2004. The effects of low-dose ultraviolet light-C treatment on polygalacturonase activity, delay ripening and *Rhizopus* soft rot development of tomatoes. Crop Prot. 23, 551–554.

Suffo, A.K.L, Ashish, R., Tedonkeng, P.E., Kuiate J.R., 2016. Effect of processing methods on chemical composition and antioxidant activities of two *Amaranthus* spp. harvested in west region of Cameroons. J. Nutr. Food Sci. 6, 1–9.

Tang, G., 2010. Bioconversion of dietary provitamin A carotenoids to vitamin A in humans. Amer. J. Clinic. Nutr. 91, 1468–1473

Tarek, A.R., Rasco, B.A., Sablani, S.S., 2016. Ultraviolet-C light sanitization of English cucumber (*Cucumis sativus*) packaged in polyethylene film. J. Food Sci. 81, 1419-1430.

Terry, L.A., Joyce, D.C., 2004. Elicitors of induced disease resistance in postharvest horticultural crops: a brief review. Postharvest Biol. Technol. 32, 1–13.

The Enonomist, 2017. Kenya tries to ban plastic bags—again. Acessed on 5-6-2017 at http://www.economist.com/news/middle-east-and-africa/21719471

Thompson, J., Hodgkin, T., Atta-Krah, K., Jarvis, D., Hoogendoorn, C., Padulosi, S., 2007. Biodiversity in agroecosystems farming with nature: the science and practice of ecoagriculture, pp. 46–60, in: Scherr, S.J., McNeely, J.A. (Eds.). The science and practice of ecoagriculture., Island Press, Washington, DC.

Tobiska, W.K., Nusinov, A.A., 2000. Status of the draft ISO solar irradiance standard. Physics and Chemistry of the Earth, Part C: Sol., Terr. Planet. Sci. 25, 387–388.

Tomás-Barberán, F.A., Espín, J.C., 2001. Phenolic compounds and related enzymes as determinants of quality in fruits and vegetables. J. Sci. Food Agric. 81, 853–876.

Tomás-Callejas, A., Otón, M., Artés, F., Artés-Hernández, F., 2012. Combined effect of UV-C pretreatment and high oxygen packaging for keeping the quality of fresh-cut tatsoi baby leaves. Innov. Food Sci. Emerg. Technol. 14, 115–121.

Turtoi, M., 2013. Ultraviolet light treatment of fresh fruits and vegetables surface: A review. J. Agroaliment. Proc. Technol. 19, 325–337.

Underwood, B.A., Arthur, P., 1996. The contribution of vitamin A to public health. The J. Fed. Amer. Soc. Exp. Biol. 10, 1040–1048.

Van Soest, P.J., Goering, H.K., 1963. Use of detergents in the analysis of fibrous feeds. II. A rapid method for determination of fibre and lignin. J. Assoc. Off. Anal. Chem. 46, 829–835.

Van Soest, P.J., Robertson, J.B., Lewis, B.A., 1991. Methods for dietary fibre, neutral detergent fibre, and non-starch polysaccharides in relation to animal nutrition. J. Dairy Sci. 74, 3583–3597.

Virchow, D., 2003. Leipzig declaration on conservation and sustainable utilization of plant genetic resources for food and agriculture. Efficient conservation of crop genetic diversity, Springer Berlin Heidelberg, Bohn, Germany.

Voutilainen, S., Nurmi, T., Mursu, J., Rissanen, T.H., 2006. Carotenoids and cardiovascular health. Amer. J. Clinic. Nutr. 83, 1265–1271.

Wafula, E.N., Franz, C.M.A.P., Rohn, S., Huch, M., Mathara, J.M., Trierweiler, B., 2016. Fermentation of African indigenous leafy vegetables to lower post-harvest losses, maintain quality and increase product safety. Afr. J. Hortic. Sci. 9, 1–13.

Wang, M., Zheng, Q., Shen, Q., Guo, S., 2013. The critical role of potassium in plant stress response. Int. J. Mol. Sci. 14, 7370–7390.

Wangolo, E.M., Onyango, C.M., Gachene, C.K.K., Mong'are, P.N., 2015. Effects of shoot tip and flower removal on growth and yield of spider plant (*Cleome gynandra* L.) in Kenya. Am. J. Exp. Agric. 8, 367–376.

Ward, R.G., 1996. The influence of electric currents on the growth of tomato plants. Acta Physiol. Plant 18, 121–127.

Weaver, J.C., Chizmadzhev, Y.A., 1996. Theory of electroporation: a review. Bioelectroch. Bioener. 41, 135–160.

Williams, C., 2007. Research methods. J. Bus. Econ. Res. 5, 65–72.

Yadav, S., Sehgal, S., 2002. Effect of domestic processing and cooking methods on total, HCl, extractable iron and in vitro availability of iron in spinach and amaranth leaves. Nutr. Health 16, 113–20.

Yadoo, A., 2012. Delivery models for decentralised rural electrification: Case studies in Nepal, Peru and Kenya. International Institute for Environment and Development, London.

Younis, M.E.-B., Hasaneen, M.N.A.-G., Abdel-Aziz, H.M.M., 2010. An enhancing effect of visible light and UV radiation on phenolic compounds and various antioxidants in broad bean seedlings. Plant Signal. Behav. 5, 1197–1203.

Zhang, J., Yuan L., Liu, W., Lin, Q., Wang, Z., Guan, W., 2016. Effects of UV-C on antioxidant capacity, antioxidant enzyme activity and colour of fresh-cut red cabbage during storage. Int. J. Food Sci. Technol. 52, 626–634.

Zimmermann, U., Pilwat, G., Riemann, F., 1974. Dielectric breakdown in cell membranes. Biophys. J., 14, 881–899.

Zvitov, R., Schwartz, A., Zamski, E., Nussinovitch, A., 2003. Direct current electrical field effects on intact plant organs. Biotechnol. Prog. 19, 965–971.

13. Acknowledgements

I thank my academic advisors; Dr. Susanne Huyskens-Keil and Prof. Dr. Dr. Christian Ulrichs, from Humboldt-Universität zu Berlin, Faculty of Life Sciences, Division Urban Plant Ecophysiology, Germany, and Dr. Arnold Opiyo from Egerton University, Department of Crops, Horticulture and Soils, Kenya, for their constructive critic and guidance, without which this study would have been a huge task.

I am very grateful to Susanne Meier from Humboldt-Universität zu Berlin, Faculty of Life Sciences, Division Urban Plant Ecophysiology, Germany, who was very resourceful during the biochemical analysis.

I express my sincere gratitude to the German Government (BMBF/BMZ) for providing the scholarship which gave me the opportunity to study in Germany.

I thank my wife, children, parents, siblings and friends, who were very supportive during the study. Last but not least, I solemnly acknowledge the hand of Almighty God for the health and energy to accomplish the study.

14. List of abbreviations

ABTS	2,2'-azino-bis (3-ethylbenzothiazoline- 6-sulphonic acid) diammonium salt
AC	Alternating electric current
ADF	Acid detergent fibre
ADL	Acid detergent lignin
AIVs	African indigenous leafy vegetables
ANOVA	Analysis of variance
AOAC	Association of official analytical chemists (now AOAC International)
AVRDC	Asian vegetable research and development centre (now world vegetable centre)
BMBF	German federal ministry of education and research
BMZ	German federal ministry of economic cooperation and development
DC	Direct electric current
DM	Dry matter
EFSA	European food safety authority
GlobE	Securing the global food supply (global food security)
GPOX	Glutathione peroxidase
GRAS	Generally recognized as safe
HIV/AIDS	Human immunodeficiency virus/ Acquired immune deficiency syndrome
HORTINLEA	Horticultural innovation and learning for improved nutrition and livelihood in East Africa
HPLC-FLD	High-performance liquid chromatography: fluorescence detection
ICP-AES	Inductively coupled plasma-atomic emission spectroscopy
ICP-OES	Inductively coupled plasma-optical emission spectrometry
IDC	Intermittent direct electric current
LA	Leaf area
NDF	Neutral detergent fibre
PAR	Photosynthetically active radiation
proc GLM	Procedure for general linear model
REML	Restricted maximum likelihood
RH	Relative humidity
ROS	Reactive oxygen species
SAS	Statistical analysis system
SDGs	Sustainable development goals
SPSS	Statistical package for social sciences
TEAC	Trolox equivalent antioxidant capacity
Tukey's HSD	Tukey's honestly significant difference

In der Reihe *Berliner ökophysiologische und phytomedizinische Schriften* sind bisher erschienen:

Band 01: Mohammad Mahir Uddin (2009)
Chemical ecology of mustard leaf beetle Phaedon cochleariae (F.).
ISBN 978-3-89959-848-3.

Band 02: Ilir Morina (2009)
Entwicklung von Verfahren zur Rekultivierung der Aschedeponie des Braunkohlekraftwerks in Prishtina (Kosovo).
ISBN 978-3-89959-872-8.

Band 03: Melanie Wiesner (2009)
Veränderungen gesundheitsrelevanter Inhaltsstoffe in *Parthenium hysterophorus* L. in Abhängigkeit von der Pflanzengröße und Klimafaktoren.
ISBN 978-3-89959-880-3.

Band 04: Fransika Rohr (2009)
Variabilität aliphatischer Glucosinolate in *Arabidopsis thaliana*-Ökotypen und deren Einfluss auf die Wirtspflanzeneignung von zwei folivoren Insektenarten.
ISBN 978-3-89959-884-9.

Band 05: Jutta Buchhop (2009)
Characterization of phylogenetically diverse CLRV-isolates by RFLP and research into identification of two isometric viruses.
ISBN 978-3-89959-929-9.

Band 06: Nora Koim (2010)
Urban sprawl, land cover change and forest fragmentation – Case study Pereira, Colombia.
ISBN 978-3-89959-955-8.

Band 07: Nadja Förster (2010)
Eignung unterschiedlicher salicylathaltiger *Salix*-Klone für die Arzneimittelindustrie.
ISBN 978-3-89959-964-0.

Band 08: Jana Gentkow (2010)
Cherry leaf roll virus (CLRV): Charakterisierung ausgewählter Virusisolate unter besonderer Berücksichtigung des viralen Hüllproteins.
ISBN 978-3-89959-976-3.

Band 09: Ahmad Fakhro (2010)
Interaction of Pepino mosaic virus (PepMV) and fungal root endophytes with tomato hosts (*Lycopersicum esculentum* Mill.).
ISBN 978-3-89959-995-4.

Band 10: Stefan Irrgang (2010)
Mikro- und makroskopische Untersuchungen an Veredelungsstellen von Straßenbäumen im Hinblick auf die Beeinflussung ihrer Bruchsicherheit.
ISBN 978-3-89959-998-5.

Band 11: Julia Jahnke (2010)
Guerilla Gardening anhand von Beispielen in New York, London und Berlin.
ISBN 978-3-86247-001-3.

Band 12: Astrid Karoline Günther (2010)
Analysen zur Intensität der Pflanzenschutzmittel-Anwendung und Aufklärung ihrer Einflussfaktoren in ausgewählten Ackerbaubetrieben.
ISBN 978-3-86247-005-1.

Band 13: Milena A. Dimova (2010)
Untersuchungen zur Epidemiologie von *Pythium aphanidermatum* in Abhängigkeit von den Umgebungsbedingungen bei der Gewächshausgurke (*Cucumis sativus* L.).
ISBN 978-3-86247-033-4.

Band 14: Claudia Patricia Pérez-Rodríguez (2010)
Physiologische Veränderungen in Früchten der Solanaceaengewächse in Abhängigkeit von physikalischen Elicitoren während der Produktion und nach der Ernte.
ISBN 978-3-86247-066-2.

Band 15: Charles Adarkwah (2010)
Integrated management of the stored-product pest insects *Corcyra cephalonica*, *Cadra cautella*, *Sitophilus zeamais* and *Tribolium castaneum* by use of the parasitic wasps *Habrobracon hebetor*, *Venturia canescens*, *Lariophagus distinguendus* and neem seed oil.
ISBN 978-3-86247-077-8.

Band 16: Christoph von Studzinski (2010)
Angewandte Methoden der xenovegetativen Vermehrung.
ISBN 978-3-86247-088-4.

Band 17: Tanja Mucha-Pelzer (2011)
Amorphe Silikate – Möglichkeiten des Einsatzes im Gartenbau zur physikalischen Schädlingsbekämpfung.
ISBN 978- 3-86247-106-5.

Band 18: Diego Miranda (2011)
Effect of salt stress on physiological parameters of cape gooseberry, *Physalis peruviana* L.
ISBN 978- 3-86247-119-5

Band 19: Franziska Beran (2011)
Host preference and aggregation behavior of the striped flea beetle, *Phyllotreta striolata*.
ISBN 978- 3-86247-188-1

Band 20: Mohammed Abul Monjur Khan (2011)
Induced biochemical changes and gene expression in *Brassica oleracea* and *Arabidopsis thaliana* by drought stress and its consequences on resistance to aphids.
ISBN 978- 3-86247-203-1.

Band 21: Sandra Lerche (2012)
Untersuchungen zur Anwendung, Praxiseinführung und molekularen Identifizierung von Stamm V24 des entomopathogenen Pilzes *Lecanicillium muscarium* (Petch) Zare & W. Gams.
ISBN 978- 3-86247-248-2.

Band 22:   Carsten Richter (2012)
Entwicklung und Überprüfung eines gasdichten Küvettensystems für Experimente unter hochgradig kontrollierten Bedingungen mit Gaswechselmessungen.
ISBN 978- 3-86247-271-0.

Band 23:   Aksana Grineva (2012)
Influence of the two stored grain pest insects *Sitophilus granarius* and *Oryzaephilus surinamensis* on temperature, relative humidity, moisture content, and mould growth in stored triticale.
ISBN 978- 3-86247-279-6.

Band 24:   Carmen Büttner & Christian Ulrichs (2012)
Aktuelle Themen in Landwirtschaft und Gartenbau am Beispiel von Südtirol.
ISBN 978- 3-86247-279-6.

Band 25:   Juliane Langer (2012)
Molecular and epidemiological characterisation of Cherry leaf roll virus (CLRV).
ISBN 978- 3-86247-279-6.

Band 26:   Franziska Rohr-Doucet (2012)
AOP-Variabilität in *Arabidopsis thaliana*-Kreuzungslinien – Auswirkungen auf die Resistenz gegenüber verschieden spezialisierten Lepidopteren-Arten.
ISBN 978- 3-86247-329-8.

Band 27:   Vanessa Hörmann (2012)
Lignin als biologische Barriere gegen Schimmelpize in Innenräumen.
ISBN 978- 3-86247-330-4.

Band 28:   Jacqueline Kurth (2013)
Auswirkungen verschiedener Düngerzusammensetzungen auf den Ertrag bei Schnittrosen unter Berücksichtigung des Anbauverfahrens.
ISBN 978- 3-86247-336-6.

Band 29:   Juliane Langer, Carmen Büttner & Christian Ulrichs (2014)
Kolumbien – klimatische und politische Voraussetzungen für eine landwirtschaftliche Produktion.
ISBN 978- 3-86247-430-1.

Band 30:   Heike Luisa Dieckmann (2014)
Detection of the European mountain ash ringspot associated virus (EMARaV) in Sorbus aucuparia L. in several European contries.
ISBN 978- 3-86247-441-7.

Band 31:   Rima Marion Baag (2014)
Analyse von trans-Resveratrol in historischen Rebsorten der Weinanbaugebiete Sachsen und Saale-Unstrut.
ISBN 978- 3-86247-488-2.

Band 32:   Ayesha Rahmann (2014)
Study of the protective effects of nano-structured silica and plant derived biomolecules on nuclear polyhedrosis virus affected silkworm larvae at the behavioral and molecular level.
ISBN 978- 3-86247-495-0.

Band 33:	Bettina Gramberg (2015) Weiterentwicklung eines elektrochemischen Biosensors zum Nachweis von Pflanzenviren und Insektiziden. ISBN 978- 3-86247-512-4.
Band 34:	Wilhelm van Husen (2015) Artspezifische Aufnahme und Verteilung von Cadmium bei indigenen afrikanischen Gemüsearten und daraus abzuleitende Ernährungsempfehlungen. ISBN 978- 3-86247-523-0.
Band 35:	Jenny Roßbach (2015) European mountain ash ringspot-associated viras (EMARaV): diversity and geographic distribution in Europe. ISBN 978- 3-86247-547-6.
Band 36:	Silke Steinmöller (2015) Risikominderung der Verbreitung von Quarantäneschadorganismen der Kartoffel durch hygienisierende Maßnahmen. ISBN 978- 3-86247-550-6.
Band 37:	Christin Siewert (2016) Genomic and functional analysis of species within the Acholeplasmataceae – Phytoplasmas and Acholeplasmas. ISBN 978- 3-86247-579-7.
Band 38:	Angela Köhler (2016) Untersuchungen zur Phenolglycosidkonzentration ausgewählter intra- und interspezifischer Kreuzungen salicinreicher Biomasseweiden. ISBN 978- 3-86247-581-0.
Band 39:	Nicolas Meyer (2016) Vergleichende ökophysiologische Untersuchung verschiedener Baumarten zur Verwendung als Straßenbegleitgrün in Berlin. ISBN 978- 3-86247-586-5.
Band 40:	Stefanie Schläger (2017) Identification of variation within sex pheromone blends of various Maruca vitrata populations for refining pheromone lures and traps in Asia. ISBN 978- 3-7369-9570-3.